WAR AND SOCIETY

PARTICIPATION AND REMEMBRANCE

South African
black and coloured troops
in the First World War,
1914-1918

Albert Grundlingh

SUN PRESS

WAR AND SOCIETY: PARTICIPATION AND REMEMBRANCE –
South African black and coloured troops in the First World War, 1914-1918

First edition 2014

ISBN 978-1-920689-54-4
ISBN 978-1-920689-55-1 (e-book)

Set in Aparajita 13.5/15 pt

Cover photograph: http://www.theatlantic.com/static/infocus/wwi/wwisoldiers/ [image 24]
Cover design by SUN MeDIA Stellenbosch
Design and layout by SUN MeDIA Stellenbosch

SUN PRESS is an imprint of AFRICAN SUN MeDIA. Academic, professional and reference works are published under this imprint in print and electronic format. This publication may be ordered directly from www.sun-e-shop.co.za.

Produced by SUN MeDIA Stellenbosch.

www.africansunmedia.co.za
africansunmedia.snapplify.om (e-books)
www.sun-e-shop.co.za

In memory of the late
Professor Burridge Spies,
former colleague.

CONTENTS

ABBREVIATIONS

A.G.	Archives of Adjutant General
A.P.S.	Aborigines' Protection Society Papers
B.L.	Archives of the Magistrate Bethal
C.A.B.	Cabinet Papers (Britain)
C.G.	Archives of the Commandant General
C.M.T.	Chief Magistrate Transkei
C.N.C.	Chief Native Commissioner (Natal)
C.O.	Colonial Office Records
C.S.O.	Chief Staff Officer
D.B.A.	Departement Bantoesake
D.C.	Archives of the Secretary for the Department of Defence
1/E.L.N.	Archives of the Magistrate East London
G.G.	Archives of the Governor General
G.N.L.B.	Government Native Labour Bureau
ICU	Industrial and Commercial Workers' Union
J.	Archives of the Secretary for the Department of Justice
K.J.B.	Johannesburg Commissioner
1/L.S.M.	Archives of the Magistrate Ladysmith
M.N.I.	Archives of the Secretary for the Department of Mines and Industries
M.U.N.	Ministry of Munitions
N.A.	Archives of the Secretary for the Department of Native Affairs (Union)
O.C. Records	Archives of the Officer Commanding Records
P.M.	Archives of the Secretary for the Department of the Prime Minister
S.	Archives of the Secretary to the Government (Basutoland)
SANLC	South African Native Labour Contingent
SANNC	South African Native National Congress
S.A.P.	Archives of the South African Police
S.N.A.	Archives of the Secretary for Native Affairs (Natal)
1/T.B.U.	Archives of the Magistrate Tabankulu
T.	Board of Trade Records
U.G.	Union Government

1/U.T.A.	Archives of the Magistrate Umtata
U.W.H.	Union War Histories
W.O.	War Office Records
WWI 1914/1918	WWI 1914/1918 Group
WWI G.S.W.A.	WWI German South-West Africa Group, 1914/1918
WWI I.S.D.	WWI Imperial Service Details, 1914/1918

INTRODUCTION

Centenaries can be very seductive for historians. They spin an inviting web for scholars to reflect anew on the significance of particular events or occurrences and to showcase the depth (or absence thereof) of historical work on particular topics. Whether historians should yield to such temptations is a moot point, as centenaries can also produce gross banalities and little of substance. The current centenary of the Great War of 1914-1918 (only known as the First World War after the end of the Second World War of 1939-1945)[1] is no different. In Britain, in particular, and in parts of Europe, there has been an outpouring of books, articles, documentaries, films and theatre plays.[2] The quality varies greatly.

In comparison, in South Africa First World War centennial fever is extremely mild if not largely absent. Part of the reason is that in 2014 the country has changed more markedly from 1914 than many other countries, and in the public mind it is hard to conjure up and connect to a historical world so different and distant in terms of dominant race ideology, political power and imperial networks. To this can be added that historically South Africa has also been on the periphery of the global conflict of 1914-1918, which played out mainly on the killing fields of Europe. Yet for all of this, South African participation in the war has not been completely forgotten. Even in France, despite the commemorative deluge of reporting on the war and its remembrance, there appeared an article in a prominent French newspaper on black South African wartime participation in that country.[3]

This book then deals with that sliver of history; the swirl of politics which helped to shape the nature of South African black and coloured participation in the war, the experiences of the troops and the wider effects thereof, as well as the way in which their participation has been remembered.[4] The participation of these groups in the war

---

1   Strachan, "The First World War as a global war", 3.

2   *The World Today*, August 2014 ("Haunted by the hell of the trenches").

3   *Le Monde*, 8 July 2014 ("*L'afrique du Sud enterre la ségrégation au bois Delville*").

4   The problem of terminology remains a vexed issue in South Africa. Although it has become common practice to use 'blacks' as a collective term for Africans and Indians and coloureds, in this study 'black' is used interchangeably with 'African' to indicate a specific group.

is not only memorable in its own right, but also in terms of subsequent memory work. The emphasis will be mainly on black involvement with a chapter on coloured troops. The analysis concludes with a reassessment of the general impact of the First War on South Africa and its standing as a catalyst for change is debated.

Conceptually, the work has been informed by what has become known as a social history approach. Those familiar with the ebb and flow of historiographical developments in South Africa since the 1970s, will recognise an indebtedness to a generation of scholars who has attempted to foreground the historical experiences of ordinary people who found themselves outside the traditional power structures in South Africa. In addition, the book draws upon more recent historiographical developments dealing with the construction of historical memory.[5] The overall analysis has also benefitted from what is generally termed 'war and society' studies. Scholars active in this field have tried to look beyond the smoke of the battlefield and seek to place warfare in a broader context, focusing on war as an agent of social change and incorporating the socio-political repercussions of military service.[6]

The participation of groups other than whites in colonial warfare is a recurring theme in South African history. Since the early days of white settlement at the Cape, burgher commandos regularly employed Khoikhoi against the San, and in 1795, Khoikhoi (and 'coloureds') were also active in the fruitless attempts to defend the Cape against the British. This trend continued and a marked feature of the numerous 19th-century

'Coloured' is used to denote members from the Cape Corps. Indians were also involved in the war, but is not is not discussed here. For this, see Vahed, "'Give till it hurts': Durban Indians and the First World War", 41-61.

5   For an overview of historiographical developments, see Grundlingh, "Some trends in South African academic history" in Jeppie (ed.), *Rethinking History*, 32-47.

6   There is a large amount of literature on this in the British, European and American context. For a succinct review dealing with the First World War, see Kramer, "Recent historiography of the First World War", 155-174. For Africa and South Africa, see Killingray, "War and society in British colonial Africa: Themes and prospects", 251; Ogot, *War and society in Africa*; Katzenellenbogen, "Southern Africa and the war of 1914-1918, 107-121; Garson, "South Africa and World War I", 68-85; Willan, "The South African Native Labour Contingent, 1916-1918", 61-86; Nasson, *Springboks on the Somme: South Africa in the Great War, 1914-1918*; Lambert, "Britishness, South Africanness and the First world War; Samson, *World War I in Africa: The forgotten conflict among the European powers.* See also Frankel, *Pretoria's Praetorians: Civil-military relations in South Africa*; Grundy, *Soldiers without politics: Blacks in the South African Armed Forces*; Cock and Nathan (eds), *War and society: The militarisation of South Africa.* Written in a more popular format, are the publications by Gleeson, *The unknown force: Black, Indian and Coloured soldiers through two world wars* and Clothier, *Black valour.*

frontier wars was the military assistance rendered by coloureds and also, in certain instances, by Africans drawn into alliances with Boer or British forces.[7] Despite the widespread use of Africans in combatant and non-combatant capacities, there was a constant undercurrent of uneasiness amongst the colonists that such a policy might perhaps boomerang and in various ways jeopardise their position.

During the Anglo-Boer War, black people were extensively employed in non-combatant capacities by British and Boer alike, but there was a tacit understanding that it would be preferable not to arm them. However, military exigencies dictated otherwise. At various stages of the campaign the British had at least 10 000, and perhaps as many as 30 000, armed Africans in their service, while there are indications that the Boers also armed Africans, though in far smaller numbers.[8] Both opposing camps drew armed black people into the conflict and the same issue was destined to re-emerge during the First World War.

There were also a number of other considerations between 1902 and 1914 that had a distinct bearing on the black and coloured experience during the First World War. The outcome of the Anglo-Boer War had paved the way for the formation of a modern capitalist South African state and had set in motion a train of events that led to the political unification of the four colonies in 1910. The establishment of a unified parliamentary democracy for whites, meshed smoothly with the interests of evolving capitalism, inasmuch as it provided "the locus of resolution for the competing and disunited ruling classes in capitalism" and ultimately promoted and strengthened the economy and white rule.[9]

Members of the educated black elite – teachers, ministers of religion, lawyers, journalists, clerks and small-time businessmen – who had sought inclusion in the new state, were sadly disillusioned by the post-Anglo-Boer War settlement. While they had hoped to benefit from a British victory, the terms of the Peace of Vereeniging and the calculated indifference of the subsequent British administration, not to mention the intensification of certain aspects of legal discrimination, dispelled any such optimism. This, in turn, led to an upsurge in formal political activity after 1902, and various African organisations mushroomed during the reconstruction period in the often vain hope that they would be able to influence official decision making.

---

7   Warwick, *Black people and the South African War*, 10-14.

8   Warwick, *Black people and the South African War*, 25-26.

9   Kaplan, "The South African state: The origins of a racially exclusive democracy", *The Insurgent Sociologist*, X Fall, 1980,15.

A major blow was the constitution of the Union of South Africa. While certain Africans in the Cape continued to enjoy the qualified franchise, they were denied the right to sit in parliament. Their counterparts in the other former colonies fared even worse, remaining voteless and, in terms of formal political process, powerless. This development proved to be a further potent stimulus in promoting not only African political organisation but also unity, for the myriad of fledgling associations scattered across the country now started to cooperate formally at an intercolonial level. A manifestation of this new political activity was the deputation sent to Britain in 1909 to protest, albeit in vain, against the colour bar in the draft Union constitution. But of far greater and more enduring significance were the moves which led to the formation of a national body, the South African Native National Congress (SANNC), in 1912 to protect African interests.[10] The founding of the SANNC two years before the advent of the First World War meant that, at a formal level at least, African political opinion was consolidated. There was now one national body which could, within limits, exert itself on behalf of Africans in the subsequent tumultuous years. As will be shown, however, the SANNC represented only one strand of African opinion; outside the organised body of black politics there existed a whole gamut of often divergent viewpoints.

Immediately prior to the war, African political consciousness was also shaped by the momentous implications of the Natives' Land Act 27 of 1913. The act, which prompted a SANNC deputation to Britain, restricted black ownership of land to 7.3 percent of the total area of the Union, while the anti-squatting measures contained in the legislation caused hardships in certain areas amid the eviction of black sharecroppers and other tenants from white farms. Although the tenancy regulations of the act were not rigidly applied across the board, it had the effect of turning independent and semi-independent producers into wage labourers.[11] During the war years, the ramifications of this legislation were to surface in terms of the politics of black recruitment.

Legal restrictions relating to access to land were not the only source of African unrest. Indeed, in the immediate pre-war years there was a considerable ferment of protest activity. In the years 1912-1914, black women of Winburg and Bloemfontein launched a celebrated anti-pass campaign and a large-scale African strike occurred on the Jagersfontein diamond mines.[12] The Union government also feared possible industrial

---

10   Odendaal, *The founders: Origins of the ANC and the struggle for democracy in South Africa*, 259-286, 311-325, 455-473.

11   Bundy, *The rise and fall of the South African peasantry*, 242.

12   Simons and Simons, *Class and colour in South Africa, 1850-1950*, 136, 168.

action by blacks on the Witwatersrand gold mines. It appointed a commission during this period to investigate "native grievances" and, of greater importance, "to inquire into the control capable of being exercised over natives housed in compounds" and to suggest effective ways of coping with industrial disturbances.[13] However, there was neither African unrest nor strike action in progress when European hostilities broke out in August 1914. Had it been otherwise, it would almost certainly have complicated South Africa's entry into the war.

---

13   U.G. 37-14, *Report of the Native Grievances Inquiry, 1913-1914*, 1.

MIXED RESPONSES
TO THE
OUTBREAK OF WAR

While South Africa as a British dominion could technically not remain neutral and was therefore automatically at war with Germany once the British ultimatum had expired on 4 August 1914, the Union had the right to decide on the extent to which it was prepared to render to the imperial war effort. The government was faced with this decision three days after the declaration of war. On 7 August 1914, Britain approached South Africa to invade German South-West Africa (currently Namibia), to occupy Swakopmund and Luderitzbucht and to take over the German radio stations in the interior. The South African parliament was not in session at the time, but after initial differences of opinion in the cabinet, the Union government informed Britain on 10 August 1914 of its willingness to accede to the request. A month later at a special session of both houses of parliament the decision was confirmed by 92 votes to 12 in the Assembly and by 24 votes in the Senate. Various factors informed General Louis Botha's decision to invade German South-West Africa, perhaps the most important of which was the prospect of including the territory in the Union, though this was never openly acknowledged. Black people, of course, had no say in the decision to participate in the war, but in several other respects the decision had a direct bearing on them and was also to elicit varied responses.

White apprehensions

In parliament, National Party members were unanimous that country's participation in the war would weaken the dominant position of whites and present black people with an ideal opportunity of forcefully challenging the *status quo*. Amongst others, P.G.W. Grobler, member for Rustenburg, voiced this concern when he asked: "What would be the position if the able-bodied men went to war and a native rising took place?"[14] The National Party also had other reasons for opposing South Africa's entry into the war, including a marked reluctance to assist Britain, a sworn enemy in the Anglo-Boer War twelve years earlier, against Germany, which was sympathetically inclined toward the republics. It may therefore be argued that they only raised the possibility of an African uprising to strengthen their case. However, it is significant that even within Botha's cabinet similar fears were expressed. F.S. Malan, Minister of Mining, Industry and Education, initially maintained that besides other considerations, the Union would require the full extent of its military power to defend the whites against possible black insurrections.[15]

Outside of parliament a persistent and pervasive atmosphere of apprehension and insecurity amongst both Afrikaans and English speakers is even more pertinently recognisable. As far as Afrikaans speakers were concerned, these fears were best reflected in the misgivings of a Boer woman from the Marico district in the Transvaal:

> Our defence force is being sent to GSWA, and here we sit amongst all the black people ... Already the servant girls are talking amongst themselves, saying that the kaffirs [sic] are only waiting till the majority of menfolk are away from the farms and then they would use the opportunity.[16]

Such views were echoed by Afrikaans speakers throughout large parts of South Africa; from Senekal, Ficksburg and Ladybrand in the Free State to Barkly East, Klipplaat and Postmastburg in the Cape Province. Some English speakers in Johannesburg and Port Elizabeth were similarly concerned, whilst in Natal, where the white population was outnumbered ten to one, fears that "the natives will use the opportunity to rise and murder the whites in their houses" were particularly pronounced.[17] White perceptions in this respect were based on what they considered to be historical precedents: thus Afrikaans speakers referred to attacks by blacks on Boer commandos during the

---

14 *House of Assembly Debates*, 10 September 1914, col. 82.

15 F.S. Malan Collection, 65, Notes on 'De Brits-Duitse Oorlog', 7 August 1914.

16 *De Volkstem*, 25 September 1914 ("Vrees voor de Kaffers"). Translation.

17 P.M. 1/1/145, C.J. Lotter to Botha, 6 August 1914 and A.J.H. Vorster to Botha, 25 August 1914; P.M. 1/1/148, A.H. Lamprecht to Botha, 25 September 1914; S.A.P. 6/245/14/16, Assistant Commissioner of Police Bloemfontein to Secretary South African Police Pretoria, 10 August 1914; D.C. 623/194/9199, Secretary of the Divisional Council Barkly East to Provincial Secretary Cape Town, 12 September 1914 (copy); J.X. Merriman Collection, 560, E. Sheppard to Merriman, 30 December 1914; *Church Times*, 11 September 1914 ("South Africa and the Empire"); S.N.A. 1/4/25/c/13/1914, Magistrate Estcourt to Chief Native Commissioner, 12 September 1914. (The quotation is from the last document.)

Anglo-Boer War of 1899 to 1902, and English speakers turned to the Bambatha rebellion of 1906 in Natal to justify their apprehensions.[18]

Although black people, as will be indicated later in this chapter, were not completely quiescent at the outbreak of war, fears of conspiracies "to drive the whites into the sea"[19] were grossly exaggerated and gained greater currency through persistent rumour. "Of course", J.C. Smuts as Minister of Defence remarked, "one hears a good many rumours, but in times like the present one was always bound to hear rumours [to] which one could not attach too much attention".[20] Rumours are common in times of war and stress, serving as an early warning system to pre-empt possible threats and to maintain existing patterns of social cohesion.[21] Some black commentators interpreted these rumours in their own way; S.M. Makgatho of the Transvaal Native Congress observed: "The white men often say there will be native risings. It is because of their consciences and the sin in the hearts of whites."[22] Others objected to being made the focal point of what they regarded white insecurities, and publicly protested against the "unfair and unjustifiable action on the part of the Europeans always to invoke 'native unrest' whenever there are disturbances amongst themselves".[23]

While the Union government as such was not unduly concerned about the possibility of an African uprising at the outbreak of war, it nevertheless sought it prudent to monitor and influence African reactions where possible. In a confidential circular to all the officials of the Native Affairs Department, magistrates and district commandants of the South African police, Botha emphasised the importance of keeping black people peaceful. These officials were instructed to move about among the people and to notify the government immediately of "any untoward occurrences".[24] A perfunctory attempt was also made to soften the blow of the Natives' Land Act 27 of 1913 by a belated directive that, where legally possible, farmers should refrain from evicting

---

18 *House of Assembly Debates*, 10 September 1914, col. 82; S.N.A. 1/4/25/c/13/1914, Magistrate Estcourt to Chief Native Commissioner, 12 September 1914.

19 J.X. Merriman Collection, 560, E. Sheppard to Merriman, 30 December 1914.

20 *House of Assembly Debates*, 10 September 1914, col. 88.

21 Brown, *Understanding race relations*, 58.

22 N.A. 108/521, Report on a meeting of the Transvaal Native Congress, 19 June 1921.

23 *Tsala ea Batho*, 6 June 1915 ("A native protest").

24 S.A.P. 6/245/14/17, Confidential and urgent circular, 12 August 1914; J. 205/474/14, Confidential and urgent circular, 15 August 1914; G.N.L.B. 192/1329/14/48, Message to the Native population, 21 August 1914; *Imvo Zabantsundu*, 25 August 1914 ("Natives and the War").

Africans from their farms. Furthermore, numerous posters and handbills were printed for distribution amongst the African population, informing them that any movement of South African soldiers which they might witness was only to protect the interests of blacks and whites alike. This was obviously intended to counteract possible African expectations that white influence in the country was being diminished by the withdrawal of troops. In addition, Africans were urged to believe only in "true government messages" and to discount any untruthful reports which might cause "unrest in their minds".

It is difficult to assess the overall effect of these measures on African perceptions at the outbreak of war, but at least some prominent members of the educated black elite welcomed these initiatives. J.L. Dube, president of the SANNC, interpreted it as a hopeful sign that the government was concerned about the welfare of the African population and that Africans were regarded as sufficiently important to be taken into its confidence. He commented:

> The native mind has been composed at a juncture when it might be parti-
> cularly susceptible to vague alarms, but the black population has received
> the assurance of the Government's readiness to afford every information as
> to events, and to take natives into their confidence regarding any measures
> affecting them ... Perhaps a good deal of trouble might have been averted
> in the past if such measures had been more systematically adopted, since it
> has always been the complaint of the intelligent natives that they have been
> kept in the dark on subjects of national concern: but the Government are now
> carrying out a less reticent policy.[25]

However, other educated Africans had their reservations. With a vague sense of unease an anonymous African newspaper correspondent from Natal questioned the government's motives. "It is not often that the Government takes the trouble to give the Natives general news about what is taking place", he wrote. "The natives naturally ask, why this ... time?"[26]

Responses of the African elite

As an indication of the more general response of the educated black elite at the outbreak of war, the position adopted by the SANNC is of particular interest. The SANNC was in session in Bloemfontein when the news was conveyed that hostilities

---

25 *Ilanga Lase Natal*, 28 August 1914 ("Native tranquillity").
26 *Ilanga Lase Natal*, 25 September 1914 ("Unsettled Native minds").

had broken out in Europe. Congress immediately affirmed its loyalty to the British king and empire, pledging to suspend all public criticism of the Union government and to desist from agitation in connection with the Natives' Land Act 27 of 1913. A delegation further assured the authorities of African support for the duration of the conflict.[27] This policy, as well as the outbreak of war itself, of course meant that the work of the deputation in Britain protesting against the Natives' Land Act 27 of 1913 was terminated. Although it was abundantly clear even before August 1914 that the British government was not prepared to pressurise the Union cabinet, the wistful belief nevertheless persisted for a considerable period amongst certain SANNC members that the deputation "might have had a real effect had not the First World War been declared in the midst of that agitation".[28]

At the time though, the SANNC's conformist stance was not shared by everyone. J.T. Gumede, a more militant member, considered it essential to keep up criticism of the South African government despite the war. He argued in March 1915 that such a policy would be more beneficial to African interests "than the present attitude of folding their hands in idle talk of the war, which they have no right to claim as theirs ..."[29] Later, the SANNC's policy was subjected to even more scathing comment. For Albert Nzula, writing in 1933 as a member of the South African Communist Party, the decision of the SANNC to remain loyal during the war was the first act of betrayal by the "chiefs and petit bourgeois native good boys" which weakened the "liberationist struggles of the native people".[30]

The arguments advanced by Gumede and, particularly, Nzula illustrate the precarious position of a body like the SANNC Since it operated through constitutional channels, it was ultimately dependent on official goodwill and could hardly have afforded to alienate the authorities on such a major issue as the war. It would be misguided though to construe this loyalist response and cooperative stance simply as an indication of passive acceptance of a subservient position. Given their limited range of options to bring about constitutional change, the SANNC leaders regarded loyalty during the war as an additional method to be utilised. In openly proclaiming a common allegiance to the British crown, they expected in due course to be rewarded for their loyalty. They

---

27 G.N.L.B. 187/1217 /14/D 110, SANNC to Minister of Native Affairs, 6 August 1914; *Tsala ea Batho*, 22 August 1914 ("SANNC resolutions"); Plaatje, *Native life*, 260-61; Walshe, *African nationalism*, 51-52.

28 *Contact*, 3, 7, 2 April 1960, Interview with Selby Msimang.

29 *Izwe La Kiti*, 17 March 1915 ("The Native question").

30 A.T. Nzula and others, *Forced labour in colonial Africa*, 205.

also hoped that such an attitude might enable them to pressurise the South African authorities into granting meaningful recognition. In this respect, they were given a degree of assurance by the government. F.S. Malan, acting as Minister of Native Affairs at the time, approvingly told a delegation from the SANNC in October 1914 that they had taken a "very wise step" at the outbreak of war "which would be likely to impress Parliament to consider their cause sympathetically".[31] Moreover, they had implicit trust in the ability of the British government to effect favourable change. This clearly influenced their view that an event as cataclysmic as the First World War would change the nature of the empire, with corresponding benefits accruing to the African population.[32] The African elite, as Dube explained later, "were not loyal because their treatment was good in South Africa, but because they wanted to show that they were loyal and that they were deserving of fair and just treatment".[33] He claimed that the African elite was "far too loyal to England to entertain for one moment the idea of active resistance to the laws of this country".

The African elite furthermore came under the spell of British war propaganda, which claimed that Britain was fighting on behalf of the oppressed and weak (Belgium), as well as for the protection of democratic ideals like personal freedom and equality. Members of the SANNC were quick to equate this with their own position in South Africa and to express the hope that once the freedom of Europe had been guaranteed, Britain would also demand an alleviation of the plight of Africans in the Union.[34] War propaganda, however, is seldom translated into reality and, moreover, the propaganda during the war was intended for a European and not an African audience.

In another respect, though, the black elite drew sharper conclusions from the European conflagration. In considering the devastation wrought by the war, they voiced criticism of the assumed cultural and moral superiority of whites, often invoked in South Africa to justify racial dominance. The outbreak of the war brought into sharp relief the weaknesses of the much vaunted white civilisation and culture. Hence, its credibility as a model to which every educated African should aspire became somewhat tarnished. D.D.T. Jabavu, son of the well-known newspaper editor, Tengo

---

31   G.N.L.B. 187/1217/14/D 110, Report of a meeting with the acting Minister of Native Affairs, 31 October 1914.

32   *Ilanga Lase Natal*, 5 March 1915 ("The native disposition"); *Ilanga Lase Natal*, 9 October 1914 ("Native loyalty"); *Tsala ea Batho*, 12 December 1914 ("Native loyalty").

33   *Cape Times*, 17 March 1917 ("Mr. Dube's speech").

34   Qualter, *Propaganda and psychological warfare*, 55-58; *Ilanga Lase Natal*, 6 April 1917 ("A worthy defence").

Jabavu, later pointed out that "the Bantu were taken by surprise that the European nations who led in education and Christianity should find no other means than the sword and accumulated destructive weapons to settle their diplomatic differences".[35] Consequently, the hope was expressed amongst the elite that "perhaps, when the war is over there will be less boasting of the supposed civilisation that lays so great a burden on the people".[36]

Dissenting African views

Black reactions to the outbreak of war must not only be gauged in terms of the over-whelming loyalist rhetoric from the educated elite. They were a small fraction of black society and their views did not necessarily reflect opinions and perceptions of the majority of illiterate and semi-literate blacks. In addition, as has been demonstrated for the rest of Africa during the First World War, the relative passivity of the educated black elite during the war often concealed the "ferment in the rest of society".[37] It is therefore essential to explore the way in which other African social groupings in South Africa responded to the outbreak of war.

In contrast with the loyal response of the educated elite, dissenting views were expressed by the African working class on the Witwatersrand gold mines. They were quick to draw their own conclusions from the European struggle and relate them to their experiences on the mines. Britain was associated with the oppressive system in which they found themselves and therefore Germany was seen as worthy of their sympathies. On the Nourse mines, L. Ralitane informed his fellow labourers that "the Germans are beating the English, and you boys are foolish to work for the English when the Germans are giving them a hiding" (Ralitane's "inflammatory" views earned him the option of a £25 fine or six months' imprisonment).[38] Another labourer expressed his animosity even more trenchantly. "God be with Germany and clear out all Englishmen on earth", was his fervent wish. "Indeed", he continued, "if the German came out in South A.[frica] we shall be glad if we can help them too".[39]

---

35   Jabavu, "Native unrest in South Africa", *International Review of Missions*, 1922, 254.

36   *Ilanga Lase Natal*, 27 November 1914 ("Civilization demands").

37   Rathbone, "World War I and Africa: Introduction", *Journal of African History*, XIX(1): 5.

38   G.N.L.B. 192/1329/14/D 48, Copy of a report by the compound manager, 18 November 1914; *Tsala ea Batho*, 21 November 1914 ("Seditious language").

39   G.N.L.B. 192/1329/14/D 48, Anonymous letter intercepted by Native Affairs Department, 6 September 1914.

Moreover, some mine workers also perceived that the war held out opportunities for resistance against the repressive system in which they found themselves. The chief compound manager at the Crown mines reported in September 1914:

> I notice a great change the last weeks in the attitude of the natives towards Europeans, the natives being very cheeky and insubordinate. They appear ... to have the idea that the Government are in difficulties owing to the war and are in consequence weak and frightened of the natives ...[40]

Occasionally, such perceptions also contributed to explicit acts of resistance on the mines. On the Geduld mine, for example, black mine workers withdrew their labour, or deserted as the management viewed it, at a rate of 60 men per week during October 1914. A subsequent investigation revealed that these actions were inspired by rumours that South Africa's war involvement had weakened the government's hold over Africans and thus presented mine workers with a chance of escaping from a hostile environment.[41]

Outside the Witwatersrand, in gold mining areas like Pilgrim's Rest, the attitudes of mine workers towards the war were likewise being shaped by the harshness of their daily experiences. From Pilgrim's Rest "extreme dissatisfaction amongst the natives" was reported, "due to the treatment meted out to them over a period of many years by the Transvaal Gold Mining Estates Ltd". As a result, the report continued, "the sympathies did not seem very much against the idea of the British regime being deposed (a feeling which is shared by many natives who have suffered at the hands of the Transvaal Gold Mining Estates Ltd)".[42] The attitude of these mine workers was a far cry from the stereotype that Africans generally favoured and supported Britain at the outbreak of the war.

Amongst other categories of workers, too, the outbreak of war was perceived as an appropriate occasion to voice anti-white sentiments and to demonstrate the lack of black support for the war effort. In response to the government's circular that Africans should be loyal during the war, an anonymous manual labourer from Johannesburg wrote: "We are no friends of the whites. When you, the whites, are in a fix you begin to recognise us as your friends ... The war is not ours but yours." He regarded it as preposterous that whites who treated Africans "more or less like dogs" should

---

40 S.A.P. 6/245/14/37, copy of a report by the compound manager, 4 September 1914.

41 G.N.L.B. 192/1329/14/D 48, Rex versus T.M. Paulsen, 10 November 1914; *Transvaal Leader*, 13 November 1914 ("Fruits of sedition").

42 J. 196/3/317/14, J. Cullen and others to Assistant Magistrate Pilgrim's Rest, 22 May 1915.

suddenly in a time of crisis be concerned about black friendship.[43] Some black male domestics, the so-called houseboys in colonial parlance, harboured similar feelings. They pinned their hopes on British defeats "all along the line", which they argued would mean an increasing number of white men leaving Johannesburg for the front and a corresponding weakening of white control over African lives.[44] At a later stage, Ben Machumela, a waiter in Rosebank, interpreted the war in even more drastic terms. In April 1917, he declared unequivocally: "If we rise against the white people now we shall triumph over them, because the Germans too are drowning them in the water."[45] Although such an interpretation of war time occurrences was obviously mistaken, the way in which these black workers perceived and experienced such events is of some significance.

A more militant pattern of response was not confined to the largely urban proletariat. In rural Natal, for example, there were peasants who viewed the war as a source of new opportunities to be exploited. The wartime predicament of Britain and South Africa meant little to them – they were more concerned about ways in which the war could possibly alleviate their own plight. Decidedly pro-German sympathies surfaced rapidly. Some peasants associated the British with the white colonisation of Natal; if Britain could be defeated, it was argued, their position might also change. From their perspective any change in the established order was regarded as preferable to the existing dispensation. In the Harding district, for instance, it was a "current topic of conversation ... that a German force is coming here and the consensus of opinion is that the natives should assist them to fight the English. It is said that if the natives help the Germans to kill the English, they will give natives back the land".[46] Likewise, in the Umzinto district "it was common talk at beer drinking parties that the Germans were to land and that they would restore to them the Natives the lands the English had taken from them, and for this reason the natives ... should assist the Germans ..."[47] Furthermore, an elderly Zulu in Durban was quite explicit that the Germans were "fighting for the right, because the Germans say that the English are taking all the

---

43 G.N.L.B. 192/1329/14/D 48, Anonymous intercepted letter, date stamped 3 September 1914.

44 G.N.L.B. 192/1329/14/D 72, H.E. Mathie to J.C. Smuts, 27 October 1914.

45 S.A.P. 6/499/17/2, letter from Ben Machumela intercepted and translated by the Native Affairs Department, 9 April 1917.

46 J. 205/14/467/14, Sworn declaration by S. Sincuba, 26 September 1914.

47 S.N.A. 1/4/25/.c/2/1915, Magistrate Umzinto to Chief Native Commissioner Natal, 26 January 1915.

native places away. It is true what the Germans say ... because our place has been robbed by the English people."[48]

Clearly, there was a groundswell of opinion that stood in contradistinction to the position which the elite adopted. But one must also be careful of reading too much radical intent into these statements. Ultimately, the belief in German salvation was not that far removed from the belief in elitist circles that support for Britain would yield dividends. Both points of views, in different ways, were based on hope rather than reality.

African responses at the outbreak of the war also found expression in millenarian fantasies. These combined religious and political strands in African life and were manifested in prophecies about the second coming and the commencement of a golden era in which Africans would be delivered from white domination. In the Pieter-maritzburg district, one S. Nkabindi gained a considerable following as a prophet, predicting that the whites in South Africa would be annihilated by the Germans, who would then restore the land to its rightful African owners.[49] Somewhat different in content, though not in spirit, was the prediction of an anonymous prophet in the Dundee district who claimed that Dinuzulu (former head of the Zulu royal house who had died in 1913 after being deposed in 1909 and sentenced to four years imprisonment for his part in the Zulu rebellion of 1906) was still alive and that the Germans would bring him to South Africa and reinstate him as the supreme African ruler.[50] Millenarianism also surfaced on the Witwatersrand, where prophets interpreted the outbreak of the war as an omen that Africans should rid themselves of acquired Western customs in preparation for the dawn of a new era in which they would once again rule in their own land.[51] These manifestations of millenarianism are of interest since such movements usually reflect a pessimism about the efficacy of human agencies and a belief that social transformations can only come about by cataclysmic means.[52] It was the politics of the last chance.

---

48   *Rand Daily Mail*, 10 August 1914 ("Zulu gives his version of how the war started").

49   C.N.C. 247/1196, Chief Native Commissioner Natal to Attorney General Natal, 10 August 1914.

50   S.A.P. 6/245/14/37, District Commandant Dundee to Commissioner of Police, Pietermaritzburg, 6 September 1914 (copy).

51   *Transvaal Leader*, 8 April 1915 ("Native prophets").

52   Shepperson, "The comparative study of millenarian movements", 44.

Others had less faith in outside intervention or salvation, and perceived the war as an opportunity to deliver themselves from bondage. The magistrate of the Greytown district in Natal declared explicitly:

> Certain natives are going amongst the tribes ... saying that now the English are at war with another nation, you have a good chance to fight them, as England cannot send men to assist. Why should you forever be under a contract to a white man? What are you to do? Your chance to ease your burdens is to fight the white man and get your country back.[53]

From the same district, the police reported towards the end of August 1914 that "there have been several remarks passed by the Natives ... here to the effect that 'Now is the time' ..."[54] Of course it must be kept in mind that at the outbreak of the war whites were prone to exaggerate the possibility of African uprisings, but in these particular cases there is no reason to doubt the veracity of the reports. Nevertheless, to have implemented these ideas would have required a sustained level of organisation and mobilisation, as well as a focussing of discontent on some central issue. In the absence of such prerequisites, no widespread concerted mass action occurred in 1914, but this does not detract from the logic of African perceptions that the outbreak of war weakened the state and thus offered an opportunity to strike at the system.

On one particular occasion, African peasants did in fact attempt forcibly to exploit the situation brought about by the war. Between 12 and 19 November an uprising occurred in the Matatiele, Mount Fletcher and Mount Frere districts of East Griqualand (the northernmost part of the then Transkeian territories) when two to three thousand peasants destroyed cattle dipping tanks and burnt and looted a number of trading stores. The situation seemed critical at the time and the whites in the countryside hastily fled into the town for protection. The chief magistrate, W.T. Brownlee, immediately acted to reassert white dominance in the district; every available member of the Citizen Force was called out, armed, and rushed by motor car to the scene of disaffection. Confronted by the armed might of their white overlords, open resistance on the part of the peasants petered out. A subsequent report revealed that they were seriously aggrieved at the way in which the authorities applied compulsory cattle dipping regulations against the tick-born disease East Coast fever. Although the area was not declared fever stricken, African peasants were nevertheless forced to comply

---

53   J. 205/4/467/14, Report of the Magistrate of Greytown, 18 August 1914.

54   S.A.P. 6/245/14/37, District Commandant Greytown to Commissioner of Police Pretoria, 31 August 1914.

with the dipping regulations. In addition, they had to make weekly payments for such dippings, whilst white farmers of greater financial means managed to evade these regulations with impunity. Moreover, opposition to cattle dipping also had a political dimension in that peasants experienced compulsory dipping as a drastic intervention in traditional rural life, which emphasised their inability to exercise control over the way in which they were governed.

Dipping regulations were admittedly the focal point of the revolt, but the timing of peasant resistance to these measures is of considerable significance in assessing African responses. The revolt took place at a time when white authority in the Transkei was particularly vulnerable, since many policemen had been drafted into the South African Defence Force. From a series of meetings held prior to the revolt, it is clear that the withdrawal of a substantial section of the police had not gone unnoticed amongst the peasants. With the attention of the authorities diverted by hostilities elsewhere, the opportunity for meaningful resistance had presented itself. Though more armed men turned out to quell the revolt than they had anticipated, it is still significant that they considered the outbreak of war as an opportune time to attempt to rid themselves of the obligations imposed by the authorities.[55]

Conclusion

Responses by Africans to the outbreak of the war ranged, then, from declarations of loyalty through to expressions of anti-white sentiment, millenarianism, and contemplated or actual revolt. Reflecting the complex diversity of African society, these responses all began in a general awareness of a possible shift in power relationships due to the war. However, not all African groups demonstrated this awareness of the changing situation. For some, the war was merely a white man's quarrel. It was reported that: "The feeling came to be pretty common amongst them

---

55   This account is based on C.M.T. 3/926/778/2, Official government report, 8 December 1914 (published as 3-15, *Union of South Africa, Senate, Report of the Government's Special Commissioner*, April 1915); S.A.P. 6/245/14/209, Police and Magistrate's reports, 31 October, 10 to 21 November, 1914; C.O. 551/62/45389, Buxton to Harcourt, 17 November 1914; S.N.A. 1/4/25/c/16/1914, Chief Native Commissioner Natal to Native Affairs Department Pretoria, 19 November 1914; *Imvo Zabantsundu*, 15 November 1914 ("Matatiele troubles"); *Territorial News*, 28 November 1914 ("Matatiele matters"); *Cape Times*, 25 November 1914 ("Unrest among the natives"); *Cape Times*, 26 November 1914 ("The native unrest"); W.T. Brownlee, *Reminiscences of a Transkeian*, 3; Bundy, "Dissidents, detectives and the dipping revolt: Social control and collaboration in East Griqualand in 1914", Centre for Southern African Studies, University of York, Seminar paper, 1982.

that this was only one more of those wars to which the Europeans, who ought to know better, were accustomed, and that it was not in any vital sense a Bantu concern".[56] In as far as these Africans were informed about the war, the possible implications passed them by. They had, outwardly at least, come to terms with white dominance and the forms of government under which they had to live. Whatever happened in the war, it would not really affect them. In a resigned way, a Transkeian chief explained: "The Umlungu [white man] has come here to stay, and we know well enough by this time that nothing will move him".[57]

---

56   Shepherd, *Lovedale, South Africa: The story of a century*, 323.

57   Callaway, "Umlungu: or the European in South Africa", 196.

POLITICS OF
BLACK PARTICIPATION
IN THE WAR

In the past, as indeed in the present, military establishments have assiduously cultivated the image of non-partisan concern with the protection and defence of all layers of society. Although the organisation and composition of the armed forces may stem in part from specific military requirements, ultimately their nature is determined by the power structures and prejudices prevalent in the society from which they emerge. Particularly in critical times of war, when the armed forces assume a central role and there is a greater fusion between military and civilian affairs, military establishments become even less immune from wider social tensions. It is against this background that the interactive process between the military and society is explored, by focusing on the discourses surrounding the involvement of South African black people and war, and by analysing the nature of the responses it gave rise to.

To arm or not to arm?

Article 7 of the South African Defence Force Act 13 of 1912 specified that Africans could be called upon to enrol as non-combatants, but the obligation to do armed service was restricted to persons of European descent.[58]

The decision that whites alone should carry the burden of defence was not, as implied by certain parliamentarians during the discussion of the bill in 1911 and 1912, inspired by magnanimity.[59] On the contrary, the exclusion of blacks was a direct result of the apprehensions which permeated white society. If black men were allowed to join

---

58   *Acts of the Union of South Africa*, 1912, Act 13 of 1912.

59   *House of Assembly Debates*, 23 February 1912, col. 651 (Colonel C.P. Crewe).

the Defence Force on a basis of equality in an armed capacity, it was feared that the existing nature of social relations might be threatened, and the position of the white minority jeopardised by black people who had been trained in the use of firearms. During the parliamentary debate on this act, it emerged clearly that the training of black troops "would only be a menace" and that it "would be an immoral thing in South Africa to place black and white troops on the same footing".[60] J.B. Wessels (National Party Member of Parliament for Bethlehem) explained this so-called immorality of the issue at a later stage in parliament when he asked: did they realise that the coloured man, when he donned uniform, said to the white man, "I am now your equal – the equal of your wives and children"?[61] And from a 'security' point of view, P.A. Silburn, a contemporary military writer and Unionist Party member of parliament for Durban Point, maintained that "to teach and encourage the use of the rifle by native races may result in trouble if not disaster".[62]

Intimately related to these concerns were the perceived objectives and functions of the Defence Force. The military was not merely conceived in terms of a safeguard against external threats, but was also seen as a force to be deployed in the event of black insurrection. Although the Committee of Imperial Defence, in a memorandum on the defence of South Africa in 1911, considered the possibility of a black uprising as remote, the "danger of internal native disturbances" could not be lost sight of.[63] Major General G. Aston, the British military adviser involved in formulating the Defence Force Act, largely saw the role of the Defence Force in this light, whilst General J.C. Smuts as Minister of Defence declared explicitly when the bill first came up for discussion in March 1911: "If they had a scheme of defence, by which they insured themselves against those internal native troubles which might arise in South Africa, they would have done a good day's work".[64] Right from the outset the establishment of the Union Defence Force was in part an effort to maintain and bolster the established domestic order.

The nature and implications of South Africa's first Defence Force Act did not go unnoticed in black political circles. Exclusion from the Defence Force was regarded as yet another discriminatory act and was one of the grievances cited at the time of

---

60   *House of Assembly Debates*, 8 March 1911, col. 1658 (T. Smuts).

61   *Cape Times*, 21 March 1917 ("Parliamentary debates").

62   Silburn, *The colonies and imperial defence*, 193.

63   C.A.B. 512179-C, South Africa, Memorandum by the Committee of Imperial Defence, 3 May 1911.

64   *House of Assembly Debates*, 1 March 1911, col. 1473.

the founding of the SANNC in 1912.[65] Furthermore, according to T.L. Schreiner, Unionist member of parliament for Tembuland who often tried to act as a spokesman for black people in parliament, unspecified newspapers were perturbed about the projected role of the Defence Force as an additional coercive arm of the state in its relations with Africans.[66] Indeed, some showed a keen awareness of the significance of defence developments. *Ilanga Lase Natal* pointedly commented: "The Defence Force Act ... was originally intended to terrorise the Natives who had been all along looked upon as enemies of the peace. Of course, we have never been deceived, and we know why this Force was organised."[67]

With the advent of the war, the African elite hoped that the exigencies of war would create sufficient openings in the Defence Force edifice to allow the entry of blacks, but in the event the foundations and structures of the military establishment were to remain firmly intact. Thus, an offer by the honorary president of the SANNC, W.B. Rubusana, to raise 5 000 black men for combatant army service, elicited the following candid reply from the secretary of defence:

> I am to refer you to the Provision of Section 7 of the South African Defence Act 1912, and to state that the Government does not desire to avail itself of the services in a combatant capacity, of citizens not of European descent in the present hostilities. Apart from other considerations the present war is one which has its origin among the white people of Europe, and the Government are anxious to avoid the employment of coloured citizens in a warfare against whites.[68]

The underlying meaning of the unspecified "other considerations" is not hard to detect in the light of the preoccupations which informed the Defence Force Act; in all likelihood it referred to white perceptions of the possible 'harmful' repercussions of arming blacks. Such sensibilities amongst South African whites were well recognised by A. Bonar Law, the secretary of colonies in 1915, who stated that

> no proposal for training Natives upon a large scale is likely to be acceptable to ... the British and Dutch inhabitants of the Union, as the return, after peace, of

---

65 Walshe, *African Nationalism*, 30-31.

66 *House of Assembly Debates*, 26 February 1912, cols. 673-674.

67 *Ilanga Lase Natal*, 8 October 1915 ("A scandal").

68 D.C. 623/190/9199, W.B. Rubusana to Minister of Native Affairs, 20 October 1914, and Secretary of Defence to W.B. Rubusana, 6 November 1914. A copy of the letter appears in Plaatje, *Native life*, 281.

a large body of trained and disciplined men would create obvious difficulties and might seriously menace the supremacy of the whites.[69]

It might be argued that had the war impinged more tangibly on white South Africans, perhaps to the extent that they had to face German domination in the country, the authorities might well, in order to bolster defence, have given greater thought to arming black men. This, however, is speculative. In 1916, when the Colonial Office, urged by the War Office, did tentatively approach the South African government on the possibility of raising an armed black corps for service in Europe, the South African reaction was predictable: under no condition would the government allow a black combatant force to proceed to Europe, as this could endanger white South Africa. The Colonial Office accepted this reply without demur and the War Office acquiesced.[70] This response is perhaps not surprising, for although the British government was hard pressed for manpower, there were strong reservations in relevant quarters in Britain which echoed South African concerns that

> there would be no more peace for South Africa if it were to be put in the power of the natives to say to the Whites there: 'You tried to beat your White enemies in Europe without us, but you failed and had to call us in to finish the war'. The moral effect throughout the Union of sending native contingents to fight on the battlefields of Europe would be incalculably disastrous to the prestige of the Whites there.[71]

The issue of non-combatant participation

In contrast to objections against the arming of blacks, their use in a non-combatant capacity in South-West Africa and German East Africa did not provoke any criticism. In part, this can be ascribed to the established precedent that blacks, as unarmed workers, had previously and without any qualms on the part of the authorities, been employed in South African wars like the Anglo-Boer War, where both sides utilised non-combatant blacks.

Moreover, the structure of the division of labour between black and white in the Union also offered a partial 'explanation'. "To plough, to dig, to hoe, to fetch and carry, to

---

69 C.O. 537/604/46680, Secret memorandum by A. Bonar Law for the Cabinet on the raising and training of Native troops, 18 October 1915.

70 C.O. 616/64/60190, Memorandum on steps taken to increase the supply of Coloured troops and Coloured labour, 14 December 1916.

71 *South Africa*, 18 November 1917 ("As labourers only").

cook – all laborious and menial toil is the duty of the black man. The average white man would consider it degrading to be seen doing any of these things", according to Maurice Evans, a contemporary sociologist of the time.[72] This assumption shaped military policy to the extent that in the German East African campaign General Smuts considered it imperative to employ blacks as labourers, "as white men cannot be asked to perform work associated with Natives".[73]

Furthermore, the use of blacks as non-combatant labourers, as opposed to armed soldiers, in colonial territories was also ideologically acceptable. Not only did the orthodox black-white relationship remain undisturbed, but there was also less of a chance that black men might lay claim to political and social equality on account of having served in the same armed capacity as whites. Sol Plaatje recognised this when he stated that "it seems to have occurred to the authorities that the best course is to engage the Natives in a capacity in which their participation will demand no recognition".[74] Of course, service in the colonial territories also meant that there was little chance of black South Africans being exposed to significantly different ideological influences so that the risk of posing a threat to white supremacy was considerably reduced.

Nevertheless, a major feature of black South African involvement in the war was the employment of Africans as labourers outside colonial territories in the main theatre abroad. The initiative for this development came from the imperial government and at first consideration was given to the use of South African black people in Britain, but eventually France was decided upon.

On account of the enormous loss of life on the Western Front, more and more voices were raised in Britain in 1916, advocating that Africans be enrolled to alleviate the threatening manpower shortage. The intention was that blacks should replace labourers in Britain and France so as to release more whites for active service. In some quarters, the raising of an auxiliary arm of a million black troops from Africa was mooted and the idea was widely discussed in influential British newspapers.[75]

---

72 Evans, *Black and white in South East Africa*, 155.

73 WWI I.S.D. 6/43, Smuts to Buxton, 28 August 1916 (copy).

74 Plaatje, *Native life*, 268.

75 *Daily Chronicle*, 27 October 1916 ("The Empire's native races and the war"); *Daily Chronicle*, 30 October 1916 ("Manpower from Africa"); *The Times*, 29 July 1916 ("Natives and the war"); *The Times*, 4 August 1916 ("Natives as labourers"); *The Times*, 22 November 1916 ("Native labourers"); D. Stuart-Stephens, "Our million black army!" in *The English Review*, October 1916, 353-360.

In the House of Commons none other than Winston Churchill, then a Liberal Party member of parliament, argued:

> Consider all the services in the Army which might be rendered by natives, thereby releasing white men in full efficiency for the fighting line. Their interests are identified with ours. The result of this War will settle the fate of the African population as much as it will our own.[76]

Another Liberal Member of Parliament, Josiah Wedgwood (who had been a magistrate in the Eastern Transvaal after the Anglo-Boer War) strongly supported Churchill on this issue and his views were also publicised in the South African press.[77]

However, in the Colonial Office these suggestions met with little enthusiasm and the idea of employing black South African labourers in Britain was given short shrift; objections were raised on the grounds of race, discipline, efficiency and housing. In addition, British trade unions were implacably opposed to the possible displacement of their members by foreign workers.[78]

Although South African black people were not to be used in Britain, large-scale military offensives in France during 1916 and the urgent need for manpower to maintain the infrastructure required for these operations decisively influenced the decision to use African labour in France. In March 1916, the commander of the British forces in France, General D. Haig, emphasised the dire shortage of labour:

> It is not possible for us to work the quarries and forests in this country until we get more Labour Battalions for this purpose. Labour is our great difficulty, and it is an increasing one, owing to the very extended front recently taken over by me from the French.[79]

The British military authorities estimated in August 1916 that they needed an additional 60 900 labourers in France. With the War Office continuously clamouring for more manpower, the Colonial Office reluctantly agreed, after obtaining the approval of the French government, to the use of South African blacks as workers in France. H. Lambert, a senior Colonial Office official, regarded "the whole thing

---

76 *British Parliamentary Debates (House of Commons)*, col. 2024, 23 May 1916.

77 *British Parliamentary Debates (House of Commons)*, cols. 495-96, 1530-37, 25 July and 3 August 1916; *Rand Daily Mail*, 16 August 1916 ("Use of black troops, Major Wedgwood's views").

78 C.O. 551/90/31484, Notes on proposed Native Labour for England, 4 July 1916; C.A.B. 42/46/7, Memorandum on the importation of labour from abroad, December 1916.

79 M.U.N. 4/6527, General D. Haig to W. Runciman, 26 March 1916.

as an experiment and a very doubtful and hazardous one"; he considered it "a pity that we could not have managed without employing them [black South Africans] in Europe".[80]

If the Colonial Office was perturbed about the scheme, it is not surprising that the South African government was even more so. The government recognised the wartime need for labour, but to send black people to a European country in the turmoil of war meant that they might be exposed to less inhibited contact between black and white. It was considered an undertaking fraught with danger for the existing ideological order. Whereas service in colonial territories presented no problem, white South Africans were, as H. Sloley (a former resident commissioner in Basutoland and at the time of the First World War a member of the Aborigines' Protection Society) explained

> particularly concerned with the question of whether the natives, by their experience in the new environment and under new political and social conditions, would not be entirely unfitted to return to their homes and resume, contentedly and usefully, their former status and position in the South African community.[81]

In his negotiations with the British government, Prime Minister Botha emphasised that "the employment of Natives in Foreign parts may result in social evils or difficulties on their return by reason of the freedom of social intercourse with other races". The cabinet thus viewed the scheme "with great interest and no little anxiety".[82]

The South African government clearly had deep-seated reservations, but nevertheless informed the British that they were willing to raise a black labour contingent for service in France. Why did they agree to such a scheme, despite the fact that they were extremely uneasy about its possible ramifications? In order to explain this apparent paradox, it is necessary to look at the underlying reasons which prompted their decision.

An important factor was the acceptance of the precondition for participation insisted on by the South African government. The proposed contingent had to be housed in close compounds in France similar to those on the diamond mines of Kimberley –

---

80   W.O. 32/11345, Notes on a conference to consider proposals that African and Chinese labour be employed in France, 12 August 1916, and War Office to Colonial Office, 14 August 1916; C.O. 616/64/57352 and 44419, Marginal notes by H. Lambert, 15 September and 2 December 1916. (Emphasis in the original.)

81   Sloley, "The African native labour contingent and the welfare committee", 200.

82   G.G. 549/9/93/56, Botha to Buxton, 19 August and 5 October 1916.

the Union government would otherwise have been unable to support the plan. Botha considered such a measure as an essential

> safeguard against the possible manifestation in this country in the future of undesirable consequences calculated to flow from their too familiar social intercourse with Europeans of both sexes in a country where colour prejudice is less marked than in South Africa.[83]

The imperial authorities readily agreed and the South African government's fears about 'social contamination' were assuaged.

A further consideration was Botha's concern that the imperial government could possibly bypass the Union authorities by enlisting blacks from the surrounding protectorates of Bechuanaland (Botswana), Basutoland (Lesotho) and Swaziland – an alternative that was actually raised by the British government.[84] Botha, however, maintained that for the benefit of the region as a whole South Africa should take the initiative, and was particularly concerned that South African, as opposed to British officers, should be in command. He explained that the Union government "had undertaken the recruiting of the contingent because they desired to keep the subject under their control and so that the officers should be South Africans who knew the country". He was explicit that the association of blacks "side by side with British soldiers who have not been accustomed to deal with them, is regarded as dangerous from the South African point of view".[85]

The South African government's approval of the scheme was thus dependent on gaining full control of the contingent in order to protect what they considered South Africa's interests. Besides these considerations, it must be borne in mind that through the South-West African and German East African campaigns, as well as the presence of a white South African brigade in Europe, Botha had already committed himself firmly to the war effort. His decision to assist the British government further in their quest for manpower therefore dovetailed with his general policy.

---

83   G.G. 549/9/93/56, Botha to Buxton, 19 August 1916.

84   *De Volkstem*, 8 September 1916 ("Z. Afr. naturellen dokwerkers na Frankrijk"); *De Volkstem*, 26 September 1916 ("Gen. Botha toespraak"); *Cape Times*, 21 March 1917 ("Parliamentary debates"); C.O. 616/64/54173, Colonial Office to Buxton, 29 August 1916; G.G. 549/9/93/56, Buxton to Botha, 12 September 1916.

85   *Cape Times*, 21 March 1917 ("Parliamentary debates"); G.G. 547/9/93/120, Botha to Buxton, 2 April 1917.

It has also been suggested that the authorities in South Africa might have realised that the scheme provided an ideal opportunity for testing in what would, it was hoped, be carefully controlled conditions the practicability and effects of the implementation of certain segregatory devices of social control; the lessons and results of this experiment could possibly be utilised in South Africa itself.[86] While the general climate of the time was undoubtedly segregationist, it is doubtful whether this was a primary consideration, though it may well have been perceived as a useful spin-off of a policy which was dictated by more pressing military requirements.

White reactions to black non-combatant service abroad

In the field of white party politics, the government's decision to send a labour force to France became a thorny issue. The National Party, already opposed to Botha's policy of supporting the war effort, roundly condemned the scheme as irresponsible and detrimental to white South Africa, and at congresses of the party it was even suggested that those blacks who enrolled for the contingent should not be allowed to return to South Africa.[87] In parliament, National Party members castigated Botha for once again giving preference to imperial instead of South African interests and for not consulting parliament before embarking on such a 'dangerous' course. In the face of such opposition, Botha could obviously not openly admit to any reservations that would add grist to the Nationalist mill. He counterattacked by claiming that the National Party criticism was inspired by pro-German sentiments, and that their fears were unfounded because black troops would be placed in closed compounds and under the strict control of South African officers. He also felt under no obligation to have consulted parliament since the whole undertaking would be financed by the British and not the South African government.[88]

Although the National Party was the most vociferous in its opposition to the scheme, members of other political parties had similar criticisms. While the predominantly English-speaking Unionist Party could not, in view of its fervent, almost jingoistic support of the British war effort, object in parliament to a scheme designed to promote the British cause, rank-and-file members nevertheless voiced their concern. In two staunchly Unionist cities, Durban and East London, the letter columns of the local

---

86   Willan, "The South African Native Labour Contingent, 1916-1918", 71.

87   *De Burger*, 29 September 1916 ("Nationale Partij Kongres"); *Het Volksblad*, 13 October 1917 ("Vergadering O.V.S. Nationale Partij Kongres").

88   *Cape Times*, 14 and 21 March ("Parliamentary debates").

newspapers were filled with anguished attempts to reconcile loyalty to the empire with opposition to the contingent. A common rationalisation was the claim that blacks in France would not substantially contribute to the war effort and that the perceived negative effects of the scheme outweighed its doubtful military advantages.[89] "To sum up the effect of these expressions of opinions", the *Natal Mercury* declared, "it has to be said that the weight of authority in this part of Union is not favourable to the sending of a large body of Natives overseas".[90] As for the Labour Party, T. Boydell, member of parliament for Durban-Greyville, agreed with this groundswell of Unionist opinion, considering the whole venture a "ghastly mistake".[91]

Even some prominent members of Botha's ruling South African Party objected to the scheme. None other than John X. Merriman, the high priest of Cape liberalism, cautioned in private that "anything that tends to lessen or break down the almost superstitious regard that the native races have ... for the European makes for evil". He also informed Smuts that the matter was one of concern to politicians of all persuasions: "It is not only the professional mischief maker who views the experiment with disfavour, but some of our wisest and most solid friends who regard the introduction of our Natives to the social conditions of Europe with the *greatest* alarm".[92] With this statement, paternalistic Cape liberalism firmly drew the line at what was deemed a development which might involve the possibility of loss of control and authority over Africans.

Although there was no formal cooperation between the various political parties on the matter, there was a considerable degree of tacit understanding that the undertaking was not in the interest of white South Africans. Despite other sharp differences of opinion on the Union's war policy, particularly between the South African Party and the Unionist Party on the one hand and the National Party on the other, the politics of involving blacks in the war was the one issue which, at grass-roots level, tended to blur party lines. In the general discussion on the subject, support for the war effort

---

89 *Natal Mercury*, 20 September 1916 (Letter from 'An old veteran'), *Natal Mercury*, 12 September 1916 ("Native contingent, local opinion"); *Natal Mercury*, 20 September 1916 (Letter from 'Y.O.B.'); *Natal Mercury*, 3 October 1916 (Letter from 'A colonist of 35 years standing'); *Natal Advertiser*, 13 September 1916 ("Natives for Europe"); *East London Daily Dispatch*, 11 September 1916 ("Native labourers for France"); *East London Daily Dispatch*, 25 September 1916 (Letter from the Reverend J.W.W. Owen).

90 *Natal Mercury*, 12 October 1916 ("The proposed native contingent").

91 *Natal Mercury*, 12 September 1916 ("Native contingent, local opinion").

92 Merriman Papers 444, Merriman to Buxton, 5 December 1916; Hancock and Van der Poel, *Smuts papers III*, 413-14, Merriman to Smuts, 20 November 1916. (Emphasis in the original.)

abroad had to give way to the importance of maintaining the existing order at home. To appreciate the depth of opposition to the scheme, it is necessary to move beyond the confines of party politics to the ideological constructs which helped to forge such beliefs.

Central to white objections was the argument that the venture would, in general terms, be harmful to South African 'interests'. The specific content of these so-called interests must be unravelled and defined in order to understand more precisely and comprehensively the various strands of the issue. A core element in the ideological perceptions of whites was the firm belief that service overseas would raise black political consciousness. "It seems well to point out", the *Natal Mercury* commented, "that 10 000 more or less unsophisticated boys will come back to this country after contact with an altogether new environment very different individuals from what they were when they left". Therefore, the "political change that might come over the native when he returns to this country" was a matter of grave concern.[93] The nature of the perceived political change was spelt out by J.G. Keyter, member of parliament for Ficksburg, at a party congress. He predicted that "when the kaffir [sic] returned, he will pretend to be a major or colonel and the white man his underling, he will have ideas above his station, he will work for no white man and incite his people to agitate for equal rights".[94] Advocate O. Pirow of the National Party went to the heart of the matter when he declared: "On their return from Europe, the kaffirs [sic] will demand the vote".[95]

Such considerations held powerful sway and in a rather unexpected way nearly wrecked the undertaking. Before recruitment of the contingent commenced, the government asked for medical opinion on the possible effect of the cold in France on Africans and, upon receiving a negative report from Doctor George Turner, a specialist on diseases amongst Africans, reconsidered the whole scheme. However, Doctor F. Arnold, head of the Union's health services, had no objections and commented that Doctor Turner "allowed himself perhaps unconsciously, to be influenced by considerations other than medical when he gave his unfavourable opinion". Arnold was too charitable and understated his case; medical evidence was indeed wilfully distorted to fit political views. E. Dower, secretary for Native Affairs, informed Botha:

93   *Natal Mercury*, 15 September 1916 ("The native labour contingent"); *Natal Mercury*,
      12 October 1916 ("The proposed native contingent").

94   *Het Volkblad*, 13 October 1916 ("Vergadering O.V.S. Nationale Partij Kongres"). Translation.

95   *Ons Vaderland*, 8 December 1916 ("Pirow over de kaffer kwestie"). Translation.

As regards Dr. Turner's condemnatory report he has frankly admitted to me that he was influenced not so much on the purely medical side as from his opposition to the venture on political and other grounds. As a South African he strongly objects to the move (because of its possible bad after effects).[96]

An additional strand of this question, related to the perceived political repercussions, was the fear, expressed in general terms, that blacks might be "socially and morally contaminated" in France. This specifically implied that, to the detriment of white South Africa, members of the contingent might associate and consort with white women abroad. In the Cape Province, *De Burger* held that the "cancer of immorality would spread over the breadth and length of South Africa and that our women and children would no longer be safe on their farms".[97] In Natal, a newspaper correspondent declared the scheme an "outrage against humanity", in consequence of which "hundreds if not thousands of Natives will indulge in an intercourse which in this province is considered one of the gravest crimes against our social life". He further predicted: "Truly, we shall be letting loose a boomerang, the force which on its return, will strike at the root of our social life". Another equally distressed correspondent asked: "Should the native have social intercourse with a white woman, what effect will it have on the native mind?" To him it was a foregone conclusion that "our fair daughters will be degraded".[98]

Among the organisations which took up the issue, were the white middle-class feminist Women's Enfranchisement League and the Dutch Reformed Church.[99] Since the contingent was to be housed in closed compounds in France, the authorities felt that these fears were exaggerated. "The South African public may be quite sure", was the official response, "that no untoward results will eventuate".[100] White fears, however, were not allayed and it was argued that "despite compounds and the rest, on their arrival in Europe every black man will have a woman on each arm".[101]

---

96   D.C. 768/80/1997, F. Arnold to E. Dower, 15 October 1916 and E. Dower to Botha, 15 October 1916.

97   *De Burger*, 18 September 1916 ("De Tienduizend"). Translation.

98   *Natal Mercury*, 20 September 1916 (Letter from 'Y.O.B.'); *Natal Mercury*, 3 October 1916 (Letter from 'A colonist of 35 years standing').

99   P.M. 1/1/19, Women's Enfranchisement League to Botha, 28 October 1916; P.M. 1/1/302, the Reverend I.J.A. de Villiers to Botha, 29 September 1916.

100 D.C. 768/40/1917, Secretary of Defence to T. Orr, 26 September 1916.

101 *Het Volksblad*, 13 October 1916 ("Vergadering O.V.S. Nationale Partij Kongres"). Translation.

Although the authorities had insisted on the closed compound system because they shared exactly the same reservations, in some quarters the intensity of public concern clearly surpassed even the government's own misgivings. Such responses were not uncommon in South Africa. Before the First World War, between 1890 and 1914, public outcry against the 'dangers' of affairs between black and white was a persistent feature of the collective mentality of a section of white society. This trend was particularly visible on the Witwatersrand and can be related to periods of marked instability in society. Especially from 1912 to 1913 there was a widespread fear that Africans would assault and rape women at random. Incidents that did occur were exaggerated, but a parliamentary commission was nevertheless appointed in 1913 to investigate what was called the "black peril scare".[102] Once again, in these unsettling war circumstances, opposition to the contingent was on one level a continuation of the 1913 'black scare peril'.

Besides these kind of objections, the inevitable question of the impact of the contingent on the labour situation in the country arose. The Chamber of Mines, was decidedly uneasy about the prospect of a large number of potential workers leaving the country. However, the mine owners did not experience an acute labour shortage at the time (1916) and were further relieved by government assurances that the scheme would not materially affect their labour supply.[103] In Natal, though, the "scarcity of native labour" weighed heavily with those who were dependent on cheap black labour for their prosperity and they did not hesitate to register their protest. Sir Liege Hulett, the wealthy sugar baron, condemned the undertaking as "absolutely unnecessary" and was convinced that Natal could not "spare any native labour".[104] Likewise, Sir Marshall Campbell, who had extensive interests in the sugar industry, declared that the "requirements of our industries imperatively dictate the retention of all available native labour in Natal".[105] There can be little doubt that the profit motive took precedence over patriotic considerations. Governor General Buxton caustically remarked that the capitalist class in Natal

> want the labour and they are afraid that if they allow the Zulu to go and
> assist the Empire, they will suffer in their pockets. The Natal Britisher is a

---

102 Van Onselen, *Studies in the social and economic history of the Witwatersrand, 1886-1914: 2 New Nineveh*, 45-54.

103 *Sunday Times*, 10 September 1916 ("Imperial impi").

104 *Natal Advertiser*, 13 September 1916 ("Sir Liege Hulett's views"). See also *Natal Mercury*, 10 October 1916 ("Natives for war work").

105 *Natal Mercury*, 12 September 1916 ("Native contingent, local opinion").

great man to talk of Natal as British to the backbone, but when it comes to helping the Empire in the concrete he pauses if his own interests are involved or affected.[106]

Clearly the facade of patriotism crumbled under the threat of reduced financial gain. Employers were not only concerned about the possible loss of labour, but were also perturbed that those Africans who went overseas might be exposed to socialist ideas, and as a result develop an increased sense of class consciousness and a new awareness of their position as subjected labourers. Contact with such "undesirable elements", some employers argued, would mean that on their return these so-called natives would no longer be "prepared to do the work which they had done in the past".[107] The spectre of a less tractable and servile work force obviously loomed large.

In contrast to the political, moralistic and economic objections, there were those sections of the white community who approved of the government's decision to send a contingent to France. Missionary opinion in the Eastern Cape, for instance, rejected the "political creed which would deny to the Bantu any place in the Empire's service lest they should thus secure political and social recognition", and further stressed that "one of the lessons South Africa would do well to learn is to lay aside racial prejudice". Similarly, this view condemned criticism of the "purely selfish kind which grumbles because there will be so much less labour available in South Africa". However, not surprisingly, the compound system was welcomed as a safeguard against "the temptations to debauchery".[108] While these contemporary liberals thus summarily dismissed two widely held objections, they were unable to shed certain paternalistic and moralistic beliefs. Black men stood in need of protection from the 'moral dangers' abroad and, according to missionary insight, were especially vulnerable to such temptations. Moreover, paternalistic assumptions also explain why they gave their blessing to the scheme. There was no consideration of the possible benefits (or disadvantages) of the undertaking as far as the Africans themselves were concerned, other than that "the call would bind them to the Union and to the Empire in active loyalty, a result perhaps not less valuable than the actual labour they will provide".[109] Loyalty to the Union and empire was automatically assumed to be in the best interests of Africans, and the overriding concern was clearly to strengthen black commitment to the existing dispensation.

106 W.H. Long Papers 947/602/65, Buxton to Long, 5 June 1917.

107 *Cape Times*, 21 March 1917 ("Parliamentary debates").

108 *The Christian Express*, 2 October 1916 ("The native labour contingent").

109 *Ibid.*

Others whites sanctioned the scheme because they saw possible advantages accruing. To certain farmers, particularly those relatively untroubled by labour shortages, it was a way of demonstrating to blacks the military power and capability of white society. In less than subtle terms, they argued that service in war-torn Europe "could give the Natives such a graphic description of what they would be up against, should they ever dream of rising, that that phase of the native question in South Africa would be finally settled".[110]

In some respects, the dividing line between those who opposed the scheme and those who supported it was for all intents and purposes very thin. Ideological overlays aside, both camps had one fundamental concern in common: how and to what extent did the undertaking affect the vested power structures in South Africa? Ultimately, despite widely different views, there was considerable consensus that the established order must not be disturbed.

African responses

Whereas the concerns which determined the degree and nature of black participation are outlined above, it remains to consider the way in which Africans responded to the delineation of their role as non-combatants.

Despite the fact that Defence Force Act 13 of 1912 precluded Africans from armed military service, at the start of the First World War there was a strong body of black elite opinion which argued that they should fight for the right to fight. Congress demanded active participation in the war and, according to Sol Plaatje, "threw themselves into the vortex of the martial enthusiasm that was then sweeping the country".[111] Black newspapers claimed that "it was the wish voiced by a larger number of Natives in South Africa to fight in this war".[112] And, as has been mentioned before, W.B. Rubusana in vain offered to raise 5 000 black combatant troops.

There were several reasons for the enthusiasm to secure participation in the war. To some degree at least, some Africans were influenced by the fact that other "coloured races" of the British and French colonial empires were involved in hostilities; the black press in South Africa was filled with the wartime exploits of Indian troops who

---

110 WWI I.S.D. 36/1595, B. Buchan Brown to Smuts, 22 November 1916.

111 Plaatje, *Native life*, 263.

112 *Ilanga Lase Natal*, 8 January 1915 ("The South African native as a soldier"). See also *Tsala ea Batho*, 17 October 1914 ("Return of native deputation").

had enrolled in the British army and blacks from North and West Africa who fought for the French.[113] To some extent, also, they echoed the patriotic rhetoric of the day that "it was a duty to fight: out of loyalty to the British flag".[114] Of greater importance, though, was the realisation that a wider political protest could be registered. It was recognised that since combatant service was a symbol of full citizenship, the government's refusal to allow blacks to participate in combat duty really reflected their subjected and colonised status. Insistence on armed military service was therefore a way of challenging the creed which relegated them to an inferior position, and it was hoped that entry into the armed forces would provide an opportunity of increasing their bargaining power and bolstering their claim to citizenship. Congress made this linkage clear:

> If at the conclusion of the war we were able to point to a record of military service, the Constitution would inevitably have to be altered in order that brave soldiers of the Empire might be put in possession of the fullest rights and privileges of citizenship and all that pertain to *Subjects and Soldiers* of the British Empire.[115]

Others essentially made the same point using more vivid imagery. "Without the Natives' shedding of blood for the King as all his subjects", argued A.Z. Twala, "there is no emancipation from the many unscrupulous laws until the millennium".[116] While such considerations were uppermost in the minds of the educated elite who were struggling to be accommodated in the white dispensation, other classes in society showed little or no concern. To them, there were more immediate and pressing battles than a white man's war in foreign countries.

Nevertheless, the possibility that armed participation in the war might spark off renewed political demands was, of course, precisely the reason why the government refused to arm blacks. This was a double blow for the black elite advocating combat duty: their loyalist sentiments were, in effect, snubbed, and their wider political

---

113 *Tsala ea Batho*, 26 September 1914 ("Champion fighters to go to war"); *Tsala ea Batho*, 24 October 1914 ("France's sepoy army"); *Tsala ea Batho*, 7 November 1914 ("Black forces of the Empire"); *Imvo Zabantsundu*, 22 September 1914 ("Natives and the war"); *Ilanga Lase Natal*, 16 October 1914 ("Natives and the war"); *Ilanga Lase Natal*, 10 September 1915 ("Natives at arms").

114 *Imvo Zabantsundu*, 17 May 1917 (Letter from R.M. Tunzi).

115 *Ilanga Lase Natal*, 30 April 1915 ("South African Native National Congress"). Emphasis in the original.

116 *Ilanga Lase Natal*, 12 November 1915 (Letter from A.Z. Twala).

expectations arising from the war were also frustrated. The SANNC felt aggrieved and adopted a resolution expressing its "disappointment" and regret that "the natural demand of the returning soldier to the rights of citizenship has been excluded by anticipation".[117]

Although at the time much was made of the exclusion of black men from the fighting corps, in retrospect it is worth briefly probing the issue of why, apart from the soldier-citizen link, armed service was allocated such an exalted status. It was, after all, exceptionally daunting and extremely risky to willingly declare one available to be shot at. If it were not for the discriminatory fact that black men were not given a choice in the matter, one might even argue that they were spared the imposition of and induction into a male warrior culture with potentially lethal consequences. But perhaps precisely because armed service was embedded in such notions of masculinity and prestige, it was accorded a status that ultimately went beyond logic.

Such concerns were not part of the SANNC's thinking. In the light of the government's rejection of their offer of armed service, the announcement to send a labour contingent to France was received with mixed feelings. "Responsible African opinion might be said to have been in a state of mingled bewilderment and anxiety", it was later recorded.[118] The SANNC nevertheless accepted the contingent as the second best option to combat service. Now that a black combatant unit was out of the question and the political potential of such a unit had evaporated, they hoped that the labour contingent might serve the same purpose. Although they realised that the non-combatant status of the contingent reduced its political potential, it was still regarded as a possible chance "for the natives to acquire a just and recognised status as loyal subjects of the Crown".[119] There were, however, less sanguine views. Reflecting an understanding of the ultimate interests involved, L. Ndondela of East London, who was apparently not a member of the SANNC, commented: "Of course it won't be to the natives' good, because whatever they will do will be for the good of the Imperial Government and the Union. Whether they go or remain here, they will not get any good."[120] The SANNC, as will be shown later, objected to some organisational aspects of the contingent, but never questioned the reasons for its formation or the assumption that it was necessarily in the interests of Africans.

117 *Ilanga Lase Natal*, 30 April 1915 ("South African Native National Congress").

118 *Izwe Lase Afrika*, 5 December 1941 ("South African Natives in World War One").

119 *Ilanga Lase Natal*, 3 November 1916 ("The Native Contingent").

120 *East London Daily Dispatch*, 13 September 1916 (Letter from L. Ndondela).

The class position of the black elite and their accommodationist strategy under-pinned their support for the contingent, and this policy was perhaps paradoxically reinforced by opposition to the scheme voiced by many whites. The argument that the undertaking was "politically dangerous", was considered in the black press as "the best proof that this contingent is a good thing for the natives".[121]

Other objections voiced by whites were given short shrift. Fears that blacks in France would be involved with white women were dismissed as a figment of the white imagination, and the one-sided nature of the 'black peril' syndrome caused one commentator to ask: "What do all the half-castes bear witness to the black or white peril?"[122] In turn, the criticism that the contingent would lead to a labour shortage was regarded as opportunistic and as an example of the perception of blacks as mere units of labour. The sincerity of the "British element", which was supposed to make willing sacrifices during the war, was therefore called into question since they were only aiming "to use the natives as means to enrich themselves very quickly".[123]

Conclusion

The issue of black participation in the war has demonstrated how the concerns, interests and prejudices in society impinged on military matters. Precisely because of such wider influences, the role of blacks in hostilities was neatly circumscribed. However, it remained to implement this policy, and the first hurdle to be crossed was to find the necessary manpower.

121 *Ilanga Lase Natal*, 3 November 1916 ("The native contingent").
122 *Natal Mercury*, 11 October 1916 (Letter from 'H.N.').
123 *Ilanga Lase Natal*, 3 November 1916 ("The native contingent").

RECRUITMENT AND REASONS FOR ENLISTING

During the war, approximately 74 000 Africans were recruited for service in South-West Africa, East Africa and France.[124] Various methods were used to assemble such a large number of men for military service and the recruits also had their own reasons for enlisting.

Recruitment for German South-West Africa and East Africa

Africans were first drawn into the war through the demand for railway workers and transport drivers during the South-West African campaign. The Government Native Labour Bureau (G.N.L.B.), under the auspices of the Native Affairs Department, was responsible for providing the Defence Force with the necessary recruits, and the bureau in turn depended on local magistrates and native commissioners to initiate the recruiting drive. Furthermore, local white notables deemed by the authorities to possess influence amongst the African population were also called on to assist.[125]

However, more than official and semi-official white channels were needed to complete the recruiting network. S.M. Pritchard, director of the G.N.L.B., regarded it as imperative to gain the support of the black elite. To this end he organised a meeting with delegates of the SANNC in Johannesburg, inviting their comments

---

124 This figure is based on O.C. Records 93/139/2, Recruiting Statistics, 1914-1918;
     G.N.L.B. 187/1217/14/D 110, undated (probably 1918) memorandum by Colonel
     S.M. Pritchard. The statistics which appear in pages 218-219 of the *Official History of the Union of South Africa and the Great War* are incomplete.
125 D.C. 625/67/205/9199, Pritchard to Native Labour Bureau, 20 and 22 March 1915.

on the conditions of service and emphasising the need to obtain the cooperation of the SANNC. The delegates were suitably impressed by these overtures. President J.L. Dube commented that Pritchard was "the one official of the Government who was administering Native Affairs in the right direction, namely by consulting the Natives in matters in which they were interested and for not hesitating to take them into their confidence".[126] The SANNC was clearly not concerned with the motive for consultation, which was not to confide in them or accord them any form of recognition, but merely to obtain their help in a time of need. Nevertheless, from their point of view some consultation – even if there was an ulterior motive – was better than none, and they optimistically chose to regard the meeting as "but a stepping stone to still closer cooperation between the Government and the Natives". In addition, the SANNC used this opportunity to demonstrate their assumed influence and importance to the authorities. Dube, for example, claimed that "the people looked to them for advice and if they approved of this scheme and they explained it to the people, men would soon be forthcoming to volunteer for service in German S.W. Africa".[127]

In the event, it proved to be more difficult to find recruits than the SANNC had anticipated. Dube was instrumental in arranging numerous recruiting meetings on behalf of the government in Natal, but neither he nor the officials who addressed those present were able to make much headway. Those who attended the meetings suspected the government's motives in sending them to South-West Africa, arguing that on arrival in the war zone they would be "put in front of the Troops to explode mines which had been laid by the Germans". Dube's assurances to the contrary had no effect; he was regarded as a mere "catspaw", being paid by the government and therefore not to be trusted.[128]

Outside Natal, Africans were equally wary and expressed similar doubts about the government's intentions. A dismayed magistrate from the Mount Ayliff district in the Transkei reported that the "Natives will not go to German Africa. Could not get a single man or driver or leader. They will have it we are beaten and simply want

---

126 *Ilanga Lase Natal*, 22 January 1915 ("South African Native National Congress").

127 *Ilanga Lase Natal*, 22 January 1915 ("South African Native National Congress"). See also *The Christian Express*, 1 February 1915 ("Natives and the war"); Willan, "South African Native Labour Contingent, 1916-1918", 65.

128 D.C. 626/205/2441, Report by H.M. Taberer, 2 February 1915.

to put them in front of the firing line".[129] Magistrates and other recruiting agents, however, did not relax their efforts and the constant demands for recruits became increasingly an irritant in African social life. Thus, J. Sipika, a migrant worker from the Witwatersrand mines, resented official harassment during his spell at home in the Matatiele district. Sipika regretted being home "on account of these recruiting meetings" and he, along with other Africans in a similar position, therefore decided to choose the lesser of two evils and to return to the goldfields instead of running the risk of being pressurised into military service.[130]

Indeed, confronted with African apathy, government officials soon started to exert pressure. In the Mahlabatini and Harding districts of Natal, the magistrates threatened to arrest and fine headmen who failed to produce a certain number of recruits. Under duress they complied, even though it meant some alienation between them and the commoners.[131] Similar tactics were employed in parts of the Transkei and caused an anonymous African to comment that "war methods are bad out here" and "Natives are made by force to join for the front".[132] Under such circumstances African enlistment can hardly be described as voluntary. This happened despite Pritchard's assurances to the SANNC that "the system of obtaining labourers ... would not be compulsory [and] no pressure or other influence would be exercised in order to induce Natives ... *The system would be voluntary*".[133] What was promised officially and what happened in practice were clearly two different matters.

Coercive recruiting methods coincided with an increasing need for labourers in South-West Africa, and in January 1915 the demand assumed critical proportions. Anxiously, Smuts wired from the front: "Very gravely concerned about the serious position created by formidable shortage of transport natives which threatens virtual suspension [of] real progress [in the] campaign".[134] H.R.M. Bourne, the secretary of

---

129 G.N.L.B. 192/1329/14/D 48, Magistrate Mount Ayliff to Secretary of Native Affairs, 27 November 1914.

130 G.N.L.B. 192/1329/14/D 48, Intercepted and translated letter from J. Sipika, 30 October 1914.

131 S.N.A. 1/4/25/L5/1915, State of Native feeling in the Mahlabatini district, report by Chief Native Commissioner in Natal; S.A.P. 6/245/14/308, Report by Sub-inspector H. Jones, 3 April 1915.

132 G.N.L.B. 192/1329/14/D 48, Anonymous intercepted letter, 27 October 1914.

133 *Ilanga Lase Natal*, 22 January 1915 ("South African Native National Congress"). (Emphasis in the original.)

134 D.C. 46/15/993, Smuts to Defence Headquarters, 23 January 1915.

defence, was also perturbed and feared that if the supply of labourers did not improve, "a breakdown with lamentable results is inevitable". Bourne even considered the drastic step of conscripting Africans under martial law regulations.[135] This suggested solution, however, was not implemented.

Instead, the government turned for help to the largest employer of Africans in Southern Africa, the Chamber of Mines. Since the gold mining industry was in the unusual position of having a surplus of labourers, the request to aid the government's war effort was not incompatible with the interests of the Chamber. It was therefore agreed that African labourers recruited from Mozambique to work on the goldfields would be employed for the first three months of their annual contract on railway construction in South-West Africa. The approval of the Portuguese governor general was obtained before the decision was acted upon.[136] In addition, a considerable number of Africans engaged by the railway administration in the Union were summarily transferred to South-West Africa, for similar service in that territory.[137] It would appear that these arrangements eased the labour situation and satisfied the demands of the South African military. By the end of the campaign, approximately 35 000 labourers (mostly Africans, but also some coloureds) had served in South-West Africa.[138]

Besides assisting in South-West Africa, Africans were also required as labourers for the South African military expedition to East Africa. Information on the recruiting aspects of this campaign is scant, but it can be assumed that the authorities also experienced difficulties in securing African recruits for this venture. Indeed, some recruiting agents became so desperate that, to the annoyance of the military authorities in East Africa, even children aged fifteen or sixteen and physically infirm Africans were signed up.[139] In total, 18 000 South African blacks served in East Africa during 1916 and until April of the following year.[140] The gold mines did not provide labourers for this campaign. However, after Portugal had abandoned its neutrality in 1916, the staff of the Witwatersrand Native Labour Association (WNLA) in Mozambique was

135 D.C. 625/205/9199, Bourne to Secretary of Native Affairs, 2 November 1914.

136 D.C. 625/205/9199, Governor General Pretoria to Governor General Lourenzo Marques, 22 January 1915, and Secretary of Native Affairs to Pritchard, 25 January 1915; P.M. 1/1/35, Governor General Lourenzo Marques to Governor General Pretoria, 28 January 1915 (copy).

137 D.C. 625/205/9199, General circular, 10 December 1914.

138 O.C. Records 93/139/2, Recruiting statistics, 1914-1918.

139 B.L. 4/3/25, General circular, 26 February 1917.

140 O.C. Records 93/139/2, Recruiting statistics, 1914-1918; D.C. 851/219/22714, Statistics on South African blacks in East Africa, 1916.

expanded to recruit not only workers for the gold mines, but also labourers for war purposes in East Africa.[141] This was done independently of recruiting in South Africa.

Africans constituted almost one third of the total number of South Africans (161 000 men) involved in the South-West African and East African campaigns.[142] In terms of manpower, it certainly was a significant contribution – one which received no recognition at the time and has subsequently remained largely ignored in South African historiography.

Recruitment for France

The demand for African manpower increased dramatically with the decision to send labourers to France and resulted in the most intensive recruiting drive conducted during the war. For different reasons, the formation of the South African Native Labour Contingent (SANLC) was a controversial issue for whites and blacks alike, which compounded the problem of raising recruits in sufficient numbers. Moreover, the Chamber of Mines declined to assist; it was not prepared to allow black workers to leave the country for a period which would extend the annual contractual terms.[143]

The scheme to mobilise Africans for service abroad generated a wide range of issues, reflecting conflicting ideological and material interests. Once again, as in the case of the South-West African campaign, the authorities tried to obtain the support of the SANNC. This time, however, the SANNC was not prepared to render unqualified support. In return for its cooperation, it expected the authorities to abolish the projected closed compound system in France and also requested the appointment of more black non-commissioned officers. The Native Affairs Department replied that the arrangements for the SANLC had already been finalised and that the demands made by the SANNC were received too late for consideration.[144] It is, however, inconceivable that the authorities would even have considered abolishing the compound system. As shown earlier, Botha had only agreed to the imperial request for a black labour contingent on the clear understanding that compounds would be provided.

---

141 Henriksen, *Mozambique: A history*, 107; A.G. 205/412, General scheme of recruiting natives for East African campaign, 1917.

142 *Official history*, 218-19.

143 *Sunday Times*, 10 September 1916 ("Imperial impi").

144 *Natal Mercury*, 9 October 1916 ("Native contingent for Europe"); *Ilanga Lase Natal*, 20 October 1916 ("Native contingent").

Despite this rebuff and its initial reservations, the SANNC nevertheless decided to cooperate with the government. In line with their thinking at the outbreak of war and their response to the announcement of the scheme, its leaders persisted in the view that support for the war effort could increase their bargaining power and ultimately exert more pressure on the government. "It would be folly not to comply", it was argued, "for surely if we do not, then our future ... and general welfare cannot be assured".[145] In addition, Sol Plaatje, according to his biographer, reasoned that it was important for the SANNC to support the scheme, since "recruitment for the Native Labour Contingent would bring the war to a swifter conclusion and thus make it possible to attend to their grievances".[146] Clearly, for the SANNC the possible further advantages of such cooperation outweighed the fact that their demands had been rejected by the Native Affairs Department.

Not surprisingly then, some of the leading members of the SANNC became actively involved in the recruiting campaign. In Kimberley, for example, Sol Plaatje organised and addressed meetings while, in Natal, John Dube sought to fire the Zulu with enthusiasm for the war across the ocean.[147] Others followed their example and publicly declared their support for the venture. Thus, F.Z.S. Peregrino – a flamboyant Capetonian and, at the turn of the century, editor of the *South African Spectator* newspaper – published a special brochure, painting the contingent in glamorous colours. To serve in it was the ideal way for Africans to demonstrate their loyalty to Britain.[148] And in a somewhat similar vein, an anonymous African clergyman from East London issued a general appeal to his "countrymen" urging them to "give heed to the call of duty".[149]

In government circles, the recruiting drive was considered to be of such paramount importance that Botha as prime minister and Buxton as governor general became

---

145 *Ilanga Lase Natal*, 27 October 1916 ("The 10 000 for France").

146 Willan, "The role of Solomon T. Plaatje (1876-1932) in South African society", 195. An expanded and revised version of the thesis was published in 1984 under the title *Sol Plaatje: A biography*.

147 *Diamond Fields Advertiser*, 28 June 1917 ("Native recruiting meeting"); Willan, "South African Native Labour Contingent, 1916-1918", 66-67; *Natal Mercury*, 19 October 1916 ("Arise ye Zulu"). A Zulu version of Dube's article also appeared in *Ilanga Lase Natal*, 20 October 1916.

148 Peregrino, "His Majesty's black labourers: A treatise on the camp life of the SANLC", 40. For biographical details on Peregrino, see Saunders, "F.Z.S. Peregrino and the *South African Spectator*", 81-89.

149 *East London Daily Despatch*, 6 October 1916 (Letter from 'A Native Minister').

personally involved. During September 1916, Botha visited the Transkei and, at every meeting he held in the territory, encouraged support for the contingent.[150] Similarly, Buxton went on a tour of the Transkei and Zululand in July 1917, ostensibly making a routine official visit but with the actual intent of stimulating recruitment. In order to demonstrate to the Africans the solemnity and importance of this aim, Buxton wore his Privy Council uniform with ribbons and medals during meetings with prospective recruits. Buxton's attempt to cast himself in the role of the "great white chief" was based on the assumption that African tribesmen were used to their own chiefs appearing in their regalia, and were easily overawed by a symbolic display of power. With the confidence of those imbued with imperial cultural arrogance, Buxton could confidently claim that it was undoubtedly the "right thing to wear uniform at these gatherings" since it "enables the Native to distinguish the Inkosi and also impresses them".[151]

At grass-roots level in densely populated black areas, it was the local magistrates, native commissioners and chiefs, aided by merchants and individual recruiters, who were primarily responsible for recruitment. In addition, the English churches were approached for assistance through their missionaries and other church members in close contact with the African population.[152] The churches readily offered their help. Besides patriotic considerations, they also visualised the scheme as an ideal opportunity for concentrated missionary work – a captive African audience, its members uprooted from their normal cultural environment and under military discipline in a foreign country, constituted conditions which any missionary might envy in furthering his own objectives. No wonder that after a visit to Rosebank in Cape Town, where the recruits were encamped before leaving for France, the Anglican bishop of Zululand was convinced that "a large number of the men belonging to the battalion who were heathens to-day, would come back Christians".[153]

---

150 *Territorial News*, 7 September 1916 ("General Botha's visit"); *Territorial News*, 21 September 1916 ("General Botha's tour"); *Territorial News*, 28 September 1916 ("General Botha's tour"); *Imvo Zabantsundu*, 26 September 1916 ("General Botha at Umtata").

151 W.H. Long Papers 947/602/84, Buxton to Long, 15 April 1917.

152 G.G. 545/9/93/56, Botha to Buxton, 25 May 1917; *Rand Daily Mail*, 9 September 1917 ("Natives wanted for France"); 1/T.B.U. 25/66/1, Circular from Botha to English churches, 11 June 1917; P.M. 1/1/480, Botha to Anglican Bishop of Cape Town, 6 June 1917; *Ilanga Lase Natal*, 13 July 1917 ("Botha's appeal").

153 *Cape Times*, 17 November 1916 ("Mission development after the war"). See also P.M. 1/1/480, Anglican Bishop of Cape Town to Botha, 20 July 1917.

Three basic themes, with some variations, were stressed in the call for black recruits. In the first place, an appeal was made to the loyalty and patriotism of the Africans. The educated African class regarded and depicted service abroad as a joint enterprise between black and white and also framed their appeal in general terms familiar to the public in wartime Britain and South Africa:

> The present war is a world war. Every nation must take part in it. Even we Bantu ought to play our part in this war. Some of you have done a great deal in German East Africa and South-West Africa already. You are still expected, even across the seas, to go and help. Without you, your white comrades cannot do anything, because they cannot fight and provide labour at the same time. So you must go and do the labour while your white fellows are doing the fighting. Please, everyone who loves his country and respects the British government, join this war without hesitation. Forward! Forward![154]

The same patriotic theme, but couched in a more paternalistic tone, is also evident in the attempts by government officials to convince Africans that they were privileged to enjoy the benefit of British rule and therefore they should show their gratitude by assisting the British in times of need. In overbearing terms, Africans were often reminded of their 'duty' towards king and country. "I have laid matters to Natal Natives in such a way", reported C.A. Wheelwright, chief native commissioner of Natal, "that they have the entire responsibility of the finger of scorn being pointed at them should they fail to come forward".[155] The harshness of German colonial rule was also enlarged upon to create the impression amongst Africans that it was in their own interest to prevent Germany from winning the war and eventually ruling South Africa to the detriment of black and white alike. "German rule is hell rule", F.Z.S. Peregrino pointed out, and for blacks it would only mean "slavery, oppression and cruelty".[156]

Secondly, the practical advantages of enlistment were emphasised: free food, a free uniform and a wage of 60/- per month as opposed to the average wage of approximately 50/- paid on the mines.[157] Plaatje, in his attempts to raise recruits, varied the pattern

---

154 Perry and Perry, *Jingoes*, 72.

155 D.C. 768/40/1997/9199, Wheelwright to Secretary of Native Affairs, 3 October 1916 (copy).

156 Peregrino, *His Majesty's black labourers*, 3, 40. See also Willan, "South African Native Labour Contingent, 1916-1918", 66.

157 *Cape Times*, 28 March 1917 ("Natives for France"); W.H. Long Papers 947/602/84, Buxton to Long, 15 April 1917; *Diamond Fields Advertiser*, 28 June 1917 ("Native recruiting meeting"). For the average wage rate on the gold mines, see Van der Horst, *Native Labour in South Africa*, 205.

somewhat. For those not to be swayed by the stock arguments of patriotism and financial benefits, he played on the notion, common amongst the aspiring black class in South Africa, that their advancement depended in part on education and that service abroad presented an ideal 'educational' opportunity. Thus, he told his audience on the diamond fields "that six months in France would teach them more than ten months in Kimberley; it was just like a great educational institution without having to pay the fees".[158]

Thirdly, in an attempt to move away from the somewhat rarefied nature of some of these appeals, the authorities obtained for propaganda purposes appropriate letters from Africans who had joined and were already serving in France. Such letters, heavily censored to create a favourable impression of conditions in France, were widely distributed in African communities in the hope that the information from compatriots abroad would carry more weight than official efforts. However, it was not that easy to lend credibility to the venture as an African concern. "These letters are regarded with some suspicion as coming through officials", it was reported.[159]

The authorities were nevertheless undeterred; if the letters were not convincing enough, then perhaps the presence of the authors themselves would be. "The best way to counteract sinister rumour, and to give confidence", Buxton argued, "is that some of those who have been with the Contingent should return and disseminate the actual truth".[160] This plan was duly put into practice and 20 carefully selected members returned to the Union and were sent to their home districts. There they dutifully organised meetings and generally followed the official line by relating tales of loyal and contented African labourers abroad, only too grateful to serve the Empire in the "great white war".[161] Some, however, felt the need to embroider on the official version, and without the knowledge or approval of the authorities, introduced a new element – more appealing to basic human nature – in their call for service abroad. "In France you will find magnificent entertainment, you will be going out with ladies of high standard and you will be eating nice food", was D.S. Makoliso's way of tempting

---

158 *Diamond Fields Advertiser*, 28 June 1917 ("Native recruiting meeting").

159 W.H. Long Papers 947/602/84, Buxton to Long, 15 April 1917. For copies of these letters, see C.M.T. 3/930/778/2, A.K. Xabanisa to Chief Magistrate, 25 May 1917; M. Mbanye to Magistrate Elliotdale, 15 May 1917 and G. Nomvele to Magistrate Matatiele, 17 June 1917.

160 W.H. Long Papers 947/602/84, Buxton to Long, 15 April 1917.

161 G.G. 545/9/93/56, Botha to Buxton, 2 July 1917; *Alice Times*, 15 November 1917 ("Returned Native labourers"); *Alice Times*, 18 October 1917 ("The native contingent").

prospective recruits.[162] In a similar vein, other enterprising recruiters created the impression that those who enlisted had "a lazy, happy life ... to look forward to: load and offload ships and trains – that is all, and the most important item is to have your meal and a rest, or go out for a stroll ... and for this you get paid £3 per month".[163] The authorities, mindful of the controversial nature of the scheme and the possible damaging effect of appeals which promised Africans the 'good life' abroad, clamped down on representations which overstepped the official mark.

Regardless of the contents of the appeals, the plan to raise recruits through returned members of the contingent failed miserably. "It was a great frost", a disappointed Buxton reported.[164] For those officials who were burdened with the task of supplying recruits, it became increasingly apparent that the strategies hitherto employed would not produce the desired results. "Our recruiting methods need to be more imaginative and elastic", urged W. Carmichael, the magistrate from Tsolo in the Transkei. "At present they take no account of human nature and ... unless we abandon our wooden methods we have not hope ..." Carmichael thought it essential that recruiting agents should be paid a *per capita* grant, over and above their fixed wage, for every labourer recruited.[165]

D.L. Smit, the magistrate's clerk in East London who was intimately involved in recruiting, also advocated such a departure "as the fact is undeniable that the average native expects an occasional 'swazi' or tip, and the amount of zeal thrown into the work too often depends on this consideration".[166] Even the chief magistrate of the Transkei favoured this proposal since "every other means of inducing Natives to go overseas has been tried with small success".[167] The Native Affairs Department declined to condone such perquisites, but since the magistrates who generally supported the idea were hard pressed to obtain recruits, it is more likely that such a system did operate unofficially. Other inducements were readily sanctioned; thus African recruiters who enrolled sufficient recruits were officially promised that they would be entitled to non-commissioned ranks in the contingent.[168]

162 *Imvo Zabantsundu*, 11 December 1917 ("France"). Translation from Xhosa.

163 D.C. 768/119/9199, Secretary of Native Affairs to Secretary of Defence, 19 January 1917.

164 Buxton Papers, unsorted, Buxton to Long, 4 November 1917 (copy).

165 C.M.T. 3/92/778/2, W. Carmichael to Chief Magistrate, 10 March 1917.

166 Smit Papers 35/17, D.L. Smit to Magistrate East London, 26 July 1917.

167 C.M.T. 3/930/778/2, Chief Magistrate Transkei to Secretary of Native Affairs, 10 August 1917.

168 S. 3/13/1/2, Resident Commissioner Maseru to Assistant Commissioner Mafeteng, 11 March 1918; 1/T.B.U. 25/66/1, Circular of the Department of Native Affairs,

As an additional strategy, the government deliberately tried to appease those sections of the African population whom they considered most likely to provide recruits for the contingent. This policy was followed in Zululand, where the government officials were sorely disappointed that the Zulu, whom they generally regarded as a martial race *par excellence*, only provided 300 recruits after seven months of intensive recruiting.[169] In an attempt to redress the situation, the government decided to appoint Solomon, son of the revered Dinuzulu, as chief of the Usuthu tribe in Zululand. Dinuzulu's trial and imprisonment after the 1906 rebellion was a controversial issue and deeply resented by the Zulu.[170] By appointing the direct successor of Dinuzulu, the authorities hoped that they could heal old wounds with a view to improve recruiting prospects. Chief Native Commissioner C.A. Wheelwright made it clear in a confidential letter that

> the government feels rather that the Chiefs, in acting independently as they have done, have failed to come up to scratch in ... assisting the Government to obtain labour for the Overseas Contingent, and that it is a question as to what extent Solomon's influence in Zululand might ... be availed of.[171]

Buxton also mentioned in this respect that the "reinstatement of Solomon ... was carried through with the hope that that might assist in recruiting".[172] The Zulu, however, were not to be swayed by Solomon's appointment. During a meeting organised by Solomon and attended by almost 12 000 men, it was reported that the appeal to join the contingent met with the following unambiguous rejection:

> One man raised a shout of 'We are no longer free agents. We belong body and soul to the Gold Mining Companies and the Government'. This declaration seemed to be a straw for which the men had been waiting, as the whole concourse took it up in one shout of 'Electu, electu' [It is our word].

The meeting then came to an abrupt and disorderly end as those present rapidly dispersed.[173] They clearly perceived that Solomon had been co-opted and as the

9 November 1916; C.M.T. 3/930/778/2, Chief Magistrate Transkei to Magistrate Tsolo, 5 September 1916.

169 S.N.A. 1/4/26/1/1917, C.A. Wheelwright to R. Fyfe King, 26 March 1917.

170 Marks, *Reluctant rebellion*, 249-303, 338-65.

171 S.N.A. 1/4/26/1/1917, Wheelwright to Shepstone, 17 November 1916.

172 W.H. Long Papers 947/602/65, Buxton to Long, 5 June 1917.

173 C.M.T. 3/930/778/2, Report by O. Fynney, 9 July 1917 (copy). See also *Zululand Times*, 8 July 1917 ("Solomon's meeting"); *Natal Mercury*, 25 July 1917 ("The Nongoma meeting"); *Natal Advertiser*, 25 September 1917 ("Natives for overseas"); *Ilanga Lase Natal*, 14 September 1917 ("Solomon ka Dinuzulu").

magistrate at Estcourt declared from his particular perspective, "disloyalty to the government is at the root of the matter and as Solomon has identified himself with the government he is ... also a casualty of the same disloyalty..."[174] Given the general attitude of the Zulu, it is not surprising that they formed a distinct minority in the contingent; up to June 1917, only 629 men from the whole of Natal enrolled.[175] Attempts to manipulate tribal attitudes were not restricted to Zululand. In the Transkei, certain magistrates played on traditional rivalries between tribes in an effort to rouse enthusiasm and a spirit of competition as to which tribe could proclaim the most recruits. To their dismay, however, the magistrates found that such contrived "games" were not at all popular.[176]

As in most wartime recruiting campaigns, inflated promises were also made to lure the unsuspecting into the recruiting net. In this respect, Major H. Dales, the officer commanding the contingent's transit and demobilisation depot in Cape Town, complained that "many of the up country commissioners and other authorities made promises to the natives which in numerous instances it was found impossible to carry out".[177] The contents and nature of these promises are difficult to ascertain because they were often made verbally by enterprising recruiters with no official authority to employ such methods. There is sufficient evidence, however, to discern some of the more extravagant promises made; certain recruits were amongst other things informed that they would be relieved from paying poll tax, be exempted from the pass laws and be given free grants of land as well as cattle.[178] These promises were, of course, never kept. While possibly securing the enlistment of some Africans, such deception also contained the seeds of possible future resentment amongst members of the contingent.

After wilful misinterpretation, perhaps the most pervasive recruiting tactic was the intimidation of African chiefs and headmen. Thus, in the Transkei, certain headmen

---

174 S.N.A. 1/4/26/1/1917, Magistrate Estcourt to Wheelwright, 19 July 1917.

175 *Ilanga Lase Natal*, 15 June 1917 ("Native contingent").

176 C.M.T. 3/926/778/2, Magistrate Matatiele to Chief Magistrate Transkei, 3, 26 November and 4 December 1917.

177 O.C. Records 44/22/81, Report on SANLC, 12 April 1918.

178 Roux, *Time longer than rope: A history of the black man's struggle for freedom in South Africa*, 113; J. 318/3/754/21, Native Congress meeting at Pietersburg, 7 September 1921; S.N.A. 1/4/26/1/1917, Captain. A.P. Graham (from France) to C.A. Wheelwright, 8 May 1917 and Wheelwright to Graham, 26 July 1917; Stanford Papers B.C. 293/F4/23, Sworn declaration by P. Seroke, 7 August 1923; C.M.T. 3/927/778/2, Report of a meeting with headmen in the Mount Fletcher District, 23 November 1922.

were told that they would be deposed if they failed to enlist men, and in some cases their subsidies were suspended for not complying with these orders.[179] "Often", as A.K. Xabanisa, a Transkeian member of the contingent testified, it was "only the fear that the government may deprive them of their Chieftainship or Headmanship" that induced them to cooperate.[180]

From intimidation to forceful commandeering was but a short step. Some magistrates, in fact, argued that a drastic approach was the only one which offered any hope of success. G. Cauvin, the magistrate at Port Shepstone, was in no doubt on this point: "It will take years to train and instruct the native mind to a proper sense of duty they owe to King and Country. The only thing they understand at present is brute force. Short of compulsion you will get no recruits." In line with this thinking, Cauvin dropped all pretence of persuasion and decided "to order them out for labour overseas".[181]

Certain chiefs, under pressure from the authorities, also resorted to coercion. Thus, it was reported that Solomon, in an effort to demonstrate that he still exercised control over his subjects, was "press ganging Natives into the Overseas Corps, and a large number of these people were being forced to go whether they liked it or not".[182] Similar tactics were also used in the Transvaal and caused the Transvaal Native Congress to complain that the "Natives were treated like sheep and driven overseas".[183]

Despite such compulsion, it would be wrong to assume that Africans were completely at the mercy of recruiters; as will be shown later, they displayed a certain resourcefulness to avoid being impressed into military service. Nevertheless, it is clear that questionable methods abounded and that some recruits did not, in the true sense of the word, volunteer for the contingent. Although the government officially disapproved of conscription,[184] in practice they turned a blind eye to the way in which recruiting was conducted. As a consequence, through the pressures emanating from magistrates, native commissioners, individual recruiters and chiefs beholden to the authorities, some prospective recruits found themselves enmeshed in a system which

179 C.M.T. 3/925/778/2, Magistrate Tsomo to Chief Magistrate Transkei, 8 and 28 November 1917; C.M.T. 3/925/778/2, Magistrate Kentani to Chief Magistrate Transkei, 27 July 1917.

180 G.G. 549/9/93/179, A.K. Xabanisa to Buxton, 12 January 1918.

181 S.N.A. 1/4/26/1/1917, G. Cauvin to C.A. Wheelwright, 21 September 1917.

182 S.N.A. 1/4/26/1/1917, W.N. Angus to C.A. Wheelwright, 1 October 1917.

183 G.N.L.B. 192/1329/14/48, Transvaal Native Congress meeting, 17 October 1916. See also J. 318/3/754/21, Native Congress meeting, 7 September 1921.

184 S.N.A. 1/4/26/1/1917, C.A. Wheelwright to G. Cauvin, 26 September 1916.

was geared to the whittling away of personal choice. In certain instances, the crucial decision to enlist was taken for them. An anonymous African tellingly described how the recruiting system operated on the ground: the recruiters "come to you, ask your name, they write it down, they tell you to prepare, you have to go over the water".[185] Thus, although official and systematic conscription was not resorted to, informal labour compulsion served much the same purpose.

Despite the variety of carrot and stick methods employed, the government was unable to find sufficient recruits. Initially, in September 1916, the imperial authorities requested 10 000 labourers, but in January 1917 the Union government was urgently requested to send 40 000 men abroad.[186] They failed to reach this target by a considerable margin; in total 25 000 recruits were secured, but after weeding out the sick and infirm 21 000 were eventually sent to France.[187] To make up the shortfall, it was at one stage even contemplated at ministerial level to release selected black prisoners from gaol to supplement the numbers. However, after consultation with the British War Office it was decided not to adopt this contentious and risky policy.[188]

Dismayed at the disappointing response, the authorities, whose attitude in this matter was distinctly paternalistic, accused the Africans of ingratitude towards the Union and imperial governments. Botha, in particular, was distressed that the "natives did not recognise more fully, by joining the Corps, all that the Imperial Government and Union Government had done for them in the past".[189] There were, however, much more cogent reasons for this situation than that suggested by Botha's accusation.

Resistance and apathy

In general, black resistance against white rule has historically assumed a multitude of forms, but its consistent object has been "the avoidance, disturbance, or destruction of one aspect or another of the system of domination".[190] For numerous black men, the call to serve abroad amounted to yet another attempt to dominate and control their lives. However, as is evident from the failure to raise sufficient recruits, many

---

185 *De Burger*, 7 May 1917 ("Opinies uit de Vrijstaat"). Translation.

186 P.M. 1/1/20, British Secretary of State to Governor General, 18 January 1917 (copy).

187 W.O. 107/37, Appendix F, History of the SANLC, 1918.

188 G.G. 549/9/93/167, F.S. Malan to Buxton, 4 October 1917; G.G. 545/9/93/56, British Secretary of State to Governor General, 29 November 1917.

189 Buxton, *General Botha*, 288.

190 Bozzoli, "History, experience and culture", 78.

managed with a considerable degree of success to withstand the pressures exerted during the recruiting campaign. In particular, they were concerned to exercise the right to choose, within limits, the working conditions which offered them the best comparative benefits. Working for the government under war circumstances was clearly not an attractive option. During a recruitment meeting in a township near East London, those present demonstrated that they were not prepared to tolerate unfettered exploitation of their labour. In a clear expression of working class consciousness, they challenged W.R. Ellis, the local superintendent of Native Affairs:

> Who is working the Gold Mines, the Diamond Mines, Coal Mines; what labour laid the Railway to G.W. Africa? Numbers of us have proceeded both to G.E. and G.W. Africa whilst a big contingent is overseas. We have our places to which we will proceed to labour where and when we like.[191]

The most common form of resistance was simply to stay clear of recruiters. "I am aware of instances where, [when] recruiting meetings were in the air, they [the Natives] have deliberately absented themselves and made into the bush", the hapless Ellis of East London reported.[192] A number of Sotho also fled across the border to the Free State where they looked for employment with white farmers in order to avoid being pressed into service.[193] Such tactics were of course the most effective way of resisting what they considered unacceptable demands.

Once recruited, however, another strategy remained – desertion. Some deserted a day or two after they had been attested, or if that was impossible, "during the train journey to Cape Town". In time though, recruiting agents discovered that the number of recruits despatched did not tally with those arriving at the mobilisation camp in Cape Town. In order to prevent desertion, all recruits were then placed under stricter supervision immediately after they had been enrolled.[194]

A further form of resistance is revealed in the tactics of chiefs and headmen who were not prepared to cooperate with the authorities. In order to diminish official pressure, they feigned an interest in recruiting. "Hence you get the familiar impasse, common enough in native territories", one frustrated recruiting officer reported, "of

---

191 1/E.L.N. 71/16/16, W.R. Ellis to Magistrate East London, 26 June 1917.

192 *Ibid.*

193 *De Burger*, 7 May 1917 ("Opinies uit de Vrijstaat").

194 S.N.A. 1/4/26/1/1917, Magistrate Port Shepstone to Wheelwright, 21 September 1917; D.C. 851/253/22714, Magistrate East London to Quartermaster General, 21 June 1917; *Natal Mercury*, 25 July 1917 ("An obstinate native").

the chiefs' polite disdain, sultry indifference, cordial but insincere promises, or even underground thwarting of the Government's proposals".[195] Of course the pretence could not be kept up indefinitely, since the authorities would soon press for tangible results, but in the short term such a delaying strategy was certainly effective.

As well as evoking passive resistance, the recruiting drive also led to the consideration of more drastic action over a wide front. From the Lydenburg district in the Eastern Transvaal it was reported that Africans were stocking up on "assegais and if the Government wants to send them ... to Europe they will use the assegais and make an attack".[196] Likewise, in Griqualand East and Natal some Africans threatened to resist violently any efforts to force them to join the contingent.[197] Furthermore, in the township of East London a protest meeting was held and a motion accepted "that any persons sent by the Government to recruit for the Contingent should be assaulted".[198] As far as can be ascertained these threats were not carried out, but they nevertheless demonstrate the unpopularity of wartime recruitment and the intensity with which some were prepared to resist being dragooned into military service.

Recruitment also generated divisive tensions within black communities, as one speaker at a recruitment meeting in Pretoria revealed:

> When we speak of joining the overseas contingent our women curse and spit
> at us, asking us whether the Government, for whom we propose to risk our
> lives, is not the one which sends the police to our houses at night to pull us and
> our daughters out of bed and trample upon us.[199]

Similarly, in the Bulwer district in Natal it was reported that certain women "made a terrible row" upon learning that their husbands contemplated supporting the Union war effort.[200] It is evident that those who were prepared to consider enlistment ran the risk of being branded collaborators, and it would also appear that women played a pivotal role in dissuading men from enrolling. Although the intransigence of these women may have been prompted by the possible detrimental financial effects of an

---

195 S. 3/13/1/1, Lt. J.N. Fraser to Government Secretary Basutoland, 15 October 1917.

196 J. 255/3/527/17, Commissioner of Police to Secretary of Justice, 24 October 1917.

197 S.A.P. 6/496/17, Lieutenant C.F. Bluett to Officer Commanding Durban, 11 June 1917;
     S.N,A. 1/4/26/1/1917, Magistrate Nongoma to Wheelwright, 10 September 1917.

198 D.L. Smit Papers 36/17, D.L. Smit to State Prosecutor East London, 26 July 1917.

199 Scully, "The colour problem in South Africa", 85.

200 N.A. 9130/69/363, Sworn declaration by Chief Ntshibela, 1 August 1917.

absent breadwinner, the evidence from the meeting in Pretoria certainly suggests that their opposition was also politically inspired.

The recruiting drive caused tension not only between men and women, but also between chiefs and commoners. Those chiefs who cooperated with the authorities, and often formed the cutting edge of the campaign, found that they did so at the expense of alienating their followers. In one particular case, the Pedi chief, Sekhukhune II, was openly confronted by a group of tribesmen who refused to proceed to war after they discovered that he had enlisted them under false pretences. They had already arrived at Germiston station when they learnt that they were about to entrain for war service and not, as the chief had made them believe, for road construction in Mozambique. The authorities tried in vain to persuade them and in desperation Sekhukhune II was called to Germiston to convince them. Even this had no effect. Upon his arrival the chief was told in no uncertain terms by Mpsamaleka, one of the ringleaders,

> that he was teaching him, the chief, a lesson, a lesson to tell the truth ... [and] that in future, when whites tell you something, do not connive with them. We are the tribe, tell us the truth. We should not be herded like goats; that is not right. I am not afraid to go to war, I am not afraid to die. What I want is that you tell us the truth in future. You must tell whites that our people want to be told the truth. We are not going to war.[201]

Turning from the nature of black resistance to the reasons for African apathy, a whole range of considerations unfolds. At one level the government failed to make the war a live issue to Africans, for many of whom the European conflict was a remote event which did not threaten them in any immediate way. Under such circumstances it certainly was a formidable task to convey a convincing appeal to a largely illiterate people. This problem was compounded by the government's refusal to adapt and relate Allied war propaganda in such a way that it might have some relevance for the African population. This is not surprising: the oft-repeated claim that the war was being fought for the rights of oppressed nations could hardly have been conveyed to subject people without arousing in them expectations of greater freedom. The price of the government's enforced silence on this topic was that Africans could neither identify themselves positively with the war aims nor with the war propaganda. Indeed, the government's silence spoke volubly to some Africans who, as a prerequisite for participation, insisted on drastic change within South African society. Thus, Chief Mangala of Western Pondoland declared during a recruiting meeting (though he must

---

201 African Studies Institute, University of the Witwatersrand, Oral History Project, Transcript of an interview with S. Phala, a member of the SANLC, 6 September 1979.

have realised the futility of his demand) that "the Union Government should do away with the colour bar before we go overseas".[202]

Recruitment was further hampered by the perceived inferior role allocated to black men in the South African war effort. Certain educated men argued that since the authorities refused to grant them combatant status and the equality which this implied, they were not prepared to participate in a lesser capacity as labourers. In parts of the Eastern Cape, it was said that if the government "distrusts us so much that it cannot put rifles into our hands when we ask for them in order to fight for the Empire; well then, we are a disloyal, dangerous people; we cannot do anything; we might be a danger to the army in France".[203] This does not, however, imply that blacks would necessarily have enrolled in greater numbers had the government decided to arm them. Their objection to the role assigned to them was only one of a wider range of objections which accounted for African apathy.

The main reasons why they declined to serve are all traceable to one underlying theme, namely basic mistrust. The pervasive nature of black misgivings are perhaps best illustrated by the following conversation between two Africans as reported by a white Natalian farmer who called the speakers A and B:

A: "How are things your way?"

B: "Oh, all right, but there is a lot of talk about the natives the Government wants to go and work over the sea ..."

A: "Yes? ... Why do they want our young men to go and help them?"

B: "I don't know. I don't know what to think."

A: "I thought the white people could not be beaten. Why then do they call upon us to help them?"

B: "I don't know what to think. Why do the white people want to take them ...?"

A: "I won't go and our people won't go."

B: "I hear that the white people will ... take our boys if they don't go."

A: "Yes, then if they do that, there is going to be trouble ..."

B: "The white people will humbug us about this."

A: "Yes, they are a clever people."

---

202 C.M.T. 3/925/778/2, Report of a meeting with Chief Mangala, 10 November 1916.

203 *The Christian Express*, 2 July 1917 ("Native recruiting").

According to the farmer, this was the prevailing attitude amongst a considerable number of Africans he had been in contact with: "They all appear to have the same idea that the white man is 'humbugging' them in some way".[204]

The general lack of trust found more specific expression in a refusal to cooperate with those governmental institutions which were responsible for controlling the lives of Africans in peacetime and now, in time of war, were utilised to obtain their goodwill and support. In particular, the recruiting drive suffered from its association with the Native Affairs Department. For many Africans the Department was a symbol of oppression. "Nine cases out of ten a native goes to Native Affairs Department office and comes out of it fully convinced that it is the Native Oppression and Persecution Department", ran a black newspaper's summary of the general attitude towards the department.[205] Not surprisingly then, objections were raised because recruitment for the contingent – "an essentially Imperial Native business" – was conducted by "a narrow-minded set of officials whose outlook and methods in Native matters ... are selfish and short-sighted".[206] Blacks who involved themselves in recruitment were also confronted with this dilemma. Sol Plaatje found that his own efforts to raise recruits were hampered by the "Union's methods of administering native affairs".[207]

It was on the basis of their day-to-day encounters with unsympathetic and overbearing officials that certain Africans formed their concept of the Union government. While in a vague, somewhat utopian way, some Africans might still have considered the British government to be more liberal and therefore worthy of their support, the attitude of the Union government was often perceived to be harsh and despotic. At a recruiting meeting held in Pretoria, a speaker clearly revealed how the arbitrary conduct of officials, in this case the police, shaped African perceptions and ultimately influenced their attitude towards the war effort: "We are not against the King of England; in fact he is our only hope. But as for the Union Government, it has thrown us away like filthy rags. We are loyal, but what about those police who kick us and shove us out of the way?"[208]

Moreover, certain individuals, selected as recruiting agents, were most unlikely to secure African cooperation. In Natal, the choice of Sir George Leuchars, who was well

204 *Natal Mercury*, 3 October 1916 (Letter from 'A colonist of 35 years standing').

205 *Tsala ea Batho*, 15 August 1914 ("The administration of our native affairs").

206 *Imvo Zabantsundu*, 28 November 1916 (Letter from 'A Native').

207 *Diamond Fields Advertiser*, 22 August 1917 ("Native grievances").

208 Scully, "The colour problem in South Africa", 85.

remembered for his severe suppression of the Zulu rebellion in 1906, was generally unpopular. "That fact alone will contribute to militate against the success of recruiting natives in this province and Zululand", an African observer noted.[209]

And so it did – Leuchars subsequently admitted to Botha that he was unable to raise recruits in any considerable number but, understandably, he failed to mention that his lack of standing had any bearing on the matter.[210] Like Leuchars, other officials in Natal were also frustrated in their recruiting efforts because their past conduct in quelling the 1906 rebellion counted against them.[211]

A further and important reason for the prevailing apathy relates to African reservations and apprehensions about the government's land policy. The Natives' Land Act 27 of 1913, in particular, had generated considerable resentment and the subsequent Native Administration Bill 1917, which the government was considering at the time of the onset of war, increased African fears that they might be dispossessed of their land. Even Buxton, who was a staunch supporter of the Union's policy in this respect, had to admit that it had a negative effect on recruitment:

> The feeling of unrest which has undoubtedly followed the introduction and discussion of the Native Land Bill ... has made the natives very suspicious, and made many of them believe that they will be consequently dispossessed of their land. This makes them afraid to go away just now in case they may find when they come back that their homes have been removed.[212]

However, it was not only the implications of official policy which alarmed Africans. Certain white farmers, anxious to retain their labour, undermined the recruiting drive by intimidating those Africans who considered enlistment. Threats that their families would be evicted were a powerful deterrent. "How can a Native join the colours if he is fully aware of the fact that his house might be destroyed after his departure?" asked Daniel Hafe from Natal.[213]

In addition, some Africans were not impressed by the conditions of service in the contingent. The somewhat higher than average wage to be earned by joining was not sufficient to induce them to proceed to an unknown and strange country for the

209 *Ilanga Lase Natal*, 15 June 1917 (Letter from J. Mampumulo).

210 P.M. 1/1/482, Leuchars to Botha, 21 August 1917.

211 N.A. 9130/69/363, M. Ndabaco to Wheelwright, 6 September 1917.

212 W.H. Long Papers 947/602/80, Buxton to Long, 28 July 1917.

213 *Ilanga Lase Natal*, 26 October 1917 (Letter from Daniel Hafe).

purpose of labouring under risky wartime circumstances. As one African explained "the wage of £3 per month was not enough in France where bullets were flying about, seeing that a similar wage was obtainable on the mines in Johannesburg without the fear of bullets".[214] Moreover, the closed compound system was criticised and certain educated Africans also argued that the opportunities for advancement in the contingent were too limited. Initially they could be promoted to the rank of sergeant – called "chief induna" so as not to embarrass white sergeants – but as these appointments were in terms of authority on par with those of their white counterparts, they soon ceased and blacks were restricted to the rank of corporal. This had a detrimental effect, particularly on those educated men who might have aspired to higher positions.[215] Finally, African reluctance to proceed to France increased with the news that the *SS Mendi* – a transport ship carrying members of the contingent – had sunk on 21 February 1917 with the loss of 615 African lives, after a collision with the *SS Darro* off the Isle of Wight.[216]

In the overall evaluation, it is clear that the main reasons for African apathy were directly related to the fact that they as subordinated second-class citizens were not convinced of the need to go and serve in a foreign war. Indeed, for many the battle was at home rather than abroad. However, there were of course, also those who did join.

Reasons for enlisting

In assessing the motives of African recruits, the emphasis will be placed on those who joined the SANLC for service in France. Those who had enlisted for the South-West African and East African campaigns are excluded, partly because of a lack of information on their reasons for doing so, but also because a considerable number of those sent to South-West were either transferred from the South African Railways or seconded by the Chamber of Mines and had little or no choice in the matter. Those who enrolled for France had, albeit only comparatively, a greater degree of choice. At the same time it must be borne in mind that the question of choice was, as far as African recruitment was concerned, also a relative term.

214 *Cape Times*, 28 March 1917 ("Native Labour for France").

215 O.C. Records 447/22/81, Report on the SANLC, 12 April 1918; G.G. 545/9/93/56, Botha to Buxton, 23 July 1917; C.M.T. 3/930/778/2, Magistrate Tsolo to Chief Magistrate Transkei, 5 September 1917.

216 C.M.T. 3/926/778/2, Report of a meeting in the Matatiele district, 17 March 1917; W.H. Long Papers 947/602/84, Buxton to Long, 15 April 1917; Willan, "South African Native Labour Contingent, 1916-1918", 70.

It is of considerable interest that a disproportionately large number of recruits were drawn from the Northern Transvaal. Buxton estimated that this area contributed 66 percent of the total number, whilst Lieutenant Colonel H.P. Wolff, a senior officer in the contingent, calculated that the region produced 60 percent of the recruits.[217] Such a high percentage is surprising. In the first place, the combined African population in other regions such as Zululand, the Transkei, Basutoland, and the Eastern Cape far exceeded that of the Northern Transvaal. Secondly, Africans in these areas had been exposed to British values over a fairly long period and would conceivably have been more receptive to recruiting appeals emphasising 'loyalty and duty' to the empire. Although Africans in these parts were not necessarily enthusiastic about the British connection, it has to be explained why their contribution to the contingent was eclipsed by the comparatively less populous Northern Transvaal, where British influence was weaker.

Botha claimed it was because Africans were better treated in the Transvaal than elsewhere and therefore showed greater willingness to support the SANLC.[218] Other explanations were less disingenuous and more persuasive. H. Lambert, a senior official in the Colonial Office, made a perceptive comment on the uneven regional distribution of recruits: "I think it was simply because ... conditions in the Transvaal were less satisfactory than in the native territories that the natives were readier to leave their homes".[219]

Indeed, conditions in the Northern Transvaal (currently Limpopo province) do provide the key to understanding why this area produced such a large percentage of recruits. At the time of the recruiting drive the region experienced an intense drought. In April 1917, the native commissioner in the Soutpansberg district commented that because of the very bad drought "we expect the natives to be asking for assistance shortly".[220] This was in fact the worst drought in 26 years,[221] and severely undermined the self-sufficiency of African peasants dependent on agriculture. Moreover, other avenues of employment were restricted.[222] Consequently, military service became an

---

217 W.H. Long Papers 947/602/80, Buxton to Long, 28 July 1917; U.W.H. 89/34, Report on the SANLC by Lieutenant Colonel. H.P. Wolff, 8 March 1919.

218 *Cape Times*, 21 April 1917 ("Parliamentary debates").

219 C.O. 551/123/35976, Marginal note by H. Lambert, 16 June 1919 on correspondence between Botha and Colonial Office, 1 June 1919.

220 S.N.A. 1/4/26/1/1917, Native Commissioner Pietersburg to C.A. Wheelwright, 19 April 1917.

221 Blignaut, "Die reënval van die Pietersburg-plato", 106.

222 N.A. 99/568, Director of Native Labour to Secretary of Native Affairs, 22 March 1917.

option worth considering. Joining the SANLC meant that poverty-stricken Africans were at least assured of an income, part of which could be remitted to their destitute families. "To keep the wolf from the door", was, according to the local native commissioner, an important reason why a considerable number of Africans from the Northern Transvaal decided to enrol.[223]

It was not only the prevailing drought in this area which helped to swell the ranks of the SANLC, however. According to Buxton, it would also appear that more pressure was exerted on the African population in this region than in other parts. He suggested:

> The natives there [the Northern Transvaal] no doubt are somewhat more under the control of their Chiefs, and the Chiefs there are more under control of the Government than elsewhere, ... [and] the legitimate pressure by Officials has produced a greater result than it has produced elsewhere.[224]

Whether such pressures were indeed 'legitimate' is open to doubt, but the importance of Buxton's statement lies in his explanation of the regional discrepancy in numbers. In an article in *The Christian Express*, essentially the same point was made in somewhat more euphemistic terms. The African response was generally disappointing, it reported, "except in the Transvaal where General Louis Botha has been able to apply administrative pressure".[225]

Although the drought and official harassment in the Northern Transvaal propelled Africans into service, there were also other reasons why Africans from various regions of the Union enlisted. One important aspect to be considered in this respect is the representation of the black elite in the contingent. "Educated natives of all kinds have volunteered", noted the Reverend John Lennox of Lovedale, who accompanied the contingent as a chaplain: "They have left their schools, their businesses, their congregations to serve the King".[226] Likewise, C.A. Wheelwright of Natal mentioned that "a great proportion of Natives who have gone Overseas is of the more or less educated type".[227] The black elite was clearly well represented; missionaries who went with the SANLC calculated that they constituted 25 percent of the total[228] –

223 N.A. 99/568, Native Commissioner Pietersburg to Secretary Native Affairs, 24 October 1917.

224 W.H. Long Papers 947/602/80, Buxton to Long, 28 July 1917.

225 *The Christian Express*, 2 July 1917 ("Recruiting for the Native Labour Contingent").

226 *Alice Times*, 24 May 1917 (Letter from the Reverend John Lennox).

227 S.N.A. 1/4/26/1/1917, A. Wheelwright to Magistrate Nongoma, 27 September 1917.

228 *The Christian Express*, 1 November 1917 ("The SANLC"); *Ilanga Lase Natal*, 9 November 1917 (Letter from L. Hertslet).

a significant proportion when considered in relation to their relatively small size in the population as a whole. There is insufficient evidence to provide a statistical breakdown of the different professions practised by the educated Africans in the contingent, but from various scattered sources it appears that teachers were in the majority.[229]

Educated blacks formed a clearly defined aspiring class in South African society. They were, in the main, products of English mission schools and had integrated the values of a Christian-British education with their own African consciousness. They shared a common ideological outlook, and at the time of the First World War the effects of their socialisation were discernible in their support of the British Empire – a symbolic embodiment of "justice and fairness" – and the perception that their own future was linked to that of the empire. Moreover, integral to this was the notion of a common imperial citizenry, linked with the belief in 'progress' and that recognition depended in part on their unflagging efforts to develop and improve their own abilities. Progress and improvement were vital concepts in these African circles.[230]

The value system of this class is of central importance in determining why they joined the contingent. It made them generally more responsive to the idea of serving the empire in a time of need, while the recruiting appeals which emphasised 'loyalty and patriotism', and the notion that service abroad was an educative experience, also struck a particularly sensitive chord. J. Mtemba expressed the sentiments of his class when he wrote in a letter from France: "It is ambition that comes first when a man thinks of coming here, and then extension of knowledge and last comes patriotism and loyalty".[231] Similarly, for R.M. Tunzi enrolment in the SANLC was "a splendid chance" of "learning about the world and becoming well informed men".[232] Just how widespread the idea was that military service in France presented a chance to acquire a broader educative experience, is evident from the comment of the resident commissioner in Basutoland that most of the 1 397 Sotho who had joined "were men who had passed through school and were anxious to see the world".[233] Closely allied to the preceding notion was the self-perception of this class as standard-bearers of a

---

229 *Ilanga Lase Natal*, 10 May 1918 (Letter from 'A Native'); G.G. 549/9/93/179, A.K. Xabanisa-Buxton, 10 December 1917; C.M.T. 3/930/778/2, M.J.C. Matheson to Chief Magistrate Transkei, 29 January 1918; S.N.A. 1/4/26/1/1917, A.E. LeRoy to E. Crosse, 30 August 1917; *Native Teachers' Journal*, October 1920 (Letter from F.H. Kumalo).

230 See for instance the analysis by Willan, 'Plaatje', 36.

231 *Ilanga Lase Natal*, 7 December 1917 (Letter from J. Mtembu).

232 *Imvo Zabantsundu*, 22 May 1917 (Letter from R.M. Tunzi).

233 S. 3/13/2/3, Report of Resident Commissioner Maseru, 15 August 1917.

new breed of 'civilized' Africans; they considered it as a self-imposed task to induce others to follow their example in the quest for 'improvement'. Thus, F.H. Kumalo, a Natal teacher who had joined the contingent, declared: "Although our schools needed us, we felt that it was our duty to lead the way ..."[234]

The manner in which patriotic and loyal considerations surfaced as motives for enlistment, is clear from the following interview between a newspaper reporter and W.B. Yiba, a member of the SANLC:

> 'Was it the pay that attracted you?' 'No Sir', was the prompt reply. 'When I volunteered I was a compositor at the "Imvo" office at King [Williamstown], and I was getting the same pay as I was offered by the British government'. 'What then induced you to leave your wife and family to go to France?' Pulling himself together and looking as if such a question were quite unnecessary, he promptly replied, 'I answered the call of my King'.[235]

It can be argued, that such stylised patriotic declarations were mere rhetoric and should not be accepted at face value. It assumes greater validity, however, seen against the background of the prevailing loyalist ideology expounded by so many members of the aspiring African class.

In contrast to the 'lofty' motives of this class, there were also criminals serving with the SANLC who had joined to cover their tracks and evade arrest and punishment. H. Bulaweni, for instance, was wanted in connection with a murder case in the Engcobo district in the Transkei. He enrolled in the contingent under an assumed name and was only apprehended on his return from France. In the subsequent court case, Bulaweni was condemned to death after he had confessed his guilt; he also admitted that he had enlisted "with the idea of trying to escape the consequences of the stabbing".[236] In another case, the authorities were informed of "a Native who had offered his services and after enlistment was found to be wanted by the police in connection with a charge of murder". This man was then arrested in the mobilisation camp in Cape Town.[237] Those who had committed other crimes also perceived the contingent to be a relatively safe haven where they could establish a new identity and prevent police detection. Thus, as it transpired later, "several Natives

---

234 *Native Teachers' Journal*, October 1920 (Letter from F.H. Kumalo).

235 *Alice Times*, 20 December 1917 ("Interview with returned corporal").

236 J. 256/3/527/17 I, Rex vs. H. Bulaweni, July 1918.

237 G.G. 545/9/93/56, Botha to Buxton, 23 June 1917.

who belonged to the Johannesburg criminal class" had joined the contingent.[238] The 'criminal class' referred to by the authorities, might have had members of the Ninevite gang on the Witwatersrand – an extensive criminal organisation which, significantly, was increasingly pressurised by the police at the time of the First World War.[239]

Highly personal and individual reasons also prompted some Africans to join. Jason Jingoes, for one, was disconsolate and depressed after an unrequited romantic entanglement; war service seemed to offer a dramatic escape from the turmoil of his personal life. "But it was because of Jemina that I wanted to die in France without a wife", he explained.[240] Others, young and perhaps bored with their daily existence and the narrow confines of everyday life, considered war service as an eventful and exciting new experience. S. Phala, for example, recalled that "we were driven by adventure as young men".[241]

Conclusion

The question of African recruitment was firmly rooted in the politics of the time. Africans also joined for a variety of reasons, ranging from aspiring notions pertaining to loyalty and self-improvement to more material and pecuniary considerations. It should be emphasised though that the reasons why Africans decided to join the contingent cannot be categorised in watertight compartments; more than one reason or a combination of reasons could have influenced an individual's decision. It is therefore difficult to determine which particular set of reasons was of overriding significance. Nevertheless, when it is taken into account that the majority of recruits were drawn from the drought- and poverty-stricken Northern Transvaal it can be assumed that for a considerable number material considerations were of crucial importance.

238 G.G. 545/9/93/56, Major H. Dales to British Staff Officer, 28 June 1917.

239 Van Onselen, *Studies in the Social and Economic History of the Witwatersrand*, 192.

240 Perry and Perry, *Jingoes*, 75.

241 African Studies Institute, University of the Witwatersrand, Oral History Project, Transcript of an interview with S. Phala, 6 September 1979.

IN THE CRUCIBLE

The nature of military service

At issue here, is the wartime experience of those Africans who had enrolled for service in South-West Africa, East Africa and France. In particular, attention is paid to the travails of wartime service and the reasons for the termination of service for the labour contingent in France.

Ways of working and dying in German South-West Africa and East Africa

As far as South-West Africa was concerned, approximately 500 men worked as stevedores in Walvis Bay, where they assisted in unloading war supplies, while a considerable number were responsible for all the animal transport and served as drivers of ammunition and supply wagons. Most, however, were employed to repair rail links destroyed by the retreating Germans and particularly in the construction of new railways, linking the northern South African station, Prieska, to the southern station in the war zone, Kalkfontein (modern Karasburg), some 490 kilometres distant.[242]

The strategic importance of the railways to the South African war effort made their speedy completion imperative, and to this end relay teams of workers toiled day and night. Although the white personnel were highly praised in official reports for their part in the project, no mention was made of the important role of black labourers. It seemed that their work was taken for granted. This presumption rankled with people

---

242 *Ilanga Lase Natal*, 22 January 1914 ("German South-West African campaign");
 G.N.L.B. 190/1300/14/D 78, Lieutenant A.W. Biddell to Director of Native Labour,
 18 November 1914; N.A. 9111/36/363, Mendi Memorial Addresses, 1932.

like Sol Plaatje who commented "lest their behaviour merit recognition, their deeds and acts must, on account of their colour, not be recorded".[243]

Although blacks served as non-combatants, this did not imply that they were not exposed to the dangers of warfare. In the course of their duties, a number of transport riders came under German fire at Sandfontein (in the southern part of South-West) and were captured in September 1914. There is limited, but telling, evidence available on the manner in which the Germans treated black prisoners of war with some being tortured and mutilated.

An anonymous African later testified that those who had managed to escape and had found their way back to the Union "tell piteous stories and bear marks of their treatment by the Germans ... [s]ome had one eye scooped out, some had their ears cut off, and others were castrated".[244] It is unlikely that this was an exaggeration. In 1916, a South African commission of enquiry, though concerned with the German treatment of white prisoners of war, remarked in passing and in an understated tone that the way in which the Germans treated their black captives showed "instances of hardship and in one or two instances of what would be according to our ideas cruelty".[245] Allegedly this happened because the Germans had warned blacks not to become involved in hostilities between the 'white races'. Since the Germans themselves employed blacks in their colonial forces, this injunction must and cannot be taken at face value. It is more likely that the Germans wished to send a message to local inhabitants that they must not consider assisting the invading force. Whatever the precise motive, certain South African prisoners of war suffered badly.

During the East African campaign, as in South-West, South African blacks served as transport drivers and as dock and railway workers. The climate and terrain, however, differed markedly, and in East Africa the men also acted as porters and carriers in areas difficult to traverse by animal and wagon transport. A South African missionary who had visited the contingent was impressed by the part played by transport workers on the supply lines in conveying food, ammunition, material for bridges, wireless

---

243 Plaatje, *Native life in South Africa*, 267. See also U.G. 24-16, Report of the Board of the South African Railways and Harbours, 1915, 2-3; Beaton, "Railway construction during the campaign of 1914-15 in German South-West Africa", 1-11.

244 G.N.L.B. 192/1329/14/D 48, Anonymous intercepted letter, 27 October 1914. See also *Tsala ea Batho*, 14 November 1914 ("German South-West campaign").

245 U.G. 13-1916, Report of the Commission of Enquiry into the treatment of prisoners of war by the German Protectorate Authorities during the late hostilities, 8.

apparatus, telegraph wire, and medical stores. This prompted him to ask: "Who shall say that they are not doing their bit?"[246]

The nature of the work in East Africa was arduous, and it was also performed under adverse tropical conditions. Moreover, the workers had to contend with the ravages of disease, particularly malaria. For the troops this was probably one of the worst features of an exceptionally difficult campaign. Those who were stationed in unhealthy areas and had contracted the disease had no better than a slim chance of survival. During the first four months of 1917, when a section of the force was quartered along the coast in an area heavily infested with malaria, fully 1 600 of the 2 000 men (80 percent) succumbed, while those that survived were often broken in health for the remainder of their lives. The fatalities did not end in East Africa; of the 700 men on board the ship *Aragon*, 135 died before it reached Durban. For the contingent as a whole (18 000 men) the monthly mortality rate shot up from 5,4 per 1 000 to 22,2 per 1 000. After a visit to the war zone, a South African official recorded that many black labourers "became saturated with fever which sapped all their energy, enterprise and morale. Self-help and self-respect almost disappeared. Men lay down to die rather than combat the difficulties in the field."[247] Clearly, the human dimension behind the statistics is one of profound misery. "The suffering of these men defies description", the commanding officer, Major T.E. Liefeldt, later recalled.[248]

Disease, of course, made no distinction between Allied or German troops, or between black and white. All the troops in East Africa suffered from malaria, but blacks and whites did not suffer equally. Although there are no comparable statistics for white South African troops during the height of the disease between January and April 1917, their average monthly mortality was considerably lower than that of blacks and did not exceed 2,9 per 1 000.[249] Major General R.A. Ewart, the South African quartermaster general in East Africa, ascribed the sudden increase in black mortality during the first four months of 1917 to the inclement rainy season, and the

---

246 *The Christian Express*, 1 July 1916 ("Sidelights on the campaign in East Africa"). See also G.G. 480/9/57/19, Report on the Union Natives on Military Service in East Africa, 27 June 1917.

247 G.G. 480/9/57/19, Report on the Union Natives on Military Service in East Africa, 27 June 1917. See also D.C. 769/1997/9199, Botha to Buxton, 30 April 1917 (copy).

248 N.A. 9111/36/363, Mendi Memorial Addresses, 1932.

249 *Cape Times*, 21 February 1917 ("Parliamentary debates"); Merriman Papers 246, Botha to Merriman, 27 April 1917; D.C. 769/185/9199, Major General R.A. Ewart to Secretary of Defence, 28 May 1917.

discrepancy between the number of white and black deaths to the different kinds of work and conditions experienced during the campaign. He explained:

> During this period the European troops have been practically stationary owing to the heavy rains and, although they have suffered considerably owing to their retention in unhealthy areas ... they have not been exposed to the same hardships as the native transport personnel and porters who have had to work day after day in pouring rain over incredibly bad roads, delivering or carrying the bare requirements of the Force.[250]

In South Africa, news of the disconcerting number of deaths amongst the troops caused uneasiness in government circles. Botha, in particular, expressed his doubts whether sufficient care had been taken about the welfare of the contingent:

> However bad Malaria may be in East Africa, I am unable to believe that the death rate amongst the Native labourers can be so much higher than amongst the European and Coloured troops, unless there is much that is lamentably lacking in the military arrangements for rationing and medical and hospital treatment.[251]

In response to this situation, Botha instructed H.S. Cooke, assistant director of Native Labour in South Africa, to conduct an enquiry into the circumstances that had led to the appalling death rate amongst South African blacks in East Africa. Cooke interviewed 41 whites associated with the contingent as well as some of the black members. He concluded that although the mortality rate was particularly high, it was inevitable in view of the nature of the campaign. Inadequate hospital and medical facilities, poor organisation and negligence did not, he claimed, aggravate the situation.[252] This is doubtful. Fourteen years after the war, Major T.E. Liefeldt acknowledged that the hospital facilities for South African blacks were woefully inadequate and disorganised.[253] Moreover, Lieutenant Colonel O.F. Watkins, director of the labour bureau for all military labour in East Africa, stated at the end of the war: "Where a Medical Officer had to deal with white and with black patients in times of stress, the latter suffered. In a word, the condition of the patient was apt to be a consideration

---

250 D.C. 769/185/9199, Major General R.A. Ewart to Secretary of Defence, 28 May 1917.

251 Merriman Papers 246, Botha to Merriman, 27 April 1917.

252 G.G. 480/9/57/19, Report on the Union Natives on Military Service in East Africa, 27 June 1917.

253 N.A. 9111/36/363, Mendi Memorial Addresses, 1932.

subordinate to his colour ..."[254] In contrast to the conclusion in Cooke's report then, it seems clear that the lives of many South African blacks in East Africa were lost through the prevalence of discriminatory practices.

The soaring death rate amongst South African blacks in East Africa forced Botha to act before he had received Cooke's flawed report. Despite protests from the military authorities, in April 1917 he ordered the cessation of recruitment for East Africa. Botha appears to have been genuinely concerned about the fate of South African blacks in East Africa. "Nothing has grieved me more", he claimed in a private letter, "because apart from the dictates of humanity, if there is one thing I have insisted upon during this war it is that the treatment and well-being of our Natives who have responded to the call for labourers should be properly provided for in every possible way".[255] It is unlikely that this was the only reason for Botha's decision to stop recruitment for East Africa. He was keen that recruitment for the labour contingent in France should be speeded up and given first priority, and this consideration also seems to have played a part in his decision to call off competing recruitment for East Africa.[256]

It was not only malaria and neglect that made war services for South African blacks a particularly harsh experience. In East Africa, as well as in South-West, disciplinary measures also became an issue. Although the authorities did try with the advent of the South-West African campaign to codify the procedures to be followed, and decreed that officers should deal with minor transgressions and a provost marshal or magistrate with more serious cases,[257] these regulations were honoured more in the breach than in the observance. In fact, the white 'gang bosses' who directly supervised black labourers were a law unto themselves and frequently resorted to corporal punishment as a means of coercion or retribution. E. Dower, secretary for Native Affairs, stated that he "has received constant complaints from all parts as to the indiscriminate punishment and flogging of natives, being inflicted without any proper enquiring and by conductors and other persons in no responsible positions".[258] Similarly, the commanding officer of the labour depot at De Aar where the blacks assembled before

254 C.O. 533/216/4603, Report on Military Labour in East Africa, 31 December 1919.

255 Merriman Papers 246, Botha to Merriman, 27 April 1917.

256 D.C. 851/219/2274, Major Leifeldt to Director Native Labour, undated; J.C. Smuts Collection, CXV/100, Bourne to Staff Officer German East Africa, 2 December 1916; D.C. 768/129/1997, Bourne to Staff Officer German East Africa, 23 February 1917.

257 D.C. 625/205/9199, Director of Transport to Officer Commanding Transport, German South-West Africa, 18 December 1914.

258 D.C. 625/205/9199, Secretary of Native Affairs to Secretary of Defence, 24 February 1915.

and after service in South-West reported that "from complaints received from various parts it would appear that the men directly in charge of Natives resort to unlimited chastisement and that the Natives are subject to severe ill-treatment".[259] In this respect, the treatment of South African blacks did not differ much from that in other colonial armies in Africa where flogging was a common form of punishment. It was thought to be the most effective way of disciplining African soldiers and was only finally abolished by the British in 1946.[260] This form of punishment only applied to blacks and was never inflicted on white troops during the First World War. Indeed, the flogging of white troops in the British army had been ended decades before in 1881.[261]

The South African authorities approved of flogging as an established form of punishment, but considered it prudent to issue directives that the "flogging of natives should be restricted to punishment for very grave offences and should only be sanctioned by quite senior and responsible officers and proper steps should be taken to see that it is properly carried out without undue severity".[262] Informing these caveats of 'proper steps' and 'undue severity', was amongst other things a concern on the part of the authorities that reports of the ill-treatment of labourers might filter through to the Union and discourage other Africans from enlisting.[263]

These regulations did little to ameliorate rough wartime justice. There were simply more pressing military matters to attend to. Even in cases where Africans were actually brought to trial, it was often not for the purpose of dispensing justice. For example, in one incident in Walvis Bay, three black dock workers refused to work after their contracts had expired. A month before the time they had informed their supervisors that they did not intend to renew their contracts. They were nevertheless arrested and had to stand trial before the assistant provost marshal, who summarily dismissed the case and sentenced the workers to be horsewhipped. The commanding officer, Lieutenant A.W. Biddell, fearing that the punishment might lead to general discontent, felt obliged to make an obvious point to the officer concerned:

---

259 D.C. 625/205/9199, Officer Commanding De Aar to Director of Native Labour, 21 January 1915.

260 Killingray, "The colonial army in the Gold Coast: Official policy and local response, 1890-1947", 243.

261 Spiers, *The Army and society, 1815-1914*, 90.

262 D.C. 625/205/9199, Secretary of Native Affairs to Secretary of Defence, 24 February 1915.

263 C.S.O. 50175, Secretary of Native Affairs to Secretary of Defence, 5 January 1917; D.C. 625/205/9199, Secretary of Native Affairs to Secretary of Defence, 24 February 1915.

> Don't you think the sentence was rather severe? In cases like these where there appears to be a *bona fide* grievance as far as the natives are concerned, I think it would be better if you first of all enquired into that grievance before trying and sentencing to corporal punishment.[264]

Not surprisingly, South African black troops had to endure the same punishments and arbitrary justice in East Africa. Major T.E. Liefeldt himself admitted that he was unable to exert any effective control:

> Though indiscriminate flogging of natives ... is prohibited, I have reason to know that the practice is indulged in to a considerable extent by transport conductors and other subordinates who unfortunately are supported by their officers, thus depriving the native of any possibility of redress ... Flogging would seem to be the only recognised method of punishing the native who receives his 25 cuts with a sjambok for the most trivial offence, in most cases without any pretence of a trial, proving his guilt or otherwise.[265]

This practice was so widespread and so harshly carried out, that it stirred some Christian consciences in South Africa. During a session of the Anglican Church synod in Johannesburg, the Reverend E. Paget raised the issue. Perceptively he realised that the punishment meted out to South African blacks did not primarily stem from military procedures or demands, but that "the treatment that went on there was very largely due to the accepted attitude of the white people towards the natives in South Africa, and that they were almost treated as being of less importance than the mule or oxen". Indeed the wider values of society were crucial in determining the nature of military punishment and therefore Paget could argue convincingly that the "whole thing is due to the brutal, callous and absolutely ungodly and beastly attitude of the average white person towards the natives".[266]

This outlook also opened the door for corruption. For the most trivial offences the so-called gang bosses in South West-Africa arbitrarily inflicted fines ranging from £1 to £2, a heavy penalty considering that the average wage of African labourers was about £3 per month. Moreover, to add insult to injury, these gang bosses often pocketed the money themselves. Punishing and fining Africans thus became a lucrative way for gang bosses to supplement their own incomes. The authorities did try to stop

---

264 D.C. 626/108/9199, Lieutenant A.W. Biddell to Officer Commanding Walvis Bay, 3 March 1915 and Biddell to Assistant Provost Marshal, 5 March 1915.

265 D.C. 850/104/22714, Major Liefeldt to Director Native Labour, 3 February 1917 (copy).

266 *Rand Daily Mail*, 20 September 1917 ("How the natives are treated").

such corruption by insisting that only the paymaster could dock African wages, but since the gangbosses themselves were the ultimate authority in the day-to-day work situation it is highly unlikely that these malpractices were rooted out. As a matter of fact, senior officers with the force admitted that there was little they could do to remedy the position.[267]

It stands to reason that these circumstances must have provoked African resentment. However, the very nature of the system to which they were subjected ensured, officially at least, that the African voice remained inaudible. Thus, a labourer known as John, who was upset about a fine he had to pay, "was threatened with being put in the stocks when he wanted to make representation".[268] Moreover, in cases where Africans did manage to make their grievances known, the authorities, despite ample corroborating evidence, showed no inclination to believe information emanating from labourers and even less willingness to act upon their requests. When headman Malokoane of the Pietersburg (currently Polokwane) district approached the Defence Force for permission to investigate the situation, after he had been informed by some returning members of the treatment meted out to labourers in South-West, the request was turned down with the following comment: "Natives are prone to magnify and publish their grievances, and it is doubtful if Malokoane's impression would be of value to Defence Force interests".[269]

Others followed a more direct route to air their grievances. Several strikes occurred in South-West Africa. These were usually of short duration and often ended in the arrest of the ringleaders, with the others being cajoled or forced back to work. But on one occasion, marked by the solidarity of some 365 workers who persistently refused to return to work, the authorities were forced to accede to their demand to be sent back to South Africa.[270] Desertion was another way in which some manifested

---

267 D.C. 625/205/9199, Quartermaster General to Director of Native Labour, 29 January 1915
     (copy); U.G. 14-1916, Report on the work done by the Inspection Staff on War Expenditure
     in connection with the rebellion and the German South-West Campaign to the end of
     October 1915, 20.

268 C.M.T. 3/926/772/8, H. Lowry on behalf of 'John' to Director of Native Labour,
     24 August 1915.

269 D.C. 625/67/9199, Magistrate Pietersburg to Secretary of Defence, 15 June 1915, and
     Secretary of Defence to Magistrate Pietersburg, 12 July 1915.

270 D.C. 625/108/9199, Officer Commanding Walvis Bay to Headquarters Swakopmund,
     3 March 1915 and Secretary of Defence to Director of Native Labour, 27 November 1914
     (copy); D.C. 625/205/9199, Quartermaster Central Force to Quartermaster General Pretoria,
     21 March 1915.

their dissatisfaction. The vastness and inhospitality of the terrain in South-West did not deter prospective deserters; they hid in empty goods trains bound for the Union. At times desertion assumed considerable proportions, as is evident from a telegram despatched by a distressed officer in command of large numbers of transport workers: "Very short of Natives owing to many deserting".[271] There can be little doubt that for many workers the problems involved in deserting were of lesser importance than the treatment they had to endure in military service.

Vicissitudes in France

The 21 000 men in France formed part of an ever increasing general labour force in (consisting of Chinese, Japanese, Indian, Egyptian, French, Canadian and British labourers, as well as German prisoners of war) who had to provide the necessary infrastructure for the soldiers fighting in the trenches. In December 1916, there was a total of 42 000 military labourers; a year later in December 1917, the number had increased to 91 097 and at the end of the war it stood at 124 299.[272] In December 1917, shortly before its withdrawal from France, the SANLC constituted 23 percent, or almost a quarter, of the total labour force. Clearly, in terms of numbers they contributed significantly to the combined Allied workforce.

The contingent was divided into 42 companies of about 500 men each. Some companies were employed in laying and repairing railway lines and roads, and in lumbering in the French forests to provide the Allied forces with timber for construction work. Other companies worked in stone quarries. Most, however, were employed in the French harbours, Le Havre, Rouen and Dieppe, where they unloaded ammunition, food supplies and timber, and transferred these to trains bound for the front.[273] A military chaplain, the Reverend R. Keable, has graphically described the nature of their work in the dockyard areas. They worked in "great, gaunt, enormous sheds of iron and steel. Trains run into these and are dwarfed to insignificance. Ships of three or four thousand tons stretch in a line outside." The moment a ship had anchored, the men sprang into action: "As fast as the stores are built up into monstrous heaps in the hangar, those heaps are eaten away on the other side by boys who load the stuff into

271 D.C. 626/108/9199, Secretary of Defence to Director Native Labour, 27 November 1914 (copy) and Officer Commanding Transport Depot to Headquarters Pretoria, 9 April 1915.

272 W.O. 107/37, Report on the Work of Labour during the War, December 1918.

273 W.O. 107/37, History of the SANLC, 1918; *Ilanga Lase Natal*, 9 November 1917 "Letter from Captain L.E. Hertslet).

railway-trucks – night and day, week in and week out, for the Army in France must be fed". With more than a touch of imperialistic fervour Keable concluded that the "sons of Chaka and Moshesh have come six thousand miles to feed men from every land and island in our wide-flung Empire who make up the army in France".[274]

Only a few men were used for work which could be classified as 'semi-skilled' or 'skilled'. In the quarries, some men who had experience on the Witwatersrand mines were entrusted to do the blasting. They took the place of German prisoners of war because the authorities were reluctant to trust captured enemy soldiers with explosives. Furthermore, a small number served as clerks and interpreters, or as orderlies in the two SANLC hospitals.[275] On the question of skilled labour, an officer remarked after the war "that possibly better use might have been made of the more educated and intelligent Natives by employing more of them on semi-skilled work, even if it had entailed a certain amount of training, the time and trouble would have been well repaid by the results".[276] However, mindful of the likely political ramifications that such a step might have in South Africa and the further possibility that it might encourage African material and political aspirations, the authorities declined to use this option.[277]

Similar considerations also ensured that the companies were stationed well clear of the actual war zone. The authorities were not concerned merely about the possible loss of life. As the commanding officer, Colonel S.M. Pritchard explained "there would be considerable trouble politically if the South African natives were reported to be near the fighting".[278] Although not employed in the vicinity of the battle front, some Africans were nevertheless exposed to German air raids and occasional shelling. In a private letter, an officer mentioned that "one poor fellow got a direct hit, he was blown to a pulp and we had to bury him in his clothes".[279] There were several air raids over Rouen and some members claimed that apart from the harbour and dockyard areas, the German aeroplanes singled out SANLC compounds as targets. This is probably an exaggeration, but apparently the Germans, to alarm Africans, did drop propaganda

---

274 Keable, *Standing by*, 124-26.

275 A.P.S. pamphlet, *British Africans in Europe and the work of the Welfare Committee*, 5.

276 U.W.H. 89/34, Report on the SANLC, 8 March 1919.

277 W.O. 107/37, History of the SANLC, 1918.

278 *Ibid.*

279 N.A. 9107/8/363, H. Astouken to E. Dower, 11 August 1917.

leaflets which read: "In this war I hate black people the most. I do not know what they want in this European war. Where I find them, I will smash them."[280]

The contingent furthermore worked in extremely cold and inclement weather. One member wrote that "it has been admitted that such a winter has not been experienced for the last thirty years".[281] Those companies who had to work out in the open suffered particularly. It is possible to form an idea of what they had to endure in the cold, muddy and soggy conditions by reading the firsthand account of an officer:

> The dampness and cold of the slush first got through your boots, then through your flesh, then through your bones and when it got to your marrow you went on because you had no more to get wet, and when the snow, sleet and freezing arrived, it was really terrible. The natives ... simply had to go on. If we had stopped for one day and allowed ourselves to get stiff, I believe we would have given in.[282]

The South African government, concerned about the effect of the climatic conditions because it did not want a repetition of the high fatality rate in East Africa, called for regular reports on the health of the contingent.[283] Moreover, it insisted on suitable precautions being taken in France and, although there were occasional problems in obtaining medical supplies, the workers were regularly injected and vaccinated. The Aborigines' Protection Society in England also provided additional warm clothing. A few members did lose limbs as a result of frostbite, but they were the unfortunate exceptions. Given the conditions under which they worked, the mortality rate of the contingent was not particularly high. Out of a total of 21 000 men 331 (or 1,5 percent) died in France, mainly from pulmonary diseases.[284]

All the reports on the SANLC indicated that the contingent had performed exceptionally well under difficult conditions. For example, an engineering firm in La Havre, commenting on the work rate of the South Africans, stated: "We believe that the discharge of ... a cargo of grain in sacks at such a pace, *viz.:* nearly 170 tons per hour,

280 *Native Teachers' Journal*, October 1920 (Letter from F.H. Kumalo); Perry and Perry, *Jingoes*, 88-89; Willan, "The South African Labour Contingent, 1916-1918", 73.

281 1/T.B.U. 25/66/1, A.K. Xabanisa to Chief Magistrate Transkei, 25 May 1917.

282 N.A. 9107/8/363, H. Astouken to E. Dower, 11 August 1917.

283 These reports are in G.G. 545/9/93/56 and run from January 1917 to July 1918.

284 G.G. 545/9/93/56, Health reports SANLC, January 1917 to July 1918; A.P.S. Pamphlet, *British Africans in Europe and the Work of the Welfare Committee*, pp.6, 9-14; W.O. 107/37, History of the SANLC, 1918; Willan, "The South African Native Labour Contingent, 1916-1918", 76-77.

is an absolutely unique achievement and in spite of a great deal of experience of what can be done in handling sacks, we were ourselves utterly astonished at the result".[285] In several instances, platoons and companies were responsible for the loading and unloading of war material in a record time, and some of the British officers who witnessed this believed that the records were broken only through the efforts of the labourers themselves.[286] This impression was further confirmed by H. Sloley of the Aborigines' Protection Society, who claimed that he "had the advantage of hearing the opinions of officers of the Royal Engineers, Army Service Corps, Commisariat, Transport and Ordnance Departments, and the general estimate of the African native as a labourer appears to have been that, man for man, he is equal to any other class of labourer employed behind our lines".[287] Not surprisingly, such favourable comments met with the approval of a South African government anxious to present the venture as a success.[288]

Although the officers and others concerned were not likely to mention cases where the contingent did not meet expectations, there is no reason to doubt the general veracity of the reports. It is of greater importance though to establish the context in which the SANLC performed these feats of labour. On one level, one can accept that being in a foreign country and working under difficult, sometimes risky, war conditions, might have posed a challenge to some members and appealed to a spirit of adventure. To a certain extent, at least, they might have experienced a sense of exhilaration, camaraderie and achievement in excelling at their work and demonstrating their capabilities. This was probably true of F.H. Kumalo, who stated after the war: "I was pleased to be in the SANLC and did my best".[289]

However, this can hardly be a full explanation. It is also of particular relevance in this respect to consider the discipline and control exercised over the SANLC, a matter touched on in a pamphlet dealing with the contingent:

> Colonel Pritchard and his colleagues have adopted and insisted upon a general recognition of certain excellent methods of administration. First in order is that of getting the very best of their men, and letting them know that ... as

---

285   W.O. 107/37, Appendix H, Henry Simon Ltd. to Directorate of Labour, 19 June 1917.

286   W.O. 107/37, History of the SANLC, 1918; *Imvo Zabantsundu*, 27 November 1917 (Letter from Captain L.E. Hertslet).

287   Sloley, "The African Native Labour Contingent and the Welfare Committee", 205.

288   *Cape Times*, 27 June 1917 ("Parliamentary debates").

289   *Native Teachers' Journal*, October 1920 (Letter from F.H. Kumalo).

> regards the discharge of their duties ... the Africans are expected to be no less
> diligent in their work ... than the European subjects of the King.[290]

In practical terms, this meant that the black workers were given very little leeway or respite. Indeed, the formal disciplinary regulations were formulated in such a way that they could be punished for virtually anything except satisfactory work.[291] One worker summed it up when he said that the "golden rule was to do as you are told".[292] Of course, such discipline is not uncommon in the army, particularly during wartime; the point here is that it certainly contributed in no small measure to the labour output demanded of and achieved by some SANLC companies.

Moreover, it was insisted on that the contingent should work only under the supervision of South African staff. The reason given was that the British officers did not realise "that considerable moral deterioration resulted from failure to obtain a full day's work from the South African Natives, who were perfectly aware of the labour output of which they are capable". Pritchard maintained that the men did one third less work if they were not under the supervision of South African personnel.[293] In addition, every effort was made to prevent members of the SANLC from working with groups of other labourers, particularly those from the French, British and Canadian contingents. These white workers were considered as "being of a low physical category, work at a different pace and to a different standard output; and the native working alongside has his ideas of the white man disturbed, in addition to the natural tendency to slacken to the white man's pace". It was, in fact, firmly believed by the authorities that a largely successful policy of separation in the workplace had enabled them to "obtain the best possible results".[294]

The South African officers were not only concerned about the possible effect of white workers on the labour output of the contingent, but were also acutely aware that a common workplace and common conditions of labour might transcend racial differences and forge incipient bonds of class. Thus, Lieutenant Colonel H.P. Wolff pointed out that "the average man in the White Labour Companies had no knowledge of the Native or the conditions in South Africa, and was inclined to treat him with familiarity and on terms of equality. The native was quick to take advantage of this

290 A.P.S. Pamphlet, *British Africans in Europe and the Work of the Welfare Committee*, 7-8.

291 G.G. 545/9/93/56, Memorandum on the SANLC, September 1916.

292 *Ilanga Lase Natal*, 7 December 1917 (Letter from J.A. Mtembu).

293 W.O. 107/37 History of the SANLC, 1918 and Pritchard to Directorate of Labour, 5 July 1918.

294 W.O. 107/37, History of the SANLC, 1918.

fact."[295] Even when allowance is made for Wolff's stereotyping, the way in which Africans responded to this situation is revealing. This, however, was cause for alarm amongst the white staff since it raised the spectre of a less tractable workforce, who might assert their position not only in France, but perhaps later in South Africa as well. The policy of separation was therefore designed to stifle such potential developments and to eliminate, as one officer indicated, possible exposure to "socialist" ideas.[296]

Indeed, a central feature of the contingent's sojourn in France was the extent to which attempts were made to control the socio-political perceptions of members. By their very nature military establishments often exert a high degree of social control to ensure conformity and, depending on the particular circumstances, the level of control is often such that the military environment can approximate that of total institutions. But in the case of the SANLC, even the standard measures of control were deemed inadequate; they had to be elaborated and refashioned not only in order to meet military demands but also to provide a guarantee that the socio-political ramifications of black war service in a European country would not be detrimental to white South African interests.

Control over black troops also assumed more subtle forms. Indeed as one historian has explained in general "many social control mechanisms operate independently of any conscious manipulative process; thus control will not always be overt, and may or may not be recognised as such by controller or controlled".[297] Perhaps the best example of this in the context of the contingent can be found in an apparently insignificant matter such as the type of uniform issued to the contingent. While recruits attached particular value to a uniform as a symbol of their newly acquired status as troops in the service of the British Empire, they received a uniform that was described as "the most atrocious, vile-smelling cotton velveteen; brown, sloppy and shoddy looking".[298] The authorities did not explain the reason for this, but such a uniform could certainly not have created the impression amongst members of the contingent that they were in any way equal to white soldiers dressed in the standard and widely recognised khaki uniform. On the contrary, the unattractive uniform of poor quality visibly confirmed the inferior status of the SANLC. Whereas the authorities in all likelihood acted subconsciously, reflecting the way in which African 'inferiority' was

---

295 U.W.H. 89/34, Report on the SANLC, 8 March 1919.

296 W.O. 107/37, History of the SANLC, 1918.

297 Donajgrodzki, *Social control in Nineteenth Century Britain*, 11.

298 *Cape Times Annual*, 1919 (Article by Lieutenant F.C. Cornell, 'The SA Native Labour Contingent'). According to Cornell the uniform caused them a great deal of trouble.

taken for granted, some troops were acutely aware that the uniform actually served a degrading purpose. On receipt of his clothing, an offended member remarked: "This is only fit for convicts!" Another asked: "Why do we have to wear *this?*"[299] Yet another member went to the heart of the matter: "The suit of brown corduroy certainly lowered the status of the Native labourers in the eyes of the other troops".[300]

A particularly crucial aspect in the process of control was the appointment of the white staff to accompany the contingent. Those applying for officer rank had to be familiar with "the mentality and customs" of blacks, and had to have a "combined knowledge of the Native, Military Procedure and Labour".[301] Similar qualifications were sought in non-commissioned officers; they must have had previous experience in supervising African workers and had to be "men of the right stamp".[302] Even more explicitly it was reported in the press that the officers were "specifically selected by the Union Government with the view to ensuring that the natives should be kept in their proper sphere whilst away". In effect this meant, amongst other things, that "they were the right sort of South Africans to appreciate the danger of allowing the natives to come into contact with white women".[303] Not surprisingly, applications for posts in the contingent were carefully screened. Botha as prime minister even took it upon himself to make the final appointments. "We are sifting with utmost care the many hundred applications", H.R.M. Bourne, secretary of defence, informed Botha, "so that you will have the best possible facilities for deciding on the selection of the best among the really suitable candidates for every class of appointment".[304] Clearly, the matter of control was far too weighty to be left to chance.

The background typical of the white staff who had been appointed after such careful scrutiny is well illustrated by the career of the commanding officer of the contingent, Colonel S.M. Pritchard. He had come from England in 1894 and joined the Basutoland Mounted Police. After serving for four years, he was appointed private secretary to Sir Godfrey Lagden, then resident commissioner in Basutoland. When, in 1901, Lagden became secretary for Native Affairs in the Transvaal, Pritchard joined him as Chief Inspector of Native Labour in that colony. In 1903, he was promoted

299 *Ibid.*

300 *Ilanga Lase Natal*, 10 May 1918 (Letter from 'A Native').

301 W.O. 107/37, History of the SANLC, 1918. See also Willan, "The South African Native Labour Contingent, 1916-1918", 72.

302 G.G. 545/9/93/56, Lieutenant Colonel J. Jacobsz to Colonel S.M. Pritchard, 20 May 1917.

303 *The South African Review*, 4 January 1918 ("White women and blacks").

304 D.C. 768/31/1997, Bourne to Botha, 20 September 1916.

to assistant-director of the Native Labour Bureau of which he became the director in 1914. Shortly afterwards, during August and September 1915, Pritchard was sent to Ovamboland to report on the possible incorporation of the area into the newly acquired South-West African territory and to investigate the potential for securing labour from the Ovambo.[305] Here, then, was a man with impeccable credentials. He was well versed in "native administration", with ample experience in dealing with black labour and a commendable military background that made him eminently suitable to take command of the contingent and to ensure from the South African government's point of view that the undertaking would have no negative consequences.

Other members of the white staff had also held positions in civilian life which gave them considerable control over Africans. Most of them were attached to the Native Affairs Department and some were mine compound managers; a sprinkling of magistrates completed the complement.[306] Furthermore, to make assurance doubly sure, it was impressed upon everyone appointed that "he has a heavy responsibility placed upon his shoulders. It will be his duty as a representative of the Union not merely to discharge the duties of military commanders, but for the sake of our country to see that no ill effects arise from this undertaking."[307]

Of course, it may be argued that men who had experience in 'native affairs' were obvious choices for such an enterprise. Who else, after all, could be appointed? Nevertheless, viewed from the vantage point of the SANLC's rank and file, it meant that they were to be continually under the control of men intimately involved in the implementation of South African race policies; men who could be relied upon to minimise, if not completely eliminate, any influences construed as detrimental. In short, the social and political environment of South Africa had to be kept intact in war-torn France.

In France, the white staff did not hesitate to demonstrate the qualities for which they were appointed. Upon learning that French women, involved in providing refreshments for those engaged in the war effort, had also served tea to some black dock workers at Rouen, an officer immediately told the Africans concerned: "When you people get back to South Africa again, don't start thinking that you are whites just because

---

305 *South Africa*, 18 November 1916 (Colonel S.M. Pritchard); Donaldson, *South African Who's Who, 1919-1920*, 162; W.H. Long Papers 947/603/133, Buxton to Long, 8 January 1917.

306 *Pretoria News*, 14 September 1916 ("Names of the elect"); *Cape Times Annual*, 1919 ("The SA Native Labour Contingent").

307 D.C. 768/64/1997, Letter of Appointment, undated.

this place has spoilt you. You are black and you will stay black."[308] One veteran also recalled later that they soon learnt "to recognise two distinct factors – namely the Government who had laid down the rules and regulations, and the officers who administered them".[309] Moreover, some officers certainly enforced their authority with more than sweet persuasion or mild cajolement. As some members stated after their return to the Union, "the fact was that the treatment of labourers in France by the European officers and non-commissioned officers was brutal and barbarous".[310] The situation, however, could, and probably did, vary from company to company and within companies. There were also restraints on the part of officers as they had to be mindful that excessive force might cause a backlash, impeding work performance.

The selection of those in control of the contingent drew some criticism from black people in South Africa, mainly on account of the preponderance of officials from the Native Affairs Department and also because Africans were excluded from positions of real authority.[311] The government did not even contemplate making such appointments, but instead, after careful screening, selected twelve African chaplains whom it regarded as the highest representatives of the rank and file of the contingent. Whereas the white chaplains were ranked as captains, their African counterparts were given no military rank or status.[312] Neither, as the Reverend R. Keable disclosed, were they accorded much respect or standing by the white staff:

> We found ourselves, in the great majority of cases, up against white officers who disliked 'educated natives' and who particularly disliked natives in clerical dress. Their whole attitude was an attempt to deny all privileges. Black was black, and a boy was a boy, however dressed, educated or entitled.[313]

---

308 Perry and Perry, *Jingoes*, 92.

309 *Ilanga Lase Natal*, 10 May 1918 (Letter from 'A Native').

310 *Abantu-Batho*, 18 April 1918 ("The labour contingent"). The authorities also intercepted letters in which Africans complained of "brutal treatment". (D.C. 1136/2/1197, Chief Censor to Acting Secretary of Defence, 4 June 1918). Furthermore, Jason Jingoes declared: "We bantu are often treated like dogs here by the white people from home, yet they forget that we are all here at war against a common enemy" (Perry and Perry, *Jingoes*, 83).

311 *East London Daily Dispatch*, 30 September 1916 (Letter from H. Ziduli); *East London Daily Dispatch*, 2 October 1916 (Letter from 'A Native'); G.N.L.B. 192/1329/14/48, Transvaal Native Congress General Meeting, 11 October 1916.

312 G.G. 545/9/93/56, General report on the chaplaincy and welfare work of the South African Native Labour Corps, 31 July 1918; *Imvo Zabantsundu*, 9 July 1918 (Letter from Captain L.E. Hertslet); D.C. 768/46/1997, Bourne to Dower, 25 September 1916.

313 Keable, "African Priests in France", 54.

The black chaplains, in turn, perceived themselves to be superior to the ordinary labourers and they consciously strove to set them apart as a separate class.[314] Their self-perception was vital in determining their role in the contingent. They failed to act as committed spokesmen for the labourers, nor did they assume the role of 'honest brokers' between the staff and the workers. They were in fact, co-opted to strengthen the network of control. Thus, as stated in a general report on the chaplaincy, they supported their white colleagues in preventing "that contact with new social conditions in France should complicate the social question on the return of the Natives to South Africa".[315] Revealingly, one officer also found it commendable that "the Native parsons were always willing to assist in the cause of discipline, patriotism and good order".[316] In particular, the Reverend J.J. Xaba was singled out for praise, since "his influence was at all times used to maintain discipline and keep the natives straight".[317]

As a reward for their contribution, and also to effect an even closer identification of the African chaplains with the white power structure, four chaplains, along with a white colleague, were allowed to visit London where they were placed under the watchful care of J.H. Harris of the Aborigines' Protection Society. The purpose of the visit, as Harris indicated, was of a 'political nature', and he welcomed the opportunity of impressing on his guests the achievements and values of British civilization and assured the military authorities that the visit "will be judiciously controlled".[318] The exercise was considered an unqualified success. The black chaplains, it was reported, had been profoundly impressed by the greatness of Britain and the vast resources at her disposal. Britain, British life and character, British industry and ingenuity, British cheerfulness and kindness, and the amazing wealth ... have excited their deepest admiration and wonder, and the scheme has produced nothing but good to the men themselves, and for the future of ... South Africa.[319] The report might have been an overstatement of the actual African response, but given the role played by the chaplains in the contingent, one can readily assume that it contained more than a grain of truth.

314   *Ibid.* 56.

315   G.G. 545/9/93/56, General report on the chaplaincy and welfare work of the South African Native Labour Corps, 31 July 1918.

316   U.W.H. 89/34, Report on the SANLC, 8 March 1919.

317   O.C. Records 44/22/81, Report on the SANLC, 12 April 1918.

318   A.P.S. Papers S 23 H 2/3, Harris to Buxton, 10 September 1917 and Harris to A. Loring, 14 September 1917 (copies).

319   A.P.S. Papers S 23 H 2/3, Report by the Reverend J.W.W. Owen on the tour of native chaplains, 10 October 1917.

The chaplains found themselves, wittingly or unwittingly, in the classical collabo-rationist position of some of the aspiring black middle class of the time. They were carefully and selectively exposed to some of the values of the dominant system (even the films which the chaplains were allowed to see were vetted before the time and were described as an "admiralty official film" and "a quite good story film, nothing objectionable or even comic"),[320] and were expected to internalise those values so that they in turn could become effective agents for extending ideological control.

Certainly the clearest manifestation of control over the contingent was to be found in the insistence of the South African government that the companies must be housed in closed compounds. The closed compound system had originated on the Kimberley diamond fields in the 1870s and, with certain modifications, it was later extended to the Witwatersrand and Rhodesian (Zimbabwean) mines. As one historian has noted, in the development of mining capitalism the compound was a crucial institution in the depersonalisation of Africans and in ensuring a servile workforce:

> Everywhere in southern Africa, the compounds served to isolate, regiment and exploit the ... black working class ... It was the compound, acting as the college of colonialism, that did much to rob Africans of their dignity and help mould servile black personalities.[321]

The authorities had thus decided to transplant an exceptionally well-refined system of control from the mining to the military context to fulfil a similar function in France as it did in southern Africa.

Of all the Allied labour contingents in France – both white and 'non-European' – the SANLC was the only one to be housed in compounds. Only the German prisoners of war, who were regarded as a source of forced labour, were likewise confined. "The conditions of service for our men in France as regards freedom of movement", reported Lieutenant Colonel G.A. Godley, second-in-command of the contingent, "are similar to those applying to prisoners of war, and the camps occupied by our men and the prisoners of war are identical in every respect, except that as regards locality those occupied by the prisoners are in the majority of cases more favourably situated".[322] This situation contained its own incongruity in that captives, enemies of the British Empire, were somewhat better off than South African black troops

---

320 A.P.S. Papers S 23 H 2/3. Chapman to Harris, 1 October 1917.

321 Van Onselen, *Chibaro: African Mine Labour in Southern Rhodesia, 1900-1933*, 157.

322 G.G. 545/9/93/56, Godley to Dower, 8 December 1917.

who, as subjects of the empire, had been sent to France in support of the Allied cause against Germany.

The instructions regarding the construction of the compounds were elaborate, as were the regulations governing the conditions under which the inhabitants were to live. The members of the contingent had to be confined to an area surrounded by a stout barbed wire or corrugated iron fence or a wall which had to be at least six feet high with "a wire netting or barbed wire along the top of the screen to prevent the natives climbing over". To prevent fraternisation it was stipulated that all the exits had to be guarded. The possibility of Africans leaving the compounds and meeting local whites was not the only danger which the authorities had in mind. The reverse, that whites might enter the compounds, was also possible. Hence it was emphasised that "care should be taken to prevent unauthorised persons from entering the camp or conversing with Natives and especially to prevent all familiarity between Europeans and Natives, as this is subversive to discipline and calculated to impair their efficiency as working units".[323]

Moreover, Africans could only leave the compounds under very exceptional circumstances and then only if they were accompanied by a non-commissioned or senior officer. The staff had to ensure that they did not obtain alcohol and that they were not entertained in the homes of local residents. Under no circumstances was a member of the SANLC, unattended by a white man, allowed outside the compounds. "Under the conditions under which they are living in France", it was explained, "they are not to be trusted with white women, and any Native found wandering about ... and not under the escort of a white N.C.O., should be returned to his unit under guard, or failing this, handed over to the Military Police".[324] Limitations on the freedom of movement of troops are, of course, normal and generally accepted procedure in any military environment, but it is abundantly clear that in the case of the SANLC the regulations were unrelated to military concerns and were formulated with explicit socio-political objectives in mind.

The rationale behind the closed compound system did not go unnoticed in South Africa. At a meeting of the SANLC in Natal, J.J. Dube explained that "the reason for closed compounds was that if allowed out the Natives would enjoy the same privileges as the white man". The audience stridently voiced their disapproval of the

---

323 W.O. 107/37, Appendix G. Notes on South African Labour.

324 W.O. 107/37, Appendix G. Notes on South African Labour. See also Willan, "The South African Labour Contingent, 1916-1918", 72.

system: "It's slavery! They want to make us prisoners!"[325] While the SANNC had hoped that one result of the contingent would be "the opening of their minds to what the world is like outside South Africa", it now realised that "cooped up as they are, all this may not be possible".[326]

While the vast majority of white South Africans approved of the compound system, there was one lone voice of criticism. G.K. Hemming, an Umtata attorney who was destined to become a Native Representative in the House of Assembly in 1937, raised the issue in the press and asked: "Is it right that thousands of robust men should be herded for so long a period?" He pointed out that the "conditions surrounding them will preclude the giving of leave of absence" and commented scathingly that "they are placed on conditions which even an animal is not expected to support". This led Hemming to conclude that the "spectacle of these men herded together for so long was one of the most terrible indictments against the ruling race ever framed."[327] In contrast to Hemming's criticism, a philanthropic body like the Aborigines' Protection Society in London merely accepted and approved of the compound system as a necessary measure for the welfare of Africans in a foreign environment. Without questioning the assumptions underlying the compound system, members of the organisation, after a visit to the compounds, reported in the best traditions of paternalism that they were impressed by the way in which Africans were cared for. The only role the organisation could see for itself in this respect was to provide the contingent with additional warm clothing, sporting equipment and school books.[328]

For the effective functioning of the system, the authorities realised that they had to provide some form of outlet for those cloistered in the confines of the compounds. Tensions within the compounds had to be regulated and potentially explosive situations had to be defused. This meant that the off-duty hours of the workers had to be spent in 'healthy relaxation'. "To this end", an officer explained, "periodical sports were arranged at which they ran races, jumped, threw the cricket ball, pulled 'tug-o'-war'

325 G.N.L.B. 192/1329/14/48, Report on a meeting of Natal Natives, 27 September 1916.

326 *Ilanga Lase Natal*, 31 August 1917 ("General notes").

327 *East London Daily Dispatch*, 2 October 1916 (Letter from G.K. Hemming).

328 A.P.S. Papers S 23 H 2/1, Memorandum for the information of the Committee, 13 April 1917; and J.H. Harris to A. Steel-Maitland, 18 December 1917. It is also pertinent to note that in general the Aborigines' Protection Society had very little criticism on the direction of "native policy" in the Union (Willan, "The Anti-Slavery and Aborigines' Protection Society and the South African Natives' Land Act of 1913", 183-202).

against one another, and altogether used up their superfluous energy".[329] On one level, it can perhaps be argued that such activities at least provided the labourers with some relief from their dreary existence in the compounds and the monotony of their work. As Bill Nasson has pointed out in a study of black transport riders during the Anglo-Boer War:

> Recreation and entertainment flourished, and came to occupy an extremely important space in transport riders' lives, lending vibrancy and rich colour to war experiences, and offering ritual consolation from, and defence against, the hazards, tensions, and uncertainties of wartime living. It is arguable that recreational pastimes did not simply mushroom as a safety valve. They were a way of rolling with the punch: wartime disorder provided new spaces and opportunities for conviviality, ceremony, and displays of skill.[330]

However, in the restricted and regulated environment of the SANLC compounds, sport was not a spontaneous activity initiated by the workers themselves. It was an organised and a structural affair, dictated from above and intended to function as a mechanism of control. Traditional African war dances, organised by the authorities and attended by large numbers of invited guests, served much the same purpose. Moreover, taking their cue from the mining compounds in South Africa where such dances had become part of an early publicity programme for the mines, the military realised that the propaganda value of these performances was an added bonus. It was an opportunity to display the stereotyped view of 'happy' and 'exuberant' black warriors, obviously 'contented' with the conditions and circumstances which the authorities had created for them. This view was also processed for wider consumption; twelve out of the fifteen minutes of a contemporary war film about the SANLC dealt with traditional dances performed before numerous white spectators.[331]

Despite the enthusiasm of the authorities in organising sports meetings and traditional dances, these forms of entertainment were not really popular amongst the workers and only a small minority participated. An officer indicated that "the majority preferred to be left to their own devices and sat around their fires, talking and smoking after

---

329 *Cape Times Annual*, 1919 ("The S.A. Native Labour Contingent"). See also U.W.H. 89/34, Report on the SANLC, 8 March 1919.

330 Nasson, "Moving Lord Kitchener: Black military transport and supply work in the South African War, 1899-1902, with particular reference to the Cape Colony", 40.

331 *Rand Daily Mail*, 8 September 1917 ("Interview with Native Soldiers"); Imperial War Museum, London, Archival film on the SANLC, 1917. For the function of these dances in the mining context, see Van Onselen, *Chibaro*, 188.

their work was done".[332] Perhaps they suspected the motives of the organisers, or more prosaically they were just too exhausted after long hours of manual labour to participate in any further physical activity.

However, educational classes arranged for the workers in the evenings were far more popular and were well attended. The classes were mainly conducted by black chaplains and the teachers who had joined the contingent, and the labourers were instructed in reading, writing, translation, arithmetic and geography. These classes were preferred to the other organised activities partly because no physical exertion was required, but also because they provided the workers with an opportunity for self-improvement and the acquisition of certain basic educational skills which Africans might have hoped would benefit them once they returned to South Africa. The primary motive of the authorities was not to provide an educational service for the betterment of the labourers; like the organisation of sport and traditional dances, education was seen as a means of exercising control. "These schools", it was officially reported, "assisted in no small measure to keep the Natives content in mind and employed profitably during their leisure hours in the compounds".[333]

The bulk of the evidence relating to the way in which Africans responded to their controlled environment in France gives the impression that if they did not actually welcome the disciplinary measures and various restrictions, they certainly accepted these passively.[334] It is true that many Africans, outwardly at least, might have acquiesced, but that does not imply compliance. It is also pertinent to note that all correspondence was subjected to military censorship and, moreover, that most of the letters and other available documents were written by officers or other whites with a vested interest in the undertaking. Furthermore, it was of course only the educated members of the contingent who recorded their experiences. Their letters often reflected their class bias and, in any case, they had little option but to report favourably. Indeed, after their return some contradicted their previous correspondence and explained

---

332 U.W.H. 89/34, Report on the SANLC, 8 March 1919.

333 W.O. 107/37, History of the SANLC, 1918. See also G.G. 545/9/93/56, General report on the chaplaincy and welfare work of the South African Native Labour Corps, 31 July 1918.

334 For examples, see *Cape Times*, 1 February 1918 (Letter from 'A white SANLC sergeant'); *Cape Times*, 22 March 1917 (Letter from A. Shabane); *Alice Times*, 24 May 1917 (Letter from the Reverend J. Lennox); *Cape Times*, 22 October 1917 (Letter from Captain L.E. Hertslet); *Sunday Times*, 22 July 1917 (Letter from A.K. Xabanisa).

that "they couldn't write otherwise", and were now prepared to "corroborate the statements of those who complain of ill-treatment".[335]

Although much of the documentation is either skewed or silent on African responses, there are scattered pieces of information which suggest that workers were not as placid and docile as the authorities had wished to portray them. Occasionally, occurrences of "minor strikes" were (understandably only fleetingly) mentioned in reports.[336] While the demands of the workplace and the harsh discipline might have precipitated strike action, these factors probably also ensured that such protests were short-lived. Whether the strikes were well planned and calculated or an immediate and spontaneous expression of discontent, it was most unlikely, given the imperatives of the war effort and the nature of control over the contingent, that the authorities would have acceded to any strike demands. However, Africans also attempted in less dramatic ways to regulate and modify working conditions. Thus, certain companies insisted on doing piecework – completing a specific task instead of working long stipulated hours.[337] In some instances, this was allowed and the workers themselves could then, in some measure, determine the time they had to spend at work.

The relationship between the white supervisory staff and the workers was furthermore one of considerable friction. Bearing in mind that the personnel were specifically chosen for their ability to "control and handle Natives" or, less euphemistically and more accurately, for their willingness to use physical force in dealing with them, it is not surprising that several clashes occurred. Many Africans were not prepared to tolerate the treatment meted out to them by bullying supervisors and retaliated in kind. Reports on the SANLC were often punctuated by references to Africans who had "resisted authority" or who had "offered violence to superior officers". In fact, the war diary of one battalion reveals that over a three month period such incidents were an almost daily occurrence.[338] Such acts of resistance and retribution were not restricted to the workplace or the compounds.

---

335 *Abantu-Batho*, 14 February 1918 ("Natives and the war").

336 U.W.H. 89/34, Report on the SANLC, 8 March 1919; W.O. 107/37, History of the SANLC, 1918.

337 W.O. 107/37, History of the SANLC, 1918.

338 D.C. 1136/2/1197, List of SANLC transgressions, undated; G.G. 1282/51/49/56, Incomplete list of SANLC military prisoners with commentaries on their transgressions, 9 December 1918; G.G. 1275/51/45/56, Botha to Buxton, 11 March 1918; W.O. 95/267, War Diary of 2nd Battalion SANLC, 2 January 1917 to 31 March 1917.

On their return voyage to South Africa, ten members on board the *Militiades* were accused of "gross insubordination" in a heated exchange with the commanding officer, G. Farrar. Mutual antagonisms flared up in the open and soon developed into a particularly violent confrontation during which Aaron Monliba was shot dead, another African wounded, and the others confined to their bunks under armed guard. On arrival in Cape Town, they had to stand trial for "mutiny on the high seas", and despite a shrewd argument that their contracts had expired and that they were therefore no longer subject to military law, the judge decided to "show the Natives their position" by passing severe prison sentences which ranged from ten to twelve years. However, Buxton, the governor general, as well as Botha realised that the sentences were inappropriate and would serve no real purpose as a deterrent in the dosing stages of the war, and the men were released after only a limited time in prison.[339]

Complaints about food served as another indicator of African discontent and resentment. It is generally true that troops often complain about the quality of their fare, but in the case of the contingent, food became a focal point for registering protests of much wider import. Thus, one company refused to accept the rations given to it and insisted on receiving exactly the same as white troops.[340] The concern dearly went beyond food as such.

Although the regulations limiting freedom of movement in France were strictly enforced, the network of control was not infallible. In a few instances, some members in search of either women or drink, or perhaps simply to experience ordinary life in a foreign country, did manage to abscond from the compounds.[341] For a necessarily brief and probably somewhat uneasy period, they had the opportunity of savouring what France had to offer and what was permitted to other troops but denied to them. Furthermore, some Africans also tried to entice women to come and visit them in their quarters. Obviously, it must have been as difficult to arrange such meetings as to abscond from the compounds. Nevertheless, it is revealing to note the attempts which were made shortly before one battalion embarked for their return voyage, and

---

339 G.G. 545/9/93/56, Brigadier General A. Cavendish to Buxton, 20 December 1917; G.G. 545/9/93/175, Botha to Buxton, 27 December 1917; Juta's Daily Reporter: Decisions of the Cape Provincial Division of the Supreme Court of South Africa, 27 February 1918, 1; G.G. 1275/51/45/56, Botha to Buxton, 11 March 1918.

340 W.O. 95/267, War Diary 2nd Company SANLC, 13 December 1916.

341 Transcription of an oral interview with P. Mabathoana at Maseru, 22 April 1980; D.C. 1136/2/1997, Chief Censor to Acting Secretary of Defence, 23 April 1918, and Acting Secretary of Defence to Chief Censor, 17 January 1918; W.O. 95/4115, SANLC General Hospital Diary, 1917 (venereal disease cases).

while they were stationed in a transit camp at St. Budeaux in Devonport, England, where in the absence of a closed compound it was somewhat more difficult for the officers to exercise control. Marching through the streets on their arrival they were, along with other troops, enthusiastically welcomed by the local residents, including women, who cheered and greeted the "gallant" forces of the empire. Certain members carefully noted the addresses of some of the houses of those women who had waved at them, and once in camp tried to establish contact by means of letters delivered by children. The attempt failed when the letter was intercepted by the military authorities. Fortunately for the historian the letter has survived and reads as follows:

> Dear Lady – I am so pleased that I can't even tell anybody, and I am much anxious if this note could be received by you. Then I am kindly asking you, if possible you will be so kind to do me a favour and call round our camp tonight at 8.30. I am in the first hut by the second gate as you go down; and I will be found just on the right-hand when you get in the camp. If you too late, do cleverly come, approach the door and give a small knock. I will hear you. And I will then explain to you about my notion concerning you. I beg to remain with best greetings of love to you. God be with you till I meet you. Respectfully yours. R.V.

In response to this incident, Brigadier General F.C. Stone, commanding officer of the Devonport area, warned the women of St. Budeaux in terms that must have gladdened the hearts of some South African officers:

> It is absolutely essential that the Kaffir [sic] should regard white women as unapproachable; the mischief that can be done by merely good-natured familiarity – apart from anything worse – is incalculable: and the people who will suffer from this levity on the part of white women at home, are the wives and daughters of our settlers in South Africa.[342]

There were also persistent rumours that large numbers of Africans refused to embark for South Africa, had married British women, went to Wales as coal miners and eventually "became absorbed in the motley population settled in the dockyard areas of Cardiff".[343] This, however, seems rather far-fetched. The rumours about black

---

342 A.P.S. Papers S 23 H 2/1, cutting from the *Western Morning News*, 22 October 1917 ("White women and black men").

343 *Sunday Express*, 27 February 1938 ("They refused to return"); N.A. 9108/22/903, Secretary of Defence to Secretary of Native Affairs, 2 March 1938; *De Volkstem*, 4 October 1917 ("De Honderd Huweliken per week agitasie"); *Imvo Zabantsundu*, 16 October 1917 ("Nationalists and the natives"); F.S. Malan Collection 15/41, Malan to Buxton, 9 October 1917 (copy).

and white marriages abroad emanated from the National Party in South Africa to embarrass the government and were consistently denied by the authorities. Without any corroborating evidence, it is hard to establish the veracity of these assertions.

Not surprisingly, the main thrust of black resistance in France was directed at the closed compound system. It was seen for what it was; a discriminatory measure which applied to South African black troops only. It also left a deep impression: "The compounds where our people were housed in cannot be forgotten as they were like prisons", certain veterans remarked on their return to the Union.[344] For some resistance against the system took the form of petitions, even one to the king of England, but predictably this had no effect.[345] Others took more direct action. On Christmas Eve 1917, the Reverend R. Keble awoke to find a commotion on foot, for a party of drunken white soldiers had called to the men over the barbed wire and asked them why they did not come out and enjoy themselves like the rest. When these had moved on, the sergeants had to deal with an excited camp, ready for anything, and arguing against the compound system heart and soul.[346]

This was not an isolated outburst during the festive season. Some officers, in letters to the South African press, referred obliquely but significantly to cases of "riotous behaviour" in the compounds, and somewhat more explicitly in private letters it was revealed that many companies were giving problems because of the compound system.[347]

One particularly violent incident took place on 23 July 1917 when a labourer, known as Charlie, was arrested for attempting to do his washing in a nearby stream outside the compound. This sparked off pent-up tension and an agitated crowd soon rallied to his assistance. While some tried to free Charlie by force, others succeeded in breaking the lock of the compound gate with a pickaxe. When they emerged from the compound, they were fired on immediately and without warning by the armed guard. Four members were killed and eleven wounded. The South African authorities kept

344 *Abantu-Batho*, 14 February 1918 ("Natives and the War").

345 Jeffreys, "The *Mendi* and after: Recollections of Jacob Matli", 187.

346 Keable, *Standing by*, 134.

347 *Ilanga Lase Natal*, 9 November 1917 (Letter from Captain L.E. Hertslet); N.A. 9107/8/363, H. Astouken, E. Dower, 11 August 1917.

the matter strictly confidential, but they could not stop certain members from relating the affair on their return to South Africa.[348]

Despite this bloody confrontation, or perhaps because of it, resistance against the compound system continued unabated and even intensified. Incidents of 'unruly behaviour' became so frequent that the authorities had considerable cause for alarm. It was a perturbed Lieutenant Colonel Godley who admitted in a confidential letter towards the end of 1917 that "the temper of a large proportion of the men is distinctly nasty" and that there was an "ever constant undercurrent of feeling amongst the Natives that they of all the King's soldiers are singled out for differential treatment".[349] In fact, it had become increasingly difficult for the military to maintain the closed compound system, which was on the verge of collapsing in the face of persistent resistance.

This development led to the decision to disband the contingent. In December 1917, it was Godley's "deliberate opinion" that they were running

> a grave risk of finding it impossible to effectively carry out the Government's strict instructions in regard to close compounding and control, and that it is unfair to ask, or even allow men to bind themselves down indefinitely under conditions which are unique, as all other units in France, both *white and black* are free to move about.

Should the South African government wish to keep the contingent in France, Godley concluded, it had seriously to consider abandoning the compound system.[350]

Instead, however, the cabinet decided in January 1918 to disband the SANLC. "Having regard to the difficulties which can be anticipated in maintaining the closed compound system", Botha wrote confidentially, "Ministers are of the opinion that it will not be advisable to continue recruiting".[351] The government, increasingly under pressure from the Nationalist opposition for allowing the undertaking at all, did not make the true reason for the decision public. Officially it was only announced that

---

348 N.A. 9107/12/863, Confidential letter from Godley to Pritchard, 28 July 1917; J. 248/5/242/16, Police report of SANNC meeting on 29 March 1918 containing statements by D. Modiakgotla; *Abantu-Batho*, 14 February 1918 ("Natives and the War"); SANLC attestation forms, names of the diseased killed in the incident; Willan, "The South African Native Labour Contingent, 1916-1918", 79. Although returning members claimed that thirteen people had died, Godley established after an enquiry that eleven were wounded and four killed.

349 G.G. 549/9/93/56, Godley to Dower, 8 December 1917.

350 *Ibid.* (Emphasis in the original.)

351 G.G. 549/9/93/56, Botha to Buxton, 18 December 1917.

there was a shortage of ships, and that the contracts of members of the contingent were too short to justify the continuation of the scheme.[352] The Reverend Z.R. Mahabane, prominent in the Cape branch of the SANNC, found this explanation unconvincing and commented that "as far as the Natives are concerned, the dramatic cancelling of a pact already signed and entered into, will give rise to feelings of suspicion that the reasons for this cancellation are more of a political than of a military nature".[353] These suspicions were well founded; the government could not allow the contingent to stay in France, for fear of the possible political and social ramifications.

Conclusion

Wartime service is by definition hazardous and troops can as a matter of course be expected to deal with arduous conditions. In the case of black South African troops in German South-West Africa, East Africa and France, the normal travails of war service were compounded by an additional set of circumstances which had their origins in the nature of South African society at the time. African responses to these varied, but resistance tactics had the effect of terminating the stay of labourers in France. It now remains to consider whether wartime service also stimulated a wider political consciousness.

---

352 *Cape Times*, 29 June 1917 ("Parliamentary debates"); *Cape Times*, 18 January 1918 ("Native Labour Corps"); 1/LSK 13/9/2, Circular from Botha to all chiefs and headmen, 18 January 1918.

353 *Cape Times*, 2 February 1918 (Letter from Z.R. Mahabane).

Laying down the law?
[*Source: https://www.flickr.com/photos/nlscotland/*]

An ostensibly happy band of brothers off to work.
This kind of photo was most likely taken for propaganda purposes.
[*Source: http://digital.nls.uk/first-world-war-official-photographs/*]

"We saw him, George V, our king, with our own eyes ... To us it is a dream,
something to wonder at" (M.L. Posholi, SANLC member).
[*Source: http://sthp.saha.org.za/popups/*]

General J.C. Smuts doing what generals do — showing official interest.
[*Source: http://digital.nls.uk/*]

Man of the cloth, keeping an eye on God and the men.
[*Source: https://www.flickr.com/photos/nlscotland/*]

Tug-of-war at a time of war – a form of social control or healthy relaxation?
[*Source: Cape Archives, AG 16456*]

Happy faces – intended for those at home?
[*Source: https://www.flickr.com/photos/nlscotland/*]

Making light of frozen feet.
[*Source: http://www.flickr.com/photos/*]

Moving material – small cogs in a big war machine.
[*Source: http://www.iwm.org.uk/collections/*]

War work in the French forests.
[*Source: http://www.wessexarch.co.uk/node/734*]

MILITARY SERVICE, THE WAR AND POLITICAL CONSCIOUSNESS

Military service can have an ambiguous political impact. Depending on the circumstances, for some individuals its effects may be enduring and substantial, for others they can be ephemeral and transient. With this caveat in mind, the post-war political role of veterans as potential political catalysts for change is explored. In addition, the wider impact of the war on African political thinking is considered.

Ramifications of military service

As far as can be ascertained, the political outlook of those Africans who served in South-West and East Africa was not influenced critically by their wartime service. Although many might have resented the harsh treatment meted out to them, it must be borne in mind that they served for a relatively short period only and, perhaps more importantly, that the ideological climate in these colonial territories differed little from what blacks were accustomed to in South Africa. Thus, they were not exposed to a markedly new environment.

The SANLC, of course, completed its service in a somewhat different milieu. Nevertheless, the reports of the white officers accompanying the contingent reflect a marked tendency to present the venture as an unqualified 'success'. In this view, those who served returned to South Africa "uncontaminated" and "unspoilt" and "more useful to the state in every way".[354] However, because of their vested interests

---

354 W.O.107/37, History of the SANLC, 1918; *Imvo Zabantsundu*, 17 November 1917 (Letter from Captain L.E. Hertslet).

in the matter, the impressions of the officers are heavily biased towards a sanitised version. The African voice is only audible once it has been decoded; even then it is rarely heard.

There can be little doubt that service overseas did present Africans with an opportunity to contrast the crass or, at best, paternalistic racism prevailing in South Africa, to the way in which whites abroad behaved towards them. Although the officers tried to ensure that members of the contingent had limited contact with the civilian population, some of them did on the odd occasion manage to acquaint themselves with life outside the compounds. Such encounters with French civilians gave them sufficient reason to question in a more searching manner the rigidity of South African society. "Coming from South Africa, we had fixed ideas about black/white relationships, so we were surprised that some of the French would mix freely with us", declared R. Mohapeloa. Similarly, P. Mabatoana was impressed that "we were treated with dignity by white people".[355] Moreover, Jason Jingoes drew a fine distinction between paternalistic racial attitudes and involvement on the basis of equality. The way in which white women received them with tea and other refreshments when they stopped at Liverpool in England before embarking again for France, caused him to remark: "They were so friendly and we warmed to their concern for us ... Although white women had served us with tea in Cape Town, we know they were only doing it because we were going to war. These girls were different."[356]

As pointed out earlier, the South African authorities were particularly concerned about the possibility that members of the contingent might establish intimate relationships with French women; in fact, this was one of the main reasons for the compound system. However, some Africans devised resourceful plans to abscond from the compounds and a few were involved with French prostitutes who frequented the dockyard areas. The very nature of such affairs made them momentary and superficial, but there is also evidence to suggest that certain members formed somewhat more enduring relationships with French women that went beyond casual sexual flirtation. It is instructive to note that after the return of the SANLC to South Africa, the chief censor, J.M. Weaver, intercepted and destroyed ten letters from French women to members of the contingent. He argued that such letters "will give the natives a wrong impression as to their relative position with regard to Europeans".[357] The fact that

---

355 Transcripts from interviews with R. Mohapeloa, Maseru, 9 May 1980; and P. Mabathoana, Maseru, 22 April 1980.

356 Perry and Perry, *Jingoes*, 80.

357 D.C. 1136/2/1997, Chief Censor to Acting Secretary of Defence, 23 April 1918.

such correspondence actually took place at all reflects a certain degree of commitment between the parties and Weaver's concern is a further indication of the nature of these relationships. Liaisons between black males and white females were not completely uncommon in South Africa; they were, however, often clandestine and, when revealed, such relationships were seen as a dangerous aberration in white circles that threatened the established order.[358] In war-torn France, a relatively more permissive atmosphere prevailed amongst the civilian population,[359] and it can be surmised that particularly those members of the SANLC who were involved in black/white affairs became more acutely aware of the discrepancy and less inclined to view the prevailing ideology in South Africa as an immutable force.

Through the exigencies of wartime service certain companies of the SANLC also came into occasional contact with white labour battalions from Britain, engaged in exactly the same manual work as black troops. This exposure, which was in sharp contrast to the position in South Africa where whites left most of the hard labour for Africans to perform, did not fail to leave an imprint. What impressed some even more, though, was that the whites in labour battalions displayed little colour prejudice and treated them as equals.[360] Jason Jingoes even struck up a friendship with a British labourer, named William Johnstone, and it was in this respect that he noted: "It was our first experience of living in a society without a colour bar".[361]

In another respect, the carefully controlled labour regimentation of the SANLC in France differed from standard procedures usually followed in South Africa. Whereas it was normal practice on the South African mines to divide the labour force along ethnic lines, in France it was decided to integrate various tribes. Practical considerations dictated this course of action, and it was also argued that such an arrangement would prevent the possibility of sympathetic strikes amongst members of the same ethnic

---

358 Van Onselen, *Studies in the Social and Economic History of the Witwatersrand, 1886-1914*, 45-50.

359 The commanding officer of the Cape Auxiliary Horse Transport Company (a Coloured unit which served in France as drivers) reported in this respect that some "white women showed partiality towards the Cape men and no matter how strict the control, found means of communicating with them, as is evidenced by a number of venereal cases" (C.O. 551/1117/39492, Report on the Cape Auxiliary Horse Transport Company, 13 June 1919).

360 *Native Teachers' Journal*, October 1920 (Letter from F.H. Kumalo); U.W.H. 89/34, Report on the SANLC, 8 March 1919.

361 Perry and Perry, *Jingoes*, 93.

group.[362] This had an unintended consequence. The continuous contact between workers from the different tribes in the work situation and the fact that they were all exposed to the same conditions, meant that at least for some Africans the ethnic affiliations became blurred. In an unambiguous statement, Z.F. Zibi revealed:

> We are not here as Mfengu, Xhosa and other tribes. We are conscious of the fact that we Blacks are united in staying together ... Therefore we shall never be deceived ... Otherwise it would mean that we are like people who share a mat but quarrel – in such cases one never sleeps well.[363]

The exact degree and intensity of solidarity is difficult to determine, but it seems clear that to some extent a common consciousness of their position as workers, as opposed to members of an ethnic group, began to develop in France.

In a more general sense, the wartime experiences of some members also meant an expansion of their world view. On the way to France, several troopships called at Sierra Leone, where M. Mokwena was particularly impressed by the fact that he met "some pure black negroes of very high educational attainments equal to that of the best Europeans ..."[364] Similarly, certain Africans regarded the sea voyage and that which they were allowed to witness abroad as formative influences. D.S. Makoliso, who came from a small Transkeian village (Cala), wrote: "I am glad to say that my experiences are more than any man's in Cala ... My head is full up with new things and the wonders of the world".[365] Likewise, for an anonymous member of the contingent an astonishing aspect of his experiences in France was "to see the different kinds of human races from all parts of the world".[366]

Others again, were impressed by the agriculture and "cultivation seen in an old and settled country".[367] Despite the restrictions they had to endure, some members were convinced that they had gained by the general experience of visiting a foreign European country. E. Mdlombo, for one, did not regret his decision to enlist and he viewed the period spent in France as an education which provided him with new

---

362 U.W.H. 89/34, Report on the SANLC, 8 March 1919.

363 *Imvo Zabantsundu*, 18 September 1917 (Letter from Z.F. Zibi, translated from Xhosa).

364 J. 258/3/127/20, Report on a meeting of the Transvaal Native Congress in Johannesburg, 24 August 1921. See also Willan, "The South African Native Labour Contingent, 1916-1918", 78.

365 C.M.T. 3/930/778/2, D.S. Makoliso to Magistrate Cala, 24 February 1917.

366 *The Church Abroad*, 1917, 122 (Letter from 'An African in France').

367 G.G. 549/93/56, General report on the chaplaincy and welfare work of the South African Native Labour Corps, 31 July 1918.

insights and knowledge.[368] This exposure to a world so different from their own clearly opened up new horizons for at least some members of the contingent.

One event in France left a very marked impression. On 10 July 1917, the British king, George V, inspected and addressed the contingent. For many of the educated Africans it was an unforgettable experience to see the king in person – the supreme symbol of imperial power and British 'justice' which loomed so largely in their imagination. "We saw him, George V, our king, with our own eyes ... To us it is a dream, something to wonder at", mused M.L. Posholi.[369] What made this visit even more memorable was that the king in his address not only praised them for their labour, but also assured them: "You are also part of my great armies fighting for the liberty and freedom of my subjects of all races and creeds throughout the empire".[370] The implications of these words were not lost on Posholi. "We are indeed in the midst of great wonders", he wrote, "because we personally heard that we blacks too are British subjects, children of the father of the great Nation, trusted ones and helpers, and that we are cared for and loved".[371]

A similar noteworthy occasion was the visit by a group of French parliamentarians and other dignitaries which included a black man – in all probability Blaise Diagne, commissioner of recruitment in the French colony of Senegal and a deputy in the French assembly. His presence in such eminent white company was of considerable interest to some members. At first they had thought that he was "simply there to accompany his white masters", but after enquiries they realised that he was an important official in his own right. The significance of this fired their political imaginations and inevitably raised pertinent questions as to their own position in South Africa. "One of us asked", it was subsequently related, "'would such a thing ever happen in our country?' Some replied, 'Who knows?' But others said quietly, 'It might ...'."[372]

For some Africans, the cumulative effect of their wartime experience – what they witnessed as well as their hope that something might yet come of their assistance to the state in troubled times – found expression in greater self-esteem and a less deferential attitude towards white people. Jason Jingoes claimed that "we were aware, when we returned that we were different from the other people at home. Our behaviour, as we

---

368 W.E. Stanford Papers B.C. 293/Frr/2, E. Mdlombo to Stanford, 3 March 1918.

369 S. 3/13/2/3, M.L. Posholi to P. Griffiths, 12 July 1917.

370 Ncwana, *Souvenir of the Mendi disaster*, 26-27.

371 S. 3/13/2/3, M.L. Posholi to P. Griffiths, 12 July 1917.

372 Perry and Perry, *Jingoes*, 87. See also Willan, "South African Native Labour Contingent, 1916-1918", 79.

showed the South Africans, was something more than they expected from a Native, more like what was expected among them of a white man."[373] Jingoes was not the only one to experience a change in outlook and to adopt a more assertive attitude. The commanding officer at the demobilisation depot in Cape Town, Major H. Dales, who was in a unique position to witness the demeanour of those returning from France, also observed from his vantage point a change of attitude: "[T]he conduct of these natives left much to be desired, great laxity of discipline being apparent, and their behaviour in general being a great contrast to that of recruits in training for overseas".[374]

Although the period spent in France undoubtedly sensitised certain members, one should also consider those factors which counteracted the development of increased militancy. Apart from the fact that the impact of military service differed according to individual circumstances, temperament, personality and pre-existing degree of socio-political awareness, members of the contingent were also exposed to influences which undermined their confidence. In this respect, they had occasion to witness the almost inexhaustible armed resources of the white man and the techniques of modern warfare in France. This caused some of them to realise that in the face of the ever increasing military potential of the white overlords, an African uprising in South Africa stood even less chance than before of succeeding. One veteran summed up the situation succinctly when he said: "Our assegais are no good now; they could not reach an aeroplane".[375]

Moreover, it was the avowed policy of the South African authorities to stifle the potential 'harmful' effects of wartime service. Virtually all the factors in overseas service which had the potential to broaden the social and political perceptions of black members were consciously emasculated. Central to this policy was the closed compound system and although it was not completely successful, it nevertheless severely limited the intensity of exposure to new conditions in a foreign country. Colonel S.M. Pritchard, commanding officer of the contingent, probably had sufficient reason to declare in a self-congratulatory statement in November 1919: "Knowing as he did the conditions under which they [the Africans] were employed, knowing the restrictions placed on their movements, and the strict discipline enforced, it would be a remarkable thing if these natives came back any the worse".[376] From a different

---

373 Perry and Perry, *Jingoes*, 92.

374 O.C. Records 44122/81, Report on the SANLC, 12 April 1918.

375 *Cape Times*, 18 April 1921 ("What the Native is thinking").

376 *South Africa*, 8 November 1919 ("Natives' proud record").

perspective, what is indeed remarkable under these circumstances is that at least some Africans, as has been indicated, used the restricted opportunities in the way they did.

This analysis points to the need to maintain a fine balance in evaluating the effect of participation in a white man's war. For every participant who returned from France with a changed outlook, there may have been another who was less affected. Indeed, from Sibasa in the Northern Transvaal, an area which yielded a considerable number of recruits, C.L. Harries, an official of the Native Affairs Department, reported:

> I ... find all those who went overseas most respectful and law-abiding and in no single instance have I found that the experiences gained abroad have reacted to the moral detriment of the individual. My own cook was 18 months in France and he is still the quiet, respectful and unsophisticated native that he was before he went.[377]

Clearly, in as far as Harries' evidence can be accepted, service in France had little, if any visible effect on the perceptions of these Africans. In general then, the experience of military service abroad had an uneven impact: the black veterans ranged from those who arrived back in South Africa with an increased and more explicitly defined individual and social consciousness to those who returned with their established views on the political and social order in South Africa apparently intact.

Related to the wartime exposure of SANLC members, were grievances about the callous treatment meted out to them by South African officers in France, and resentment about the paucity of post-war recognition. Despite frequent protests, veterans received no war medals or gratuities, solely because the authorities considered it politically imprudent to acknowledge publicly that whites had required the services of blacks during wartime.[378] Furthermore, the inflated promises made to lure the unsuspecting into the recruiting net during 1916-1917 were simply brushed aside; promises that they would be relieved from paying poll tax, be exempted from pass laws and be given free grants of land as well as cattle remained unfulfilled. To add insult to injury, former members were even expected to pay poll tax for the period they had been absent from

---

377 W.E. Stanford Papers B.C. 293/Frr/5, C.L. Harries to Stanford, 7 June 1920.

378 *Cape Times*, 14 August 1920 ("Parliamentary debates"); O.C. Records 89/125, British War Office to Officer Commanding War Records South Africa, 18 October 1919; G.G. 545/9/93/56, Smuts to Governor General, 30 April 1921; C.M.T. 3/926/778/2, Secretary Department of Native Affairs to Chief Magistrate Transkei, 20 September 1922; *Izwe Lase Afrika*, 21 February 1942 ("War service medals").

South Africa.[379] For a considerable time these slights and injustices rankled among former members of the contingent. Even 20 years after the war, an anonymous veteran was still aggrieved and resentful. On the eve of the Second World War, he wrote:

> It takes my memory back to the days of the Great War in 1914-1918, when the Government of South Africa said it would do all sorts of good things for us if only we would help them in the fight against Germany. Some of us were so foolish as to give belief to what they said. We went with the Native Labour Corps ... We were a help in overcoming the Germans. But when we came back we still had to have passes and we even had to make payment of Poll Tax for the time we were away.[380]

Not surprisingly, many veterans felt misled, deflated and discarded, particularly in the immediate post-war period. "The beliefs we entertained have proved to be absolutely worthless as the Government has done and is doing nothing for us", complained E.Q. Madayi in 1921.[381]

For S.T. Zondani and E. Ntusi, the calculated indifference of the government was a vindication of their suspicion that blacks in South Africa were expendable. In bitter terms, they wrote two years after the war:

> The fact that ... after we returned from France, having sacrificed our lives, no recognition whatsoever has been shown us, assures us and confirms the fact that the natives of this country, in spite of their loyalty, are a nonentity, and are only called upon when the Government are in dire straits, and are then not recognised when their services are finished with.[382]

In a similar vein, A.K. Xabanisa echoed the sentiments of a considerable number of veterans when he explained succinctly: "I am just like a stone which after killing a bird, nobody bothers about, nor cares to see where it falls".[383] To their chagrin, these ex-members discovered that the promises made and expectations raised in the turbulent and uncertain times of war meant nothing in the more placid and tranquil times of peace. The abandonment of the interests of the veterans created the potential

---

379 J. 318/3/754/21, Report on a meeting of the Transvaal Native Congress, 7 September 1921; N.A. 9108/20/363, Secretary of Native Affairs to J. Morie, 18 May 1918; Roux, *Time longer than rope*, 113.

380 *The African Defender*, September and October 1938 (Letter from 'An African').

381 N.A. 9108/26/363, E.Q. Madayi to Secretary of Native Affairs, 20 January 1921.

382 N.A. 9108/26/363, S.T. Zondani and E. Ntusi to Magistrate East London, 24 January 1920.

383 C.M.T. 3/925/778/2, A.K. Xabanisa to Chief Magistrate Transkei, 28 December 1919.

for increased militancy. Edward Roux, in his seminal work on black resistance in South Africa, drew attention to this post-war disillusionment amongst ex-members of the contingent. "After 1918", he claimed, "there were thousands of black men in the country who were prepared to stir up their fellow Africans to revolt against the system".[384] In 1920, D.D.T. Jabavu was also convinced that the

> Native Labour Contingent ... has imported into this country a new sense of racial unity and amity quite unknown heretofore among our Bantu races. Common hardships in a common camp have brought them into close relation. They had a glimpse at Europe and even from the closed compounds they got to discover that the white man overseas still loves the black man as his own child, while on the contrary some of their white officers ... made themselves notorious by their harsh treatment and slanderous repression of them when French people befriended them. All this was carefully noted ... in this country when they returned. The result is that there is amongst the diversified Bantu tribes of this land a tendency towards complete mutual respect and love founded upon the unhealthy basis of an anti-white sentiment.[385]

How valid were those generalisations and did the veterans, in fact, act as political catalysts? We now turn to explore the links between military service in France and tangible, perceptible opposition to white rule in South Africa. The fact that some members of the SANLC returned from France with a sharper awareness of their relative deprivation and were discontented over their post-war treatment, did not necessarily mean that their feelings and insights were actually translated into active resistance. It is therefore essential to consider whether the stimuli of service abroad, and all that accompanied it, were sufficient to galvanise veterans into political action.

On a personal and individual level, some veterans did not hesitate to demonstrate their increased self-confidence in everyday South African situations. In the Pietersburg district in the Northern Transvaal, an anonymous ex-member refused to accept passively what he regarded as exorbitant prices in the local trading store. He confronted the shopkeeper, named Williams, and a subsequent police report on the incident revealed the way in which this particular veteran asserted himself:

> A native who had recently returned from France came to his [Williams's] store and stated that the Europeans were responsible for the high prices of foodstuffs. He then asked Williams to whom the ground on which he was

384 Roux, *Time longer than rope*, 114.

385 Jabavu, *The black problem*, 17.

trading belonged, on receiving a reply that the ground belonged to Williams, the Native replied, 'the ground belongs to the Natives and we will show you'.[386]

In another incident, certain members on their train journey home had an altercation with the station master at Christiana in the western Transvaal. They entered his office "in an insolent manner and used abusive language which was levelled at white people in general". Some of them were also less than deferential to white women. As the train left they shouted at the local ganger's wife, *"Wil jy saam gaan?"* [Would you like to come along?][387] Rowdy behaviour is of course common amongst returning soldiers, but in this case there was obviously an added socio-political dimension.

Certain veterans furthermore attempted to shape the perceptions of rural black communities. Shortly after his return from France, L. Molife addressed peasants in the Rustenburg district in the western Transvaal and assured them in the following terms that their plight would soon be relieved: "The Germans were building powerful airships, capable of moving an army – they must not worry, that shortly a German army would be in Africa and would help them gain their freedom". This message, endorsed by similar statements from other ex-members, was received with considerable acclamation.[388] The factual accuracy of Molife's account is beside the point; what is important is its strong millenarian element and that veterans were involved in the dissemination of such ideas. However, the significance must not be exaggerated and it appears to have been an isolated incident. There were no large-scale post-war millenarian movements in the Transvaal, nor is there evidence to suggest that veterans were in any sustained way politically active in the rural areas.

In contrast with the Transvaal, millenarianism was an outstanding characteristic of rural resistance in the Eastern Cape and Transkei during the 1920s. Here, America featured prominently as the country which would deliver Africans from bondage.[389] There is some tantalising evidence to suggest that a few former members of the

---

386 J. 225/3/527/17, District Commandant Pietersburg to Assistant Commissioner of Police Pretoria, 21 December 1917.

387 N.A. 9108/22/363, Complaints re behaviour of native overseas troops, 18 January 1918.

388 S.A.P. 6/592/18, Report from Detective P. Mokhatla, 7 March 1918.

389 For a detailed analysis of these movements, see Edgar, "Garveyism in Africa", 31-57; Edgar, "The fifth seal", 151-181; R.T. Vinson, *The Americans are coming! Dreams of African American liberation in segregationist South Africa*, passim.

contingent were involved in these movements; however, it seems as if they could only have played a very marginal role.[390]

On a more formal level, some veterans did become active in organised black politics. Shortly after the war, Doyle Modiakgotla and Ben Nyombolo joined the Industrial and Commercial Workers' Union (ICU) of Africa, and Modiakgotla later became secretary of the Griqualand West branch. In 1920, S.M. Bennet Ncwana also became a member of the ICU and in addition initiated a short-lived publication, *The Black Man*.[391] Although it is significant that they became overtly involved in politics, there is no firm evidence that their war experiences were the prime motivating force. It can only be surmised that to some extent their exposure in France must have had a contributing influence.

Veterans were also involved in working class action in Port Elizabeth during October 1920. During a campaign for higher wages, the police arrested one of the leaders, S.M. Masabalala, whereupon a crowd of approximately 3 000 gathered outside the local gaol and demanded his release. When the police refused to consider their appeal, the demonstrators attacked with sticks and stones. Retaliation was swift and bloody; after a few warning shots the police fired indiscriminately into the retreating crowd – wounding 81 and killing 22. Amongst the victims of police violence were a number of former SANLC members.[392] The participation of veterans in this protest indicates post-war dissatisfaction and militancy amongst some veterans, but their precise role in these events remains hazy and there is no suggestion in the documentation that they spearheaded the unrest or that their war service was a decisive consideration in their action. Like the other participants, they might have been swayed by more immediate concerns, unconnected with their earlier experiences.

On the basis of this, there is insufficient evidence to make huge claims that the veterans "constituted the vanguard of the emerging black working class movement

---

390 Jabavu, "Native unrest in South Africa", 250, 254. See Edgar, "Garveyism in Africa", 5; and Edgar, "The fifth seal", 159.

391 P.M. 1/1/300, Secretary of the Prime Minister to Secretary of the Governor General, 20 February 1919; Wickins, *The Industrial and Commercial Workers Union of Africa*, 35, 61, 67-68, 76, 147, 163; Willan, "The South African Native Labour Contingent, 1916-1918", 83.

392 Simons and Simons, *Class and colour in South Africa, 1850-1950*, 241; Pirio, "The role of Garveyism in the making of the South African working classes and Namibian Nationalism", 6-7.

and of radical black nationalism in South Africa".[393] The conspicuous absence of veterans in the endemic and large-scale labour unrest on which occurred on the Witwatersrand between 1918 and 1920 can only make the point that such an assertion is far-fetched.[394]

Overall then there is no satisfactory evidence that veterans were in the forefront of sustained black resistance in the post-war years. Nor does it appear that they acted as 'modernisers' in rural societies. Immediately after his return, Jason Jingoes (and one can readily assume that his was not an isolated case) found that "he was thrown back into the old traditional ways".[395]

Politics of post-war expectations

The impact of the war was not restricted only to those who actually participated. It is therefore important to delineate the wider effect of the war as it was manifested in African political thinking.

It will be remembered that the loyal stance of the SANNC at the outbreak of the war was based on the hope that such a policy would increase its bargaining power and also render the authorities more sympathetic to black aspirations. During and immediately after the war, the SANNC maintained its faith in this belief, which was further strengthened by the contribution of the labour contingent to the Allied war effort. These expectations were clearly expressed by R.V. Selope Thema, secretary general of the SANNC, in May 1917:

> We ... are now facing the enemies of our King-Emperor on the battlefields of France. When that mighty Army of Sir Douglas Haig, which is now slowly but surely marching on Berlin, shall enter that City of Destruction, it will do so through the energetic efforts of our men at the front who are building railways, making roads and unloading ships ... On such a high tide are we afloat, and we must take the current ... Never before did the Bantu people stand on such a high tide as today.[396]

Towards the closing stages of the war black participation in the hostilities had further raised the level of expectancy amongst African political leaders and they became

393 Pirio, "Role of Garveyism", 6.

394 For these developments, see chapter 8.

395 Perry and Perry, *Jingoes*, 93.

396 *Ilanga Lase Natal*, 26 May 1917 ("Under the flag of freedom").

more strident in their demands. "We expect to be rewarded for our work after the war when prizes are distributed to the brave who were in battle", insisted D.S. Letanka, an influential SANNC member, in February 1918.[397] A month later, S.M. Makgatho, then chairman of the SANNC, openly declared at the organisation's annual conference that "the blood of these sons of ours, spilled on behalf of the Empire, entitled us to claim a say ... in the Parliament".[398] Another member, L.T. Mvabasa, made a similar point in April 1918 and furthermore located African aspirations in the context of freedom and democracy – the oft proclaimed war aims of the Allied forces. Unambiguously he stated:

> That in consideration of the sacrifices the Bantu have made during this war which we are continually being told is for democracy and freedom, the British and white people of this land should redress our grievances and give the freedom for which we lost thousands of men in this struggle.[399]

Black expectations were also stimulated by the pronouncements of Allied statesmen and other dignitaries. H.S. Msimang recalled 42 years after the war that he found the address of King George V, in which the king recognised the work of the labour contingent, particularly encouraging.[400] In addition, David Lloyd George, the British prime minister, and Woodrow Wilson, the American president, propagated the idea from 1918 onwards that sufficient allowance should be made in the post-war dispensation for the self-determination of smaller and oppressed nations. This was interpreted as yet another hopeful sign. "We look upon Mr Lloyd George's declaration as a message of hope that the dawn of freedom is at last breaking forth", commented D.S. Letanka.

This view was not as naive as it may at first appear. Letanka was well aware that the policy was not formulated with South Africa in mind, but for him the post-war credibility of Britain was at stake in this matter. "It may be argued that Lloyd George's doctrine of self-determination does not apply to South Africa", he continued. "Against this, we argue that if this doctrine is not applicable to the native inhabitants of this country, then the case of the British Government falls to the ground".[401] Closer to home, the governor general, Lord Buxton, further impressed the SANNC when he

---

397 *Abantu-Batho*, 14 February 1918 ("Our position").

398 G.N.L.B. 187/1217/14/D 110, Report of the annual SANNC conference, 29 March 1918.

399 *Abantu-Batho*, 25 April 1918 ("Notes and comments").

400 *Contact*, 7 April 1960 (Interview with H. Selby Msimang).

401 *Abantu-Batho*, 7 February 1918 ("The future of the German colonies").

addressed a mass meeting of Africans during the peace celebrations in December 1918 and declared that "the war has proved to you that your loyalty was well placed; and I can assure you that it will not be forgotten".[402]

Visions of a new world order in which Africans would be elevated to their rightful place, were not restricted to the educated elite. British, and particularly American, pronouncements on the self-determination of oppressed nations were absorbed in a somewhat distorted form by Transkeian peasants and exerted an influence on the millenarian movements which surfaced during the 1920s. In 1927, W.D. Cingo, a Transkeian journalist, graphically explained this strand in millenarianism and its relation to the war:

> The Great European War also had its contribution to these illusions. The moral and military power of America came into prominence. Her declaration for the 'Self-determination of smaller nations' ... caught the tender ears of the unsophisticated natives in these parts. They regard the voice of America as that of a mighty race of black people overseas, dreaded by all Europeans ... Hopes for political and economic emancipation were revived and today the word America (iMelika) is a household word symbolic of nothing but Bantu National freedom and liberty.[403]

Whereas the hopes engendered by an optimistic post-war mood contributed to the millenarian movements in the Transkei, increased expectations led the SANNC to consider yet another deputation to Britain. The perceived need for such a deputation was further reinforced by the refusal of the Union government to include an African in the official delegation under Botha and Smuts to the Paris peace conference.[404] Initially, Dube doubted the wisdom of approaching the British government before constitutional means in South Africa were exhausted, but later on he agreed that perhaps more could be achieved in Britain than locally.[405] H.S. Msimang further suggested that they should broaden their platform and involve blacks from South-West Africa in the venture since the future of the former German colony was an important item on the agenda at the peace conference. Although the idea was considered

---

402 G.G. 1169/50/759, Petition to King George V, 16 December 1918 (copy). Buxton's address is quoted in this petition.

403 Edgar, "Garveyism in Africa", 37.

404 Walshe, *African nationalism*, 62.

405 *Ilanga Lase Natal*, 17 November 1918 ("Generalities"), 13 December 1918 ("The proposed deputation"), 28 February 1919 ("Lack of unity"), 28 March 1919 ("Off to England").

sympathetically, there was not sufficient time to act upon it.[406] Otherwise there was little to debate and the SANNC decided unanimously to send a deputation to Britain and to the peace conference in Paris.

To pave the way, a petition to the king was drawn up in December 1918 at a special session of the SANNC. The petition strongly emphasised black loyalty and participation in the war and the king's own speech to the SANLC was even quoted back at him. It was argued that their wartime record entitled them to greater consideration and that the British government should exert pressure on the Union to ensure that the position of blacks in South Africa was improved.[407] This petition, however, was never transmitted to the king; Buxton referred the matter to the South African government, which reacted in a predictable way by declaring that either black people had no reason to be dissatisfied or their complaints were exaggerated.[408] This rebuff strengthened the resolve of the SANNC, and in April 1919, three members – R.V. Selope Thema, L.T. Mvabasa and H.R. Ngcayiya – sailed from Cape Town for Britain. Later on they were joined by Sol Plaatje and J.T. Gumede.

In Britain, the Colonial Office received the news of the black deputation's mission with distinct misgivings and even antagonism. Upon learning that they sought an interview with the king, J. Reid, one of the senior officials, commented: "I don't think that H.M. should be advised to receive the deputation. Its object would be to arraign the Union Govt.; it can do no good, and would probably embarrass H.M. and annoy [white] South Africans generally."[409] Other officials in the Colonial Office were hardly more sympathetic. They refused a further request by the deputation to interview the British prime minister and, like Reid's, their marginal comments revealed their real opinions and attitudes. H. Thornton noted that such an interview would only lead to "further publicity of the deputation's grievances and that would seem all the more undesirable", while H. Lambert argued that "these people no doubt want a little advertisement and take this opportunity to try and get it".[410]

The Aborigines' Protection Society which prided itself on being 'friends of the natives', was no source of encouragement either and ultimately gave the deputation

---

406 *Contact*, 15 July 1960 (Second interview with H. Selby Msimang).

407 G.G. 1169/50/759, Petition to King George V, 16 December 1918 (copy).

408 G.G. 1169/50/759, F.S. Malan to Buxton, 20 February 1919.

409 C.O. 551/111/15305, Marginal notes by J. Reid, 4 April 1919.

410 C.O. 551/122/35102, Marginal note by H. Thornton, 19 June 1919; C.O. 551/122/35007, Marginal note by H. Lambert, 13 June 1919.

no real moral support. Their assistance was restricted to some financial aid and offers to find lodgings for the deputies.[411] Otherwise, the organisation remained aloof. Its influential secretary, J.H. Harris, had already indicated in an article written in 1916 that he was not in favour of the "native races" having any say in the possible consultations at the end of the war.[412] It is therefore not surprising that he regarded the deputation as "ill-advised". Moreover, as he revealed in a private letter, he was offended because the delegation had not consulted him before their departure from South Africa.[413]

The deputation was thus confronted either by official intransigence or unhelpful paternalism. However, through the good offices of W.P. Schreiner, the South African high commissioner in London who himself had led a deputation to England in 1909 to protest against the colour bar in the Union constitution, they succeeded in arranging an appointment with L.S. Amery, the undersecretary of state for colonies. During the interview which took place on 8 May 1919, Amery could give the delegation little solace and advised them to work patiently within the existing framework of the Union constitution. Although Amery was not prepared to take the matter any further, he was somewhat upset by what he had learnt. In his personal diary, he noted that the deputation "gave a full and not unfair recital of all the grievances suffered by the natives under Union ... I replied sympathetically ... but it was very clear to me that trouble is coming this way, possibly much sooner than we have generally thought".[414]

Meanwhile, Thema and Mvabasa had left for Paris where they unsuccessfully tried to put their cause to the peace conference. However, they did manage to meet Lloyd George, who assured them than when he arrived back in London he would find time for an interview.[415] On their return to London, the deputation submitted a detailed memorandum on the discriminatory measures in South Africa to Lord Milner, the British secretary of state for colonies. This, however, elicited the stock reply, namely that the British government was not in a position to interfere in South African affairs.[416] Nevertheless, the deputation persisted in its task and Sol Plaatje, in particular, exerted

411 A.P.S. Papers S 23 H 2/50, J.H. Harris to Selope Thema, 12 January 1920 (copy).

412 Harris, "Native races and peace terms", 752-759.

413 A.P.S. Papers S 23 H 2/50, Harris to M.E. Sadler, 12 February 1920 (copy). See also Smuts Collection CXV/8, Harris to private secretary of the South African High Commissioner, 10 April 1919 (copy).

414 Barnes and Nicholson, *The Leo Amery Diaries, I, 1896-1929*, 260.

415 C.O. 551/114/58532, H. Lambert to South African High Commissioner, 21 November 1919.

416 C.O. 551/112/30799, Deputation to Milner, 22 May 1919 and Milner to Deputation, 4 June 1919.

himself to gain general public support. He addressed numerous meetings and to some extent received a favourable response from church circles and certain factions of the labour movement.[417]

Towards the end of November 1919, despite the opposition from the Colonial Office, the long-delayed interview with Lloyd George took place and the deputation once again gave a wide-ranging account of African disabilities in South Africa. In contrast to other high ranking officials, Lloyd George was not indifferent. After he had informed them that he had also had an interview with another South African deputation – that of the National Party under General Hertzog, which called for republican independence for South Africa –, he thanked them for the contribution made by the SANLC and for the loyalty which blacks had generally shown during the war. Lloyd George was impressed by the clear way in which they had put their case and informed the deputation that he had "listened with some distress to the story you have told of restrictions which are imposed upon you in your native land". The constitutional position prevented him from taking any firm action, but he continued:

> If South Africa were under the control of the British Parliament, well, I should know exactly what to do. I should certainly take all your grievances into immediate consideration and examine them very carefully and give due weight to all you have said with the feeling that we were dealing with a population which has been very loyal to the flag.

Lloyd George also assured them that their cause should receive serious and sympathetic consideration from the South African government and that he would inform General Smuts accordingly.[418] The British prime minister remained true to his word and showed his concern by sending an official report as well as a private letter. In the official despatch, Lloyd George suggested that it was advisable for Smuts to meet the deputation himself, but in the private communication he stated that it was a matter of urgency "to redress any real grievance from which they may suffer, and to satisfy any legitimate aspirations". For Lloyd George it was clear that "if they have no effective constitutional mode of expression it is obvious that sooner or later serious results must ensue".[419] Smuts' response was predictable. He replied that the deputation had exaggerated black grievances and harmed their cause by going to Britain, and that

---

417 Willan, *Sol Plaatje: A biography*, 247-248.

418 C.O. 537/1197/1486, Transcript of an interview between Lloyd George and the deputation, 21 November 1919.

419 C.O. 537/1197/1486, Lloyd George to Smuts, 3 March and 7 January 1920.

there were sufficient constitutional means through which black aspirations could be accommodated.[420]

Lloyd George's sympathetic attitude did not mask the obvious failure of the deputation. Indeed, its abortive mission to Britain only serves to underline the realities of white domination and the close links between South Africa and Britain in this respect. As the historian Martin Chanock has noted:

> Lloyd George's letters, a random outburst from an isolated and erratic radical, could not alter the fact that ... Britain shared a common stance with South Africa ... An uninformed sense of disquiet, even in a Prime Minister, was negligible when weighed against the community of interest between the white rulers in Africa.[421]

In retrospect then, the attempts of the SANNC may appear unrealistic and even naive. This, however, would be too harsh a judgement. Viewed in their own terms and the overall historical context it is clear that in the more hopeful post-war climate their attempts amounted to a resolute move by constitutionally minded men to effect favourable change through the only avenue they deemed promising and available. "The Great War has ... opened a chance to us ... let us not lose the chance", argued L.T. Mvabasa on the eve of their departure to Britain.[422]

The failure of the deputation nevertheless left the SANNC disillusioned and eroded its earlier trust in the British government. Even Lloyd George's sympathetic attitude was no consolation. "Lloyd George said he did not know the black people were so badly treated in Africa, but Lloyd George is a white man and cannot be trusted", was the reaction of J.D. Ngoja, a Cape member of the SANNC.[423] Some members of the SANNC, though, sought solace in the fact that during the volatile post-war period the government, through the Native Affairs Act 23 of 1920, attempted to regularise 'native policy' and created a Native Affairs Commission which was intended to advise the government on matters of policy towards Africans. Although these developments failed to meet the demands and expectations of the SANNC – Africans, for example, were not included in the Commission – there were those members, like R.V. Selope Thema, who considered the establishment of such a body a hopeful sign. He argued that it vindicated their deputation to England in as far as the South African

---

420 C.O. 537/1198/17397, Smuts to Lloyd George, 12 May 1920.

421 Chanock, *Unconsummated Union: Britain, Rhodesia and South Africa, 1900-1945*, 134.

422 J. 256/3/527/17, Report of a meeting of the Transvaal Native Congress, 17 December 1918.

423 J. 257/3/527/17, Report of a meeting of the Transvaal Native Congress, 8 February 1920.

government had at least shown a willingness to establish the principle of consultation and to be informed of African interests.[424] However, even if one is to accept the dubious proposition that the commission was a step forward, it remains a moot point whether these government initiatives were in any way a result of the SANNC's mission to England.

The increased expectations brought about by the war only buttressed the aspirations of the SANNC for a limited period. The visit to England, as Peter Walshe has viewed it in his study of the ANC, represented a watershed in the history of the organisation; its constitutional efforts frustrated, the SANNC found it difficult to adopt decisive new strategies.[425] When it became clear that there would be no meaningful concessions in response to black loyalty and sacrifices, the organisation lapsed into a mood of political cynicism which contributed towards its relative stagnation in the 1920s.

However, of greater importance in its decline were the changed socio-economic conditions in which the SANNC had to operate towards the end and in the aftermath of the war. These conditions spawned new forms of consciousness and gave rise to popular militancy on the Rand and elsewhere, and also saw the birth of more populist organisations like the ICU. Although some members of the SANNC tried to meet the new challenges, the organisation on the whole became increasingly inactive.

Conclusion

War-related events had a decided, if uneven, impact on black political consciousness. While many Africans undoubtedly remained untouched by war events, for others the war brought into sharper focus the prevailing iniquities. The war left the SANNC, who had such high hopes initially, disillusioned. In evaluating the broader significance of the war though, it is important to look beyond the fluctuating fortunes of organisational politics. It is in this respect that we turn to the sinking of the SANLC contingent troopship, the *SS Mendi*, which was destined to become an enduring element in African political consciousness.

424 Willan, *Sol Plaatje: A biography*, 296.

425 Walshe, *African nationalism*, 65.

THE *SS MENDI* DISASTER

Politics of remembrance, 1917-2014

On the cold and foggy early morning of 21 February 1917, just off the Isle of Wight, the *SS Mendi*, carrying the last detachment of the SANLC to France, was rammed by another ship, the *SS Darro*, on its starboard side. The damage was severe; a gaping hole of 20 metres long and 20 metres wide opened up. The *Mendi* tilted almost immediately, took in a flood of water through the hull and began to sink rapidly. There was little time to even begin ordering the men to the deck and launch the life boats. Not surprisingly, the death toll was high: of the 882 men on board, 615 died and 267 were saved.

Of that much, historians can be sure. The subsequent history, though, of how this event has been remembered over the decades, is more complicated, with a number of twists, turns and at times apparent dead ends. What is of particular concern, is to trace how the *Mendi* disaster has been recalled and contextualised in terms of public memory at different historical junctures and how elements of the event have been mythologised to be readily consumed, particularly in the 2000s. What, however, were the circumstances of the ship's sinking?

A controversial accident

In August 1917, a court of inquiry was convened in England to investigate the matter and found the captain of the *Darro*, H.W. Stump, guilty of gross negligence. In the foggy weather, he had failed to transmit the relevant warning signals and he had also exceeded the speed limit laid down for such conditions. Moreover, in an even more serious breach of regulations, Stump had made no more than feeble attempts to assist the floundering men in the water. The court was convinced that had Stump "got the boats out as soon as he knew his vessel was safe, more lives would, in all reasonable probability have been saved". In delivering the verdict, the court declared that Stump's inaction was "inexcusable", and as a disciplinary measure his license as a ship's captain was suspended for a year.[426] Given the explicit finding of the court, the disciplinary action was surprisingly lenient. One of the British officers associated with the case, Captain A.H. Young, was of the opinion that Stump's license should have been cancelled. He argued that either Stump was

> utterly callous to all sentiments of humanity or, as a result of the collision, his nerve deserted him to such an extent as to render him incapable of rational thought and action at a time when every instinct of the trained seaman should have been brought into play. In either case it points to the necessity for a prosecution with a view to cancellation of certificate for gross incompetence or criminal neglect and so prevent him from again becoming a common danger. I consider that if inhumanity be proved he should be punished by cancellation; if incompetence through loss of nerve be the judgement then he is not a fit person to again have command of any ship.[427]

The case remained closed, but Young was not alone in condemning Stump. In South Africa, some black people maintained that for Stump's share in the "never-to-be-forgotten *Mendi* holocaust, he should not be permitted to enjoy liberty for another twenty-four hours".[428] It is furthermore of interest that despite a wide-ranging inquiry, once the court had established Stump's negligence, it did not in any systematic manner attempt to assess the reasons for his misconduct. The absence of any reliable evidence makes it impossible to provide an answer, but in view of Stump's blatant disregard for the plight of the *Mendi*'s passengers, one is certainly justified in raising the question that the court failed to probe in any depth: was Stump's indifference entirely unrelated to the fact that the *Mendi* carried black troops?

Be that as it may, the circumstances surrounding the *Mendi* disaster and a subsequent administrative delay on the part of the South African government to release full details gave rise to unconfirmed suspicions amongst certain blacks that there was "more behind it than has been revealed".[429] More specifically, from New Brighton,

---

426 T. 9/1115/6590, Finding of the Court of Inquiry, 8 August 1917.

427 T. 9/1115/6590, Statement by Captain A.H. Young, 15 August 1917.

428 *Imvo Zabantsundu*, 16 October 1917 ("The deplorable disaster").

429 W.H. Long Papers 947/601/42, Buxton to Long, 10 March 1917.

near Port Elizabeth, an Anglican missionary reported that "some mischiefmakers had created unrest by hinting that the same care was not taken in the case of natives as with white troops".[430]

Botha was aware of these rumours and in his official announcements in parliament about the collision he claimed that such "idle and mischievous stories" were unjustified. He then expressed the government's sincere regret at the loss of life and extended his deepest sympathy to the relatives of those who had died in the disaster. T. Smartt, leader of the Unionist Party, and John X. Merriman made similar speeches and a motion of sympathy was unanimously passed. The adoption of this motion witnessed the unusual sight of an all-white parliament rising to pay respect to deceased blacks.[431] The government furthermore undertook to assist the next of kin financially through a gratuity of £50 each.[432] For the authorities this was the end of the matter, but the memory of the *Mendi* was destined to live on with great potency.

Making and unmaking of memories under segregation and apartheid

Outside of parliament, the sinking of the *Mendi* elicited some heartfelt responses in the black press in South Africa. Besides lamenting the death of those on board the ill-fated ship, the newspapers also saw their demise to be of wider import in the sense that "they have died to set us free".[433] Similar wishful thinking associated the tragedy with the freedom of the empire at large and that "those who had died by drowning had given their life for the liberty of all peoples of the Empire".[434]

Such hopes, which could only be regarded as forlorn at the time given the constellation of powerful forces which militated against equality in South Africa, were nevertheless of sufficient depth to find expression in the founding of a Mendi Memorial Club in 1919, with the aim of keeping the memory of the *Mendi* alive.[435] The club seemed to have run into organisational problems, though, which is not altogether surprising as one of the main figures, S.M. Bennet Ncwana, an ex-SANLC member, had an unsavoury

---

430 P.M.1/1/483, A.T. Wijmans to Botha, 15 March 1917.

431 *Cape Times*, 10 March 19197 ("Parliamentary debates").

432 G.G. 545/9/93/56, Botha to Buxton, 8 June 1917.

433 *Abantu-Batho*, 14 January 1918 ("Wail of the Native Widows").

434 *Imvo Zabantsundu*, 27 March 1917 ("The *Mendi* disaster").

435 G.G. 1169/50/771, S.M. Bennet Ncwana to Buxton, 12 March 1919.

reputation as a devious plotter who was inclined to use organisations to further his own financial ends.[436] Apart from this short-lived attempt at commemoration, the participation of the SANLC in the war was enshrined in the course of time in a monument in France at Arque-la-Bataille, near Dieppe; the names of the deceased of the *Mendi* were recorded at the Hollybrook memorial in Southampton; and smaller memorials appeared in Umtata, Langa, Soweto and fairly recently at the lower end of the University of Cape Town campus, all bearing testimony to the participation of the SANLC in the war.

Public recollections and general consciousness of the *Mendi* disaster remained febrile and widespread enough to extend beyond the erection of monuments. This was considered too an important an occurrence "to be allowed to fade from the memory of a nation".[437] In 1928, an effort was made to harness these memories in the form of a 'living' monument. Channelling and sustaining remembrances of the *Mendi* now assumed the form of an educational fund, as well as an annual memorial day in February, close to the date of the actual sinking. The mobilisation of these memories in the late 1920s coincided with what the organisers called a new awareness of "race consciousness".[438] This was a period during which the ICU sought to promote black working class interests in a more radical albeit erratic fashion than before and even some branches of the usually sedate African National Congress (ANC) experienced a spurt of raised political energy levels.[439]

Central to this initiative was the role of the black petty bourgeoisie in providing organisational leadership. Clergymen, in particular, stood out and they dominated the various committees which were formed.[440] Church affiliations, together with family connections, education and ethnicity, were key elements in the social networks of the black elite and ministers of religion often assumed roles that moved well beyond religious boundaries. Given their positions of leadership, it was considered natural for them to act not only as guardians of the memories of the *Mendi*, but also to help

---

436 On Ncwana, see Cobley, *Class and consciousness: The black petty bourgeoisie in South Africa, 1924 to 1950*, 215.

437 K.J.B. (Johannesburg Commissioner) 409/1/14/3, H.G. Mpitso, Notes on the *Mendi* anniversary, 1946.

438 K.J.B. 409/1/14/3, H.G. Mpitso, Notes on the *Mendi* anniversary, 1946.

439 Lodge, *Black politics in South Africa since 1945*, 8; Limb, *The ANC's early years: Nation, class and place in South Africa before 1940*, 332-333.

440 K.J.B. 409/1/14/3, Mendi Memorial brochure containing the names and vocations of the various members, 1952.

shape the form and values to be associated with the historical event. In the hands of the educated elite, the *Mendi* project was to become part of the array of social and cultural associations through which these groups wished to express themselves in the larger centres during the 1930s: reading circles, debating societies, music and choral societies, drama societies and sport clubs, especially cricket and tennis. These organisations and cultural ways of self-expression had the effect of confirming identities.[441] Those associated with the *Mendi* fund and annual commemorations viewed these ventures as further opportunities to enhance their claims to equality and to demonstrate that Africans too, through those who had died on the *Mendi*, "placed the name of the black man in history books of the world".[442] The fact that this was an elite-driven initiative ensured that its shape, form and contents were also likely to reflect the preoccupations of the leadership. The concerns of the more plebeian veterans of the First World War might well have been less rarefied.

Having said that, there can be little doubt about the commitment shown by some of the individuals involved in organisational work pertaining to the *Mendi* fund and annual commemorations. H.G. Mpitso, the honorary general secretary, reported after an exhausting trip to urban centres, as well as to selected rural towns in Natal and the Free State to promote the *Mendi* bursary fund, that the tour "occupied 18 days of constant movement without resting anywhere. It imposed considerable strain; nevertheless it was enjoyable because it involved a *sacrifice* self-imposed on behalf of my fellow men."[443]

One of the main aims of such visits was to raise funds for the bursary. Donations were also collected during annual memorial days and each adult was supposed to contribute one shilling. In addition, larger sponsorships were obtained through businesses which traded on a regular basis with African customers, such as the cycling firm of Shimwell Brothers in Johannesburg, and Geen & Richards, a popular furniture store.[444] The fund, which was partially administered by the Native Affairs Department, grew slowly but steadily and in 1951 it had accumulated at least £2 000. But this was not sufficient for the large number of applications which were received.[445] Many of these applications, couched in formal and stylised English, contained as their subtext

---

441 Cobley, *Class and consciousness*, 75, 81.

442 K.J.B. 409/1/14/3, H.G. Mpitso, Notes on the *Mendi* anniversary, 1946.

443 K.J.B. 409/1/14/3, Report by H.G. Mpitso, 1948. (Emphasis in the original.)

444 K.J.B. 409/1/14/3, Secretary Shimwell to Native Commissioner Johannesburg, 13 Februrary 1948: Secretary Geen and Richard to Native Commissioner, 18 February 1949.

445 K.J.B. 409/1/14/3, Mendi Memorial Day brochure, 1951.

near-desperate pleas for "self-improvement".[446] Those who were awarded bursaries went to the University College of Fort Hare at Alice for further study.

The *Mendi* enterprise created a favourable impression among certain whites. To F.E.T. Krause, a prominent judge in the Transvaal who was asked to be a guest speaker at the 1946 commemoration, the experience was a 'real eye opener'. In a private letter to the native commissioner in Johannesburg a day after the event, he explained his enthusiasm for the project and also cautiously assumed an advocacy role:

> Those who still think that the Native is not capable of absorbing civilizing influences and cannot react to uplifting conditions ought to have been there to witness the scene. In my opinion it is up to the government to set aside a substantial sum, at least 25 000 pounds to establish scholarships for deserving but poor natives. I wanted to say so yesterday but was afraid that it might be said that I was indulging in 'subversive activities' or trying to create hostility in the minds of the Natives ... But that is the truth. It is the duty of the Native Affairs Dept or perhaps the Defence Department, as far as the *Mendi* disaster is concerned, to have sponsored the scheme and not call upon the poor harassed native to contribute to the fund.[447]

Such largesse was of course most unlikely to be forthcoming, but it is clear that casting the *Mendi* message in an educational form had the effect of creating common ground between so-called 'friends of the natives' and the black elite. Notions of "self-help", "upliftment" and the need for "responsible citizens", as well as a belief that "heaven helps those who help themselves" punctuated the appeals for fund.[448] For the Mendi Memorial Committee education was the central plank of their appeal as "it will give us inspiration and determination to help ourselves, so that of our own efforts we may climb the ladder until we reach the highest pinnacle of self-development".[449] In a wider context, the function of education as one of the main pillars of the world view of the petty bourgeoisie is well explained by historian Alan Cobley:

> Education was also a vital asset for those wishing to prosper in a period of rapid economic and social change. Education provided the basic saleable skills required by South Africa's early industrial cash economy; these included the

446 Examples of these requests are to be found in K.J.B. 409/1/14/3.

447 K.J.B. 409/1/14/3, F.E.T. Krause to Native Commissioner, 25 February 1946.

448 K.J.B. 409/1/14/3, H.G. Mpitso Notes on the *Mendi* anniversary, 1946; K.J.B. 409/1/14/3, V. Baloye to Secretary *Mendi* Fund, 14 February 1948; K.D. Morgan to Mayor Johannesburg, 11 February 1947; Secretary *Mendi* Fund to Chairman, 7 March 1951

449 *Umteteli wa Bantu*, 19 March 1932 ("The *Mendi* memorial").

ability to read and write, to understand figures, to communicate effectively in the language of the colonists, and to demonstrate what the missionaries and industrialists called the 'habits of industry'.[450]

These skills were essential for those who wished to add an additional element to an increasingly fluid African identity. It was, moreover, not necessarily a strategy of the weak as it could, if only tentatively in the initial stages, be used during the 1940s to explore the possibility of more radical departures in raising general awareness of the discrepancies built into the segregationist system. In this way, though the *Mendi* educational fund may have appeared innocuous, ideologically it did indirectly contain at least the seeds of a potentially more probing politics.

By the 1940s, the annual *Mendi* memorial days attracted up to 6 000 people in the larger venues as some of the participants caught up in the general war fever of the time and keen to recall earlier African sacrifices during the First World War. The public structuring of these memorial performances was an opportunity to showcase African absorption of Western rituals; they usually incorporated a military band, march pasts, choirs, scripture readings and speeches, while the importance of arriving punctually before the proceedings started and behaving suitably decorously during the ceremony were emphasised. Often the proceedings were broadcast.[451]

A determined effort was also made to reach out and draw in various sections of society, and on one occasion even an Afrikaans Dutch Reformed Church minister of religion appeared as the guest speaker.[452] Equally noticeable was the singing of three anthems at the close of the event: "Nkosi Sikeleli Afrika", "God save the King" and "Die Stem".[453] The hybrid nature of these events reflected not only the broad appeal which the organisers of the *Mendi* day sought to cultivate, but at its core it also mirrored the ambivalent nature of segregation itself. Segregation was an umbrella ideology which incorporated several and, at times, conflicting interests. Under the guise of "benevolent patriotism", several such strands were woven into and contained

---

450 Cobley, *Class and consciousness*, 61.

451 For example, K.J.B. 409/1/14/3, Mendi Memorial Day brochures, 1946-1949; *Umteteli wa Bantu*, 20 February 1932 ("The *Mendi*").

452 N.T.S. (Native Affairs Department) 9112/36/363, Mendi Memorial Day brochure, 1951. See also *Bantu World*, 24 February 1934 ("Loyal service of thousands of Africans".) *Bantu World*, 6 March 1937 ("Mendi Memorial Anniversary").

453 K.J.B. 409/1/14/3, Mendi Memorial Day brochure, 1949; *Umteteli wa Bantu*, Mendi Memorial Anniversary, 3 March 1945.

in an ideological maze.[454] The structure of *Mendi* days transmitted an unmistakable signal that the deaths of those on board the ship were not to be used to challenge the authorities, but rather to appease and demonstrate goodwill.

It would be misleading, however, to focus only on the outward form of memorial days. Some speakers did use the occasion as a platform to voice more critical opinions. In 1939, Doctor A.B. Xuma, who had assumed the presidency of the ailing ANC and who did much to overhaul the organisation of the movement, made it clear that the deaths of those on the *Mendi* had not been translated into any tangible benefits for those left behind and that the position of Africans in the intervening 22 years had not improved in any appreciable way. Africans needed to be free in the land of their birth and so in "honour and grateful memory of those noble dead, the African will work for these ideals so that these men will not have died in vain".[455]

The Second World War helped to bring about an important socio-economic and ideological shift. The need for increased war production and the absence of large numbers of white men, who had gone to the front, opened up opportunities for Africans and facilitated migration from the countryside to the urban areas. At the same time black political expectations were raised by the portrayal of the Allied Forces in their fight against Nazi Germany as conducting a war against tyranny and oppression which resonated readily with some blacks in South Africa.[456] Xuma plugged into these currents when he was once again given the opportunity to speak at the 1941 annual day. "It seems to me", he argued.

> that in memory of the men who died in the *Mendi* and of thousands of others
> of all races who lost their lives during the World War as well as in honour
> of white and non-white men who are keeping South Africa's boundaries
> inviolate in the North and from the high seas, South Africa can build no more
> valuable or a lasting monument for them than to maintain and operate during
> the war her democratic institutions and to grant, now, and henceforth freedom
> in the state and social justice for all her people irrespective of race, creed or
> colour. This is not merely winning the war, this is winning the peace.[457]

---

454 Compare Cell, *The highest stage of white supremacy: The origins of segregation in South Africa and the American south*, 219-220. See also Dubow, *Racial segregation and the origins of apartheid in South Africa, 1919-1936*, 37-38.

455 Gish, *Alfred B. Xuma, African, American, South African*, 101.

456 Lodge, *Black politics*, 11, 15.

457 Karis and Carter, *From protest to challenge*, 165-166, "Dr A.B. Xuma, An address at the Mendi Memorial Day Celebration, 23 February, 1941".

Apart from the ideological impact of the Second World War, a range of other factors helped to create unprecedented black political volatility on the Witwatersrand during the 1940s: increased urbanisation improved the logistical possibility of sustained political activity amongst a closely settled urban population as opposed to a scattered rural one; the ANC's gradual revival partly as a result of Xuma's organisational skills and partly because of the Youth League's newfound urgency; and greater militancy amongst workers contributed to the 1946 miners' strike.[458]

Significantly, the turbulence was not restricted to the working classes. In 1944, some 1 200 African teachers took to the streets of Johannesburg in an unusually vociferous protest to demand, and ultimately receive, higher salaries. The outcome of this campaign had a distinct bearing on the way in which certain sections of the middle classes had modified their views on the strategy of mass action. Whereas earlier on activists had described teachers as "impenetrable block-heads who lived in the clouds, over and above ordinary mortals", some teachers were now prepared to a greater extent than before to become involved in political demonstrations.[459] Of particular interest in terms of the *Mendi* commemorations is that a solid middle class core such as teachers, who had formed the backbone of the *Mendi* project, now became more confrontational. This new-found stridency was reflected in more assertive Mendi Day speeches, to the extent that officials of the Native Affairs Department who attended these meetings condemned what they considered "hot left" addresses by "extremists" and by 1947 the United Party government was decidedly uneasy about the increasingly challenging political nature of *Mendi* services.[460]

The assumption of power in 1948 by the National Party, with its more rigid notions of racial ordering, saved the United Party government from the embarrassment of adopting a firm stance against what they considered a deviant way in which blacks sought to commemorate a wartime event which occurred while Africans were supposedly loyally serving a common South African and imperial cause. Mendi Day speeches by African politicians during the first years of National Party rule reflected much the same tenor as before, contrasting black sacrifice with white intransigence.[461]

---

458 Compare Lodge, *Black politics*, 27; Gish, *Xuma*, 141-143; R. Edgar, "Changing the old guard: A.P. Mda and the ANC Youth League, 1944-1949", 149-169.

459 Edgar, "A.P. Mda : The making of an African nationalist, 1935-1944", 16.

460 N.A. 9111/36/363, Native Commissioner Pretoria to Secretary Native Affairs, 27 February 1945 and G. Mears to S.A. Rogers, 7 March 1947.

461 University of Witwatersrand Historical Papers, ANC Papers A.D. 2186/F6, S.M. Molema, Mendi Day speech, 24 February 1952. I am indebted to Hilary Sapire for this reference.

This was, however, counterbalanced by officials from the newly minted Bantu Affairs Department who, sensitive to the shifts in government policy, shared the podium with black politicians and sought to provide a different perspective.

In 1952, F. Rodseth, a high-ranking official in the Bantu Affairs Department, was the main speaker. He made much of the fact that 1952 was also the tercentenary year celebrating Jan van Riebeeck's arrival at the Cape in 1652:

> And just as all sections of the community in South Africa are this year joining in the landing of Jan van Riebeeck and the start of civilization in this country, so are we who are Europeans glad to join you Bantu in honouring those of your race who so nobly gave their lives in a cause in which the Bantu stood together.

In this vein, the message of the *Mendi* became one of reconciliation and cooperation as opposed to confrontation. In the best traditions of paternalistic discourse, Rodseth carried on:

> Those of us who were born among you, grew up among you, have some knowledge of one or more of your languages and have worked with you throughout our lives, understand – I think – your aspirations, your difficulties and your disappointments. At first glance it may seem understandable that some of you should feel that the best solution is to break with the Europeans and go your own way. But what then? And what will you benefit? It is easy to break a thing, but not to mend it. It is easy to throw something away, but not always to retrieve it. It is very easy to start a fire but often impossible to put it out.[462]

Increasingly such overtures were at odds with the hardening of political battle lines during the 1950s. As the apartheid project slowly started to take shape, the government considered it inappropriate for blacks to be reminded that they had assisted whites in a European war. Afrikaner officials in the Bantu Affairs Department argued that the 'unfortunate' involvement of blacks should best be forgotten as it could only stimulate integrationist ideas and provide a platform for "agitators".[463] The general thinking in the Bantu Affairs Department was that the *Mendi* organisation "no longer warranted the recognition that it previously received".[464] In line with apartheid thinking of promoting separate ethnic cultures, officials of the Bantu Affairs Department also

---

462 K.J.B. 409/1/14/3, F. Rodseth, Mendi Day speech, 24 February 1952.

463 N.A. 9111/36/363, Memorandum on Mendi Day, 6 March 1959.

464 N.A. 9112/36/363, T. Koller to Native Commissioner, 10 December 1958.

took offence at the Western format in which the Mendi Day commemorations were cast. This was regarded as alien to African culture and "slaughtering of cattle and the drinking of K----- beer" were proposed as being a more authentic way to remember the dead.[465]

The National Party government stopped short of prohibiting Mendi Day meetings, but actively discouraged their continuation and the organisers had to contend with official harassment and numerous obstacles in their attempts to sustain the event.[466] Not surprisingly, fewer and fewer Mendi Day services were held in the ensuing years and with the passage of time the memory of the event among black people also started to wither away. While there was still a limited awareness as late as 1984, the full symbolic significance of the episode had all but faded away.[467] Indeed, in the deeply polarised South Africa of the 1980s, with unprecedented black resistance and successive states of emergencies, the memory of black troops assisting in a predominantly white war had an incredible and dissonant ring to it. This was not a history that could be usefully deployed in the stark black versus white struggle. In certain townships in South Africa, those who were suspected of collaboration with the government could easily be killed by incensed activists. This was a kind of antipathy that was transferred to those servicemen who had participated in any of the two world wars; they were at times referred to as "old-time sellouts".[468]

Ironically though, precisely at the same time that black activists rejected the history of black participation in two world wars, it was rediscovered by the National Party in the mid-1980s. In 1986, the South African government included a bronze plaque depicting the sinking of the *Mendi* at the Delville Wood memorial in France, which till then has been dedicated to white soldiers who perished on the killing fields of the Western Front during the First World War.[469] This belated change of heart in recognising the contribution of blacks in World War I, should be seen against the

---

465 D.B.A. 10/3/2/236, General Secretary Bantu Affairs Department to Commissioner,
     24 February 1965.

466 Compare, for instance, N.A. 9112/36/363, T.D. Young to Chief Bantu Affairs Commissioner,
     18 March 1959.

467 *City Press*, 19 February 1984 ("Tragedy of the *Mendi* lingers on"); *Sowetan*, 19 February 1984
     ("Death of the *Mendi*").

468 *The Star*, 27 February 1986 ("Bitterness of our forgotten war veterans").

469 *History Today*, 2 February 2007 ("The Sinking of the *SS Mendi*"). For the discourse on
     Delville Wood in this context, see Nasson, "Delville Wood and South African Great War
     commemorations", 85-86.

background of an embattled government, desperately casting around for legitimacy in the face of mounting overseas boycotts and sanctions in the 1980s; hence, appropriating the *Mendi* event, despite its earlier hostility, to shore up its attempts at political co-option in certain black quarters and, perhaps more importantly, demonstrating to the international world a supposedly shared black/white past, as well as South Africa's earlier joint contribution to world peace. Ideologically, such a symbolic act had more to do with the politics at the time than with restitution.

Memories in the service of a new state: Myth and the need for history

For a while after the seismographic shifts in the early 1990s that heralded a new political departure in South Africa, the men who perished on the *Mendi* were allowed to rest in peace. It was not too long, however, before they were once again pressed into symbolic service. As the newly established state started to assert its authority, there was a concomitant need for a history to dovetail with its ideological requirements. "There is a new front in the struggle", it was argued in 2004, "the acknowledgement of one's history. If we don't speak up and demand this, we could end up, like many of the opponents of Josef Stalin, simply airbrushed out of history."[470] Being omitted from history has its own dangers, of course, but being inserted into history is no easy matter either. What is of interest here is the way in which the memories of the *Mendi* would be resurrected in a significantly altered context after they had been all but obliterated in the late 1980s.

It appears that whatever reservations there were before 1990 about the political usefulness of invoking an event in which blacks assisted whites in a predominantly European war dissipated with the advent of a majority black government which opened up space for fresh meanings to be assigned. Commenting on the demise of the men of the *Mendi*, Lindiwe Mabuza, South African high commissioner in London, said in 2007: "Their souls are not sitting well in the English Channel, and ours are not very healthy as long as we do not do what is right. If we do not tell and retell their story, they would definitely have died in vain."[471]

One attempted restorative cure for these restless spirits was to reinterpret their history in grandiose terms. Thus, in 2002, Doctor Dlamini Zuma, the minister of foreign affairs,

---

470 *This Day*, 16 February 2004 ("Death drill on the *Mendi*").

471 *Mail & Guardian*, 21 July 2007 ("Ninety years on, South Africa salutes 600 men left to drown in Channel").

considered a strong dose of Africanism to be appropriate. With the first sitting of the transformed Organisation of African Unity into the African Union in South Africa in mind, she was of the opinion that the "efforts of Africans to address the problems facing their continent surely resonate with the aspirations of those brave warriors who perished on the *SS Mendi* for a better Africa".[472] Such lofty goals would certainly have surprised the men of the *Mendi*, as many of the ordinary recruits joined for pecuniary reasons or were dragooned into service; it is most unlikely that anyone entertained rarefied notions of redeeming the continent when they exchanged civilian clothing for uniforms during the First World War.[473] Apart from such hyperbole, the *Mendi* event nevertheless evoked greater interest than before in the United Kingdom, where the wreck of the ship became the object of considerable archaeological attention, whilst the Commonwealth War Graves Commission popularised the participation of the SANLC in the war with a DVD distributed to schools.[474]

An outstanding feature of the resurrection of the *Mendi* is the association of the event with a dominant theme of valour and courage. Thus, in 2003, South Africa's highest decoration award for extraordinarily heroic deeds was called the Order of Mendi for Bravery. In a naval context, it was also decided to name a Valour-class frigate the *SAS Mendi* and a Warrior-class fast attack craft the *SAS Isaac Wauchope Dyobha*, named after a cleric who it was believed died a courageous death in 1917 on board the original *Mendi*.[475] The *SAS Mendi* was manufactured in Germany, and on its route to South Africa it made a special stop at the exact spot where the *SS Mendi* sank to observe a minute's silence and to lower a wreath in honour of those who had died.[476] It is not normal practice for naval craft to be named after ships that had sunk, but in this case it appears that the presumed bravery of those on board the *SS Mendi* in 1917 warranted such a departure. The "story of the *SS Mendi* is a story of supreme courage in the face of death", Zola Skweyiya, the minister of social development, claimed in 2007. "The courage displayed by these men is now legendary in South African military history".[477]

---

472   ANC Daily News Briefing, 25 June 2002, http://70.84.171.10/etools/newsbrief/2002/news0625.txt [Accessed 21 April 2009].

473   See chapter 3.

474   See Wessex Archaeological Desk-Based Assessment, English Heritage, April 2007 and Commonwealth War Graves Commission, "Let us die like Brothers". (DVD)

475   http://www.info.gov.za/speeches/2007/07080810451001.htm [Accessed 19 May 2008].

476   http://www.navy.mil.za/newnavy/syrface/mendi040918-mendi-home-article.htm

477   http://www.info.gov.za/speeches/2007/07080810451001.htm [Accessed 19 May 2008].

The discourse regarding the *Mendi* that emerged from the ANC in the 2000s differed significantly from the one that had prevailed earlier. As indicated, initially the narrative revolved around the need for education and the establishment of a Mendi Memorial Fund for this purpose, while the more overtly political dimension was to contrast the position of black people under segregation and apartheid with African sacrifices made during global conflicts. The post-1994 discourse, where the need to appeal to white magnanimity had fallen away, was much more assertive and bold; whereas earlier references to the bravery of those who died were less frequent, it now emerged as virtually the only element to be foregrounded in the quest of the new state to construct a useable warrior past.

The bravery discourse centred primarily on one alleged incident which was supposed to have taken place as the *SS Mendi* started to tilt as it began its ultimate downward spiral. In an oft-repeated story, it was Isaac Wauchope Dyobha who was said to have lead about a 100 men in a disciplined and elaborate dance of death. In a stirring address, he was said to extol the virtues of African unity among the different ethnic groups in southern Africa.

> Be quiet and calm, my countrymen, for what is taking place now is exactly what you came to do. You are going to die, but that is what you came to do. Brothers, we are drilling the drill of death. I, a Xhosa, say you are all my brothers, Zulus, Swazis, Pondos, Basutos, we die like brothers. We are the sons of Africa. Raise your cries, brothers, for though they made us leave our weapons at our homes, our voices are left with our bodies.[478]

The veracity of this claim is problematic. Contrary to the heroic version, there is firm evidence that chaos erupted as the ship was rammed; it was dark, misty and cold and to men unaccustomed to the sea and untrained in emergency procedures it must have been a terrifying experience as the ship sank quickly in only about 20 minutes after it has been rammed.[479] Given the swiftness of events, the general turmoil in a pitch-black night with a ship rapidly tilting, it is rather fanciful to think of desperate men lining up to engage in elaborate grandstanding with nationalist overtures. Certainly seasoned seafarers, including one passenger on the *Mendi* who had disembarked at Plymouth

---

478 This quote is from Clothier, *Black Valour*, preface.

479 An African survivor later recalled that he heard "a terrific bang which shook the ship, putting lights out and had everybody scrambling about. There was great panic and confusion. Below there was a sea of darkness – the men plunged into the rough, cold water, singing, praying and crying." (*The Star*, 27 February 1967, "*Mendi* disaster survivor").

before the ship proceeded further, later expressed their utter disbelief at the tale.[480] To be sure, some men, the evidence suggests, were more disciplined than others, but this still did not measure up to the elaborate spectacle associated with Wauchope.[481] Moreover, it is of prime importance to note that there was not one eyewitness account of a survivor or any other contemporary account which can substantiate the dramatic story.[482] In the absence of persuasive evidence, it would be misleading to accept the tale at face value. Nevertheless, Norman Clothier, who has written at length about the sinking of the *Mendi* in a book called *Black Valour*, has – despite some reservations about whether the incident did indeed take place – decided to come down on what he regards as the side of tradition, "believing that there may be a solid core of truth in the story".[483] Exactly what one should regard as the core, however, is not clear. Other than speculative musings, Clothier does not produce hard evidence to buttress the claim.[484] It would rather appear that, taking into account the ringing title of his book, the story was just too appealing and alluring to discard.

It is precisely from such enticing material that the tempting strands of myths are woven. The story of the sinking of the *Mendi* surely contained a number of ingredients that lend themselves to dramatisation: the dark and foggy night, the freezing cold water, the idea of men on their way to war, the completely unexpected crash, the rapid sinking of the ship, the watery grave in a sea which for most rural people at home was beyond all known limits, the fact that no remains were returned and the symbolical

---

480 Clothier, *Black valour*, 96, 185.

481 S.M. Bennet Ncwana, *Souvenir of the Mendi disaster*, 20 (Evidence of Captain L.E. Hertslet).

482 Willan, "'The South African Native Labour. Contingent, 1916-1918", 85. Similarly, in my trawling through a vast amount of material no contemporary material surfaced which could lend any credibility to the claim.

483 Clothier, *Black valour*, 98.

484 Clothier tries to build an argument on the following: 1) He claims that oral tradition in Africa must have some foundation, even if it is embroidered upon. Although this may be a plausible supposition on a general level, it still needs to be buttressed regarding the specifics of the event in question. Otherwise it just remains a vague suggestion as he does not discuss the dynamics of oral tradition in any way, nor does he provide evidence of why the story regarding the *Mendi* took a particular turn. 2) He argues that visibility was poor and that the incident could have taken place without any of the survivors witnessing it. This is a *non sequitur* – if nobody could have seen it, how could it have been transmitted? 3) He speculates that the event could have taken place in a section of the ship where the door was jammed and men trapped inside, but that some could have escaped and survived to tell the tale. There is no convincing evidence for this and even he has to admit that this is perhaps "a little far-fetched" (Clothier, *Black valour*, 97-98).

implications of that loss. All of these elements combined to create the possibility of a hyperbolic and comforting tale. Whether such a rendition was an accurate version, was of no great concern. Revealingly, even Wauchope's close family did not believe the story to be literally true. His granddaughter recalled in 1993 that "they were never sure it really happened" and to them it was more like a "fairytale".[485]

By the 2000s, the myth has already become fully entrenched and assumed the status of incontrovertible fact. In 2007, Pallo Jordan, the minister of arts and culture, boldly opened his address on the occasion of the 90th anniversary of the incident by stating that the story of the *Mendi* "is one of immense human courage and bravery". He then recounted that the men on board the ship "bravely stood to attention, performed a dance and went down with their ship in an amazing display of dignity".[486] Minister of Defence, Mosiuoa Lekota, embroidered on the significance of the assumed bravery. For him Wauchope's supposed address confirmed "the deep affirmation of the unity to be found among nations" and was "a reminder of the considerable sacrifices wrought in the forging of those democratic freedoms which we enjoy today".[487] Intriguingly, none other than President Thabo Mbeki also displayed an interest the history of the SANLC. Mbeki, known for his preoccupation with the internet, wrote a blog in 2007 where he applauded the men who had joined "with their hearts free of cowardice".[488] This president, as his biographer has revealed, strongly believed in the notion of heroes; the "revolution" needed heroes and to shrink from hero worship was a bourgeois affliction.[489] In line with this, he viewed the SANLC venture in terms of bravery and argued that it "surely must be part of the heritage on which we raise our new nation that is striving to be born".[490]

Underpinning this ready belief in, and unquestioning acceptance of, the mythological dimensions of the sinking of the *Mendi*, was the need for a legitimising military history. Such a requirement was especially acute as the ANC itself could not point to a particularly heroic military past. Although the armed wing of the organisation, uMkhonto weSizwe, had a degree of success with what they called "armed propa-

---

485   *The Weekly Mail*, 19-25 February 1993 ("Reclaiming the lost warriors of *SS Mendi*").

486   http://www.info.gov.za/speeches/2007/11080810451001.htm [Accessed 19 May 2008].

487   http://www.info.gov.za/speeches/2007/07080810451001.htm [Accessed 19 May 2008].

488   http://www.kaganof.com/kagablog/2007/10/03/sek-mqhayi-a-call-to-arms? [Accessed 31 March 2010].

489   Gevisser, *The dream deferred: Thabo Mbeki*, 283.

490   http://www.kaganof.com/kagablog/2007/10/03/sek-mqhayi-a-call-to-arms/ [Accessed 31 March 2010].

ganda", it could not even remotely lay claim to clashing with and defeating the South African Defence Force in any battle.[491] Its lack of military achievement, however, did not deter it from embracing military vocabulary in post-apartheid South Africa with the use of words such as 'cadres' and 'deployment' becoming commonplace in civilian life. The atavistic invocation of such terminology in peacetime can be seen as a compensating mechanism in the absence of a solid military record to underscore the transition.[492] Similarly, the *Mendi* had to nurture the longing for a heroic past and accordingly it was asserted that "as black South Africa has rediscovered its history, – the fame of the victims of the *SS Mendi* disaster has grown".[493]

Having discounted the veracity of the band of brothers incident on the sinking *Mendi* and relegating it to the realm of myth, however, does not imply that it can be regarded as of lesser significance. One of the central tenets of the rapidly expanding literature on historical mythology is that it represents a field of investigation in its own right and that it is not sufficient merely to demonstrate that an event is likely to be untrue and constitutes a myth. Myths can generate their own power, irrespective of their fictional nature. As Ralph Samuel and Paul Thompson have reminded us, myths "open up a history which refuses to be safely boxed away in card indexes or computer programs: which instead pivots on the *active* relationship between past and present, subjective and objective, poetic and political".[494] Embedded in the case of the *Mendi* was the need to construct a functional myth, using wartime participation and disaster to lay claims to bravery and, as suggested, to invest the event with the weight of historicity which could serve a useful purpose in the present.

Explaining the myth

This dimension alerts us to a more complex issue; if it is accepted that the famed incident on the *Mendi* did not take place, how did such a version emerge and how did it gain a life of its own? A different line of enquiry, away from the deck of the *Mendi* to the realm of oral lore in South Africa, is required here. Because of the lack of

---

491 Suttner, *The ANC underground in South Africa*, 164.

492 This notion is neatly encapsulated in Mda, *Black diamond*, 66. I am indebted to Bill Nasson for this reference.

493 *The Star*, 26 July 2007 ("*SS Mendi*: ship of brave warriors"). See also *Cape Times*, 25 July 2007 ("The brave men of the *Mendi* bring their message of courage across the decades").

494 Samuel and Thompson, "Introduction", 5. (Emphasis in the original.)

sources, it is not possible to provide a definitive explanation, but certain illuminating pointers can be established.

It is particularly instructive to turn to oral poetry in Xhosa society and especially the figure of S.E.K. Mqhayi (1875-1945), a traditional praise singer (*imbongi*). Mqhayi had a noteworthy reputation; he was regarded "as a repository of his people's history, culture, tradition and customs. His experience as an historian and a traditional bard, living close to many chiefs, made that possible."[495] The preservation of what he considered Xhosa history was of special concern to Mqhayi.[496] As an *imbongi* he had few peers. His oral poetry, according to a recent academic study, "was marked by the richness and depth of diction, and by his remarkable ability to inspire his audience". For those who heard him, "he produced poetry as we've never heard before, so that the blood coursed through men".[497] Mqhayi, moreover, was well known to the Wauchope Dyobha family, as he at times attended to the latter's infirm mother. He also had a high regard for Wauchope, though there were occasional tensions between the two relating to the merit of Mqhayi's published work.[498] Besides Mqhayi's undoubted influence as a respected Xhosa cultural figure with considerable credibility, it is pertinent to note that he took a special interest in the *Mendi* and the fate of Wauchope, whom he generally held in high esteem. Before the departure of detachments of the SANLC to France, Mqhayi actually wrote a rousing poem in 1916, using a combination of warrior images and examples of Xhosa domestic life to exhort the men to bravery.[499] What is of particular significance for this analysis is that the piece shows that Mqhayi was clearly predisposed to refract the venture through a heroic prism.

It would then appear that in his role as *imbongi*, formally or informally, he carried on from his original evocative war poem to provide a stirring sequel from whatever scraps of information or permutations of the story of the sinking that might have been available to construct a version of what he thought might have happened that fateful night, shaped by his predilection towards a heroic idiom and cast in a preconceived mould. What most likely circulated orally for a number of years eventually surfaced in written form in 1935, when Mqhayi published a glowing tribute to Wauchope in

---

495 Qangule, "Samuel Edward Krune Mqhayi", 64.

496 Peires, "Preface" in J Opland (ed.), *Abantu Besizwe: Historical and biographical writings, 1902-1944: SEK Mqhayi*, x.

497 Opland, "Introduction" (*Abantu Besizwe*), 8.

498 Opland, "Introduction" (*Isaac Williams Wauchope*), xxx.

499 http://www.kaganof.com/kagablog/2007/10/03/sek-mqhayi-a-call-to-arms/ [Accessed 31 March 2010]. This poem also appears in Cope and Krige, *The Penguin book of South African verse*, 276-278.

The Bantu World in a serialised form.[500] Although it was not the first published piece to air a version of the event, it was the most extensive, with Mqhayi in full oratorical flight. Here Wauchope appears as the "hero of Ngqika's land, descended from heroes". It was claimed that Wauchope could have saved himself, but he preferred to appeal to the "leaderless soldiers urging them to stay calm, to die like heroes on their way to war". He then, according to Mqhayi, proceeded with the legendary address.[501]

It is impossible to determine today the exact nature of the material Mqhayi used to construct his version. An academic writing on Xhosa oral poetry has remarked that even under the best of circumstances "we cannot expect explanation always to be recoverable".[502] This underscores the inherent tension and contradictions in dealing with material of this kind. In a recent extended analysis of oral tradition, David Henige has pointed to this dilemma: "For historians, oral traditions are precious – as sources; for their narrators they are no less precious – as expedients. These are twains that can seldom co-exist comfortably."[503]

Nevertheless, it was Mqhayi's version as an *imbongi* which prevailed. As such it slotted in with the general pattern of Xhosa oral poetry and praise singing, known for its degree of improvisation and its shifting nature. Mqhayi, especially, as noted, was renowned for his elaborate praise songs.[504] His tribute to the fallen reflected all the hallmarks of an excellent *imbongi*: hyperbole and a vivid imagination at work which embellished past events, casting them in a mode that spoke forcefully to the listeners. It also served a wider purpose as one analyst has observed: "The poetry becomes the dream; dreaming the ancestors".[505]

Moreover, despite the fact that the Xhosa speakers were in the minority on the *Mendi*,[506] it was the 'Xhosa-ness' of the tale that ensured its longevity. Mainly because of the early missionary influence in the area, the Eastern Cape at the time had a higher literacy rate amongst black people than elsewhere in the country. Once the oral version of the story might have faded, it was given a new lease of life in printed form, becoming a trope of war which came to serve a more explicit political

---

500 A reprint of these articles appears in Opland and Nyamende, *Isaac Williams Wauchope*, 405-411.

501 Opland and Nyamende, *Isaac Williams Wauchope*, 408.

502 Opland, "Introduction" (*Abantu Besizwe*), 11.

503 Henige, "Impossible to disprove yet impossible to believe", 133.

504 Compare J. Opland, "Praise poems as historical sources", 6-7, 26.

505 Genis, *South African Great War poetry*, 277.

506 Clothier, *Black valour*, 99.

purpose than a simple loss of human life. It was this account that was woven into the fabric of black political consciousness, appropriated by black nationalists to re-emerge in the 2000s as historical fact. Ultimately, the contents of the interpretation bear a closer relation to the remarkable ability of Mqhayi to present posterity with a view on the past that has gained considerable traction than they do to inform us about what actually happened on the *Mendi* on the fateful morning of 21 February 1917. In the long run, the fabrication was probably more significant than a prosaic version devoid of heroics could ever hope for.

Conclusion

In the wider context of World War I memorialisation, the *Mendi* commemorations can be seen on one level as part of that tradition of the 'fallen heroes' that was such a hallmark of the general remembrance history of the war. More than twice as many men perished in the First World War than in all the preceding major wars between 1790 and 1914.[507] Given the scale of human carnage the authorities of the Allied countries, sensing the public need for some form of justification and acknowledgement, resorted to symbolic solutions in terms of a variety of commemorative practices in the hope that this would at least act as a kind of soothing psychological balm and a morale booster.[508] It gave rise to what has been called "the myth of the war experience", characterised by a memorialistic view of the war, replete with omissions and distortions and perpetuated as the dominant interpretation of the war in the public sphere.[509]

While such cultural dominion held sway over death and mourning in the allied countries – and elements of this can also be detected in the *Mendi* commemorations – it has to be borne in mind that South African remembrance practices took place far removed from the epicentre of memorialisation in the West and were shielded from the full glare of historical interpretation that prevailed there. Comparatively they therefore attracted less public attention and their potential impact was also blunted by more pressing local issues which helped to shape the contours of South African history to a much greater extent than black participation in a far-off European war.

---

507 Mosse, *Fallen soldiers*, 3. There is a considerable literature on memorialisation. See for example: Winter and Prost, *The Great War in history: Debates and controversies, 1914 to the present*; Meyer, *British popular culture and the First World War*; Winter, *Sites of memory, sites of mourning: The Great War in European cultural history*; Gregory, *The silence of memory: Armistice Day, 1919-1946*; Winter and Sivan, *War and remembrance in the twentieth century*.

508 Ben-Zeev, "Public encounters: The negotiation of ritual", 45.

509 Mosse, *Fallen soldiers*, 7-8.

Unlike what happened in European countries and the United Kingdom, the First World War was not elevated to a pivotal position in South African history.

In spite of the reduced scale of commemorations in South Africa, the trajectory and mutating memories of the *Mendi* were not unusual. Bill Nasson, writing on the First World War, has made the salutary point that

> whatever their own terms, memorials and commemoration could not carry fixed or immutable meanings indefinitely over time. The experience of South African society has been no different to that of other national commemorations in which memorialisation of past war has always been subject to revision, by being contested, by being recomposed, by decomposing, or by being reanimated.[510]

In this respect, it is instructive to take note of Delville Wood in France, that other – and more prominent – memorial site of South African participation in the First World War. Out of a total force of 3 150 South African men, 750 were killed and 1 500 were wounded at Delville Wood during a particularly fierce battle on the Western Front in 1916. The memorialisation of this event, like that of the *Mendi*, also went through various permutations, closely related to the susceptibilities and ideological imperatives of new political orders.[511] Delville Wood, though grounded in far more solid historical fact than was the case with the mythical material which launched the *Mendi* version into the realm of extraordinary accounts of war bravery, nevertheless acquired its own afterlife and mythological shape, though not quite in the exaggerated form which marked the *Mendi*.

Be that as it may, with the centenary commemoration of the First World War in 2014 the porous nature of historical memory and its adaptation and propensity to be shaped according to circumstances in the present once again became apparent. This time it took the form of Vice-president Cyril Ramaphosa and Minister of Arts and Culture Nathi Mthethwa planning to visit the Delville site with a view to witness the reburial of SANLC member Myenga Beleza. Beleza was buried at Le Havre in a civilian cemetery and his reinterment at Delville Wood was deemed necessary to bridge a divided past. His reburial was seen as part of "honouring all South Africans who were involved in the battle" and "that it will go a long way towards the restoration of the

---

510 Nasson, *Springboks on the Somme*, 237.
511 Nasson, "Delville Wood and South African Great War commemoration", 82-83.

dignity of black South Africans who participated in the war".[512] Ramaphosa explained that "South Africa looks at its history for the second time" and that Beleza was now buried next to "his white brothers".[513] Symbolically this interpretation signalled not only an attempt to reverse the segregatory conditions which the labour corps had experienced in France, but can also be seen as an elevation of black participation to combatant status. This reveals more about the sensibilities and subjectivities of the current South African government than about a credible commemoration of the past. Historians can do no more than point out these features, perhaps suggesting that the factual evidence can at best temper the dynamics of memorialisation, but ultimately it is bound to find its own niche and purpose in an ever-shifting present.

---

512 http:www.news24.com/SouthAfrica/News/Ramaphosa-Mtethwa-to-attend-WWI [Accessed 4 July 2014]. See also *Cape Times*, 11 July 2014 ("Re-internment reinvents reality").

513 *Le Monde*, 8 July 2014 ("L'afrique du Sud enterre la ségrégation au bois Delville"). (Translated.)

The ill-fated *Mendi*.
[*Source: http://www.wessexarch.co.uk/node/728*]

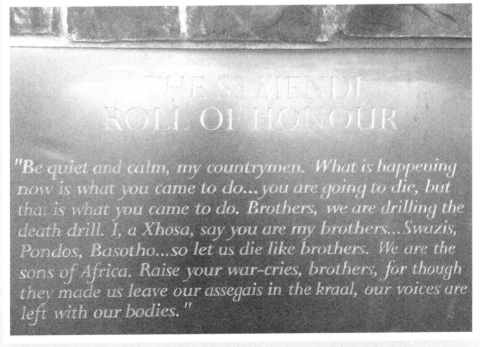

The Mendi Memorial in Rondebosch, replete with the alleged death dance speech.
The memorial is close to where members of the contingent assembled before departure.
[*Source: Author's own photograph*]

THE CAPE CORPS

Coloured participation in the war
and the
making of malleable memories

Although some of the elements of black participation in the war overlapped with those of coloureds, there were also differences, especially in terms of the nature of involvement and the dynamics of remembrance. Participation in the First World War left a legacy that took several twists and turns in the 20th century and at times attracted a surprisingly diverse group of interested parties.

Responses to the outbreak of war

News of the outbreak of war in Europe prompted a surge of pro-empire sentiments and effusive declarations of loyalty to Britain amongst many coloured people. Orchestrating and encouraging these avowals was the African Political Organisation (APO) of Doctor Abdullah Abdurahman. The APO was the main political vehicle for coloured people, and its newspaper, also by the name APO, played an influential role in disseminating political ideas. The First World War initially dominated the entire content of the newspaper.[514]

Mass meetings were further occasions to provide voluble support. One such meeting in the landmark Cape Town City Hall was described as "of an enthusiastic character with the audience, which embraced practically all sections of the coloured community, almost filling the floor of the spacious hall".[515] A motion of loyalty to the British crown was accepted with wild applause. Support for the British war effort went beyond the Cape Town epicentre, and 30 towns in the Cape countryside as well as meetings

---

514 Nasson, "War opinion in South Africa, 1914", 256.

515 *Cape Times*, 1 September 1914 ("Coloured men and the war").

in Johannesburg and Pretoria weighed in with similar declarations of loyalty.[516] To add substance to these patriotic sentiments, a special fund was established to make a contribution to war-related initiatives.[517]

The vociferous support, like that of the black elite discussed earlier, had its own internal logic. Underpinning this was the assumption that should Britain be defeated by Germany in the war, the position of coloured people might well worsen. This meant that their existing grievances had to be shelved for the greater good and to help ensure an outcome which will be in favour of Britain. Although British liberty might often be found wanting in practice, the argument at the outbreak of war was that "at present our first duty it is to see the war through".[518]

Closely related to this line of thinking, was the optimistic expectation that once the war was won, "true British liberty and justice will prevail: not the liberty and justice we have smarted under". All men of the empire, regardless of colour, had to have equal opportunities and anything short of that would have been a "sham, a mockery, a betrayal, a lie".[519] A slight variation on this theme, was the explicit hope that the war would drive home the notion that not one race has a monopoly of virtues as whites were fond of believing, while assigning undesirable traits to groups other than white. "The English", it was said, "find that the Germans are particularly base, while the Germans find the English entirely vile". On the basis of this, it was concluded that there are "fashions in thought and the war will make entirely old-fashioned the thought that a man with a white skin must necessarily be superior to a man with a brown skin".[520] Such aspirations, though wishful, nevertheless reflected the way in which the war was perceived as a possible catalyst for that change.

Apart from the politics of hope, the APO benefited inadvertently from the outbreak of war inasmuch as the organisation could ward off more radical changes from its own constituency, which claimed that their existing conservative approach, of petitioning authorities or arranging deputations for example, bore no fruit. It was with some relief that APO leaders could now claim that wartime circumstances offered them yet another opportunity and one with a greater potential than before, as they could

---

516 *APO*, 5 September 1914 ("Extracts from letters received").

517 *APO*, 19 September 1914 ("The coloured citizens' war relief fund").

518 *APO*, 7 August 1915 ("Liberty and Justice"). See also *APO*, 5 September 1914 ("Coloured people take the lead").

519 *APO*, 7 August 1915.

520 *APO*, 13 November 1915 ("White and black after the war").

now demonstrate their worth during a crisis. The chances of this yielding political dividends were considered better than embarking on rash actions which could only be construed as disloyalty to the British crown and diminish chances of any political gain.[521] Also, the APO newspaper, which had been sliding into a state of dormancy and bland reporting, was given a new lease of life by the war with the ready availability of dramatic news that could be obtained relatively easily.[522]

The issue of participation

Given the eager support for the British war effort, it is not surprising to find that many coloured men volunteered to be part of a combatant corps. "Everyone seems determined to do his duty', Abdurahman enthused.[523] A few even went on their own cost to Britain to join British regiments.[524] On the basis of this, the APO suggested to the government that the organisation would undertake to raise a corps to fight in the war.

However, in what must have been a hammer blow to the aspirations of many, Premier Louis Botha declined the offer of an armed corps. The rejection of the offer, like that of Rubusana of the SANNC which has been noted earlier, was based on article 7 of the South African Defence Force Act 13 of 1912, which stipulated that the obligation to render armed service was not applicable to people who were not from "European descent". These people could, however, be used for non-combatant manual work. The article precluding the use of black and coloured people in a fighting capacity could nevertheless be amended under war circumstances.[525] At the outbreak of the war, Botha was loath to do this. Politically, with the government already under stress as a result of the Boer rebellion, he thought it wise to avoid any possible further controversies. It was a position which the APO firmly rejected. Botha was accused of "declining the offer out of a weak deference to an irrational prejudice – the dislike of his burghers to see any Coloured men, however civilized, participate in a war between whites".[526]

---

521 Lewis, *Between the wire and the wall: A history of South African 'coloured' politics*, 85. See also Nasson, "War opinion", 258.

522 Adhikari, *Not white enough, not black enough: Racial identity in the South African coloured community*, 77.

523 *APO*, 5 September 1914 ("The APO Volunteer corps").

524 *Pretoria News*, 14 May 1917 ("Coloured men on the European front").

525 Acts of the Union of South Africa, Act 13 of 1912, 193.

526 *APO*, 24 July 1915 ("General Botha's return").

The policy of not arming coloured people so resolutely proclaimed in August 1914 was, however, completely reversed in the latter months of 1915, with the government deciding that an armed coloured corps should be recruited for campaigning in East Africa against the Germans. How is this turnaround to be explained? Of course the Boer rebellion was by then suppressed and no longer a factor in political calculations as it was when the earlier decision was taken to reject Abdurahman's offer. This though was not a particular concern; there were other justifications and considerations.

General Jan Smuts, as commanding officer of the South African forces in East Africa, sought in parliament to invoke the historical record by claiming that the decision to utilise coloured troops was not really a drastic departure of past practices, as colonial coloured troops were involved in 19th-century warfare. It was therefore not a "novel procedure" he argued.

> In almost all the campaigns waged against the natives it has been the policy of the Imperial Government and the Colonial Government to enlist coloured people to take part in the campaigns waged during the last 100 years against the natives in the Cape.[527]

Technically, Smuts was correct: coloured soldiers, known as pandours, were used in a fruitless attempt to defend the Dutch colony against the British in 1795. Subsequently, throughout the 19th century, they were grouped together in an assortment of military units such as the Cape Regiment, the Cape Corps and the Cape Mounted Rifles, to be used in the various frontier wars against the Xhosa.[528]

While Smuts' history could not be faulted, politically it was nothing more than a clever ploy to disguise more pressing reasons for seeking to enrol coloureds for armed service in East Africa. In private letters, he revealed that Germans fought with black troops called askaris, which then also justified the South African use of coloured troops. An issue of even greater importance for Smuts was climatic conditions in East Africa and that malaria had a decimating effect on white troops. East Africa, he argued, "was not a country into which to bring a force of white men, and coloureds would be admirably suited for campaigning under the conditions of hot climate and bush

---

527 *Cape Times*, 7 December 1915 ("Parliamentary debates"). See also Samson, *World War I in Africa: The forgotten conflict among European powers*, 91.

528 See, amongst others, De Villiers, "Die Kaapse Regiment, 1806-1817", 10-32. A short factual review covering the whole of the 19th century can be found in Difford, *The story of the 1st Battalion Cape Corps, 1915-1919*, 1-6.

country which obtain in East Africa".[529] Why he came to the conclusion that coloured troops would be more immune to conditions remains unexplained. The strange logic can perhaps only be understood if it is seen in the common assumption of biological determinism of the early 20th century held by many amongst the white elite. This notion proceeded from the false assumption that certain races were inherently more immune than others to certain diseases.[530]

It was then under the sway of such perverse reasoning that coloured people were allowed to participate in an armed capacity in the war. The decision was not primarily taken as a gesture of understanding or as a form of acknowledgement of the desire of coloured people to assist in the war, but rather as a result of wrongheaded, if not cynical, considerations. This, however, was not known at the time; had it been, support for the war effort on the part of coloured people might have vanished. As it turned out, despite the earlier slight of not being allowed to participate initially, the APO welcomed this change of direction. It was regarded as an important breakthrough that "the Cape Coloured men are recognised as willing to shed their blood for freedom as any other members of the British Empire".[531]

Recruitment

Although there was considerable excitement at the prospect of a fighting coloured corps, the word still had to be spread and formal recruiting had to proceed. In Cape Town and further afield, recruitment drives were launched with much military fanfare: bands, street parades, patriotic speeches at specially arranged meetings and at bioscopes where people gathered, press notices and stirring posters.[532]

In towns where there was often little else on offer in terms of entertainment, recruiting marches were popular attractions. These took the form of a march accompanied by a military band to prominent places in towns, the observation of a midday pause and the sounding of the 'last post'. These performances were attended by many and it was reported that "on all occasions opportunities were seized to gain recruits and to put

---

529 Hancock and Van der Poel, *Smuts Papers III* Cambridge, 1966, Smuts to Merriman, 27 October 1916. See also G.G. 545/9/93/56, Smuts to Buxton, 28 August 1915.

530 Dubow, "Race, civilisation and culture", 7.

531 *Cape Times*, 13 September 1915 ("Battalion of coloured men").

532 Difford, *1st Battalion Cape Corps*, 24.

forward the cause of the Allies for civilization and humanity".[533] These drives had the desired effect. A.J.B. Desmore, a member of the corps, later recalled: "If nothing else stirred the heart to patriotism, and roused the indifferent to action, these patriotic demonstrations were most successful".[534]

Recruiting propaganda was replete with patriotic notions, primarily invoking loyalty to the British Empire and secondly to the Union of South Africa. The call to arms was construed as being a major privilege and a form of recognition: "Today the Empire needs us. What nobler duty is there than to respond to the call of your King and Country."[535]

The recruitment campaign which generally proceeded smoothly did however receive somewhat of a setback with regard to the conditions under which recruits were allowed to enrol. Only those with no dependants were allowed to join, whereas in the case of white soldiers married men were inducted and a separation allowance was paid. This was, not surprisingly, considered unfair. As there were few coloured men of military age without dependants, it was argued that if this regulation had to be adhered to the whole venture should rather be scrapped. What a "sad spectacle" it was reported "to see fine strapping fellows turned away for the sake of a few shillings extra".[536] At the risk of imperilling the enterprise, the stipulation was waived after representations and coloured soldiers were placed on the same financial footing as their white counterparts.[537]

Recruits had to undergo strict medical and physical tests to ensure that they had the potential to become efficient soldiers on active service. Only one in four recruits was selected. Those that did not meet the requirements, which included dental examinations, had to return home. The chosen ones that remained were described in glowing terms by a white officer, but not without a hint of patronising prejudice; "these were fine specimens of brawny manhood. So splendidly developed were many of them that it might have been a parade of prize fighters and ugly in physiognomy as

---

533 South African Defence Force Archives, WWI I.S.D. 25/651, H. Hands to Director of War Recruitment, 13 August 1917.

534 Desmore, *With the 2nd Cape Corps thro' Central Africa*, 6.

535 *APO*, 18 September 1915 ("Duty and Honour").

536 *APO*, 30 October 1915 ("The Cape Corps").

537 Difford, *1st Battalion Cape Corps*, 23, 26.

many of them undoubtedly were, their smiles revealed dentures that many a woman would have sacrificed a good deal to call her own".[538]

As far as the composition of the corps was concerned A.J.B. Desmore provided a tantalising glimpse:

> The bulk form the labouring class of South Africa ... mainly as farm labourers and, in a lesser degree, in skilled trades in the towns. Forming part of the labouring class they have a very robust physique, they have perseverance and a power of endurance ... marked cheerfulness under extreme circumstances makes them natural soldiers.[539]

Many of these men would have been from the Cape countryside, and some from Johannesburg and Pretoria. While the recruitment drive emanated from Cape Town, the city does not seem to have provided the majority of recruits. Nevertheless, wherever they hailed from, the available evidence suggests that amidst the general war fervour patriotic considerations laced with a certain sense of touristic curiosity were the main motives for propelling men into the corps.[540] There were exceptions though. Some later claimed that they had joined because of material inducements such as promises of free land after the war or that they would automatically gained voting rights and be placed on par with whites.[541]

Intermittent recruiting during the war for the replenishment of the corps meant that in total 8 000 men were recruited to the Cape Corps. There were, however, also non-fighting coloured units who were enrolled to do manual labour in France, namely the Cape Coloured Labour Regiment (CCLR) and the Cape Auxiliary Horse Transport Company (CAHTC). In total, 4 482 men found their way into these outfits.[542] Although these units were sent to the European front, their non-combatant status counted against them and given the prevailing war fervour of the time they were regarded as less glamorous and of lower status than the armed Cape Corps.[543]

---

538 Difford, *1st Battalion Cape Corps*, 24.

539 Desmore, *With the 2nd Cape Corps thro' Central Africa*, 7.

540 Compare *Cape Times*, 26 October 1915 ("Coloured recruiting"); Difford, *1st Battalion Cape Corps*, 22. This observation is also based on an interview I had with Mr. A. Kammies, a former member of the Cape Corps at Graaff-Reinet on 13 October 1980.

541 National Library Cape Town, J.X. Merriman Papers 620, J.W. Watson to Merriman, undated.

542 G.N.L.B. 187/1217/14/D 10, Undated (probably 1918) memorandum by Colonel S.M. Pritchard.

543 WWI 1914-1918, 1st Cape Corps, F.R. Cooper to Officer Commanding, 10 August 1917.

War service

After an initial period of training, the first batch of recruits of the Cape Corps was despatched to East Africa. On 9 February 1916, they boarded the *Armadale Castle* for Mombasa. An officer poignantly sketched the scene of the departure: "Many a mother strained with tears of pride in her eyes to get a glimpse of her son; many a young coloured woman who had a very particular interest in her newly made soldier friend, moved in the crowd in the hope of a last farewell". Overall he was very taken with what he witnessed:

> With the band playing martial airs – and the sun shining upon a sea of helmets and dark skinned faces and flashing upon the trappings of the uniform, it was difficult to believe that these were the same men, who only a few months before had come to enlist at the City Hall, many ill-clad and anything but smart.[544]

In East Africa, the corps was first used at base camps and then assigned to the supply lines, but in time they were transferred to the battlefront. Hostilities in East Africa developed into an irregular war which necessitated long marches over difficult terrain in an attempt to corner the evasive German forces. The corps was involved in several armed clashes and 32 men were killed in the field and 94 wounded.[545]

A more significant threat to life, however, was the conditions under which they had to fight. Of all the South African units in East Africa the Cape Corps was stationed for the longest period during the rainy season in the particularly unhealthy swampy marshland close to the Rufiji river. Blackwater fever, dysentery and malaria were rife. In total, 126 men succumbed to disease. The corps had one of the highest malaria death rates of 8,66 per 1 000. Its extended stay of 22 months in East Africa added to the loss of life.[546]

During the campaign, Smuts was exceptionally hesitant to risk the lives of white troops in direct confrontation with the Germans and this also led to some criticism of the way in which he conducted the war.[547] Moreover, the deployment of the Cape

---

544 Difford, *1st Battalion Cape Corps*, 25.

545 For details, see Difford, *1st Battalion Cape Corps*, 45-166; Desmore, *With the 2nd Cape Corps thro' Central Africa*, 30-96; Lucas, *The Empire at war*, 497-499.

546 WW I 1914-1918, Cape Coloured Corps, vol. 5, Officer Commanding Cape Corps – Adjutant General Pretoria, 14 March 1918: G.G. 480/9/57/19, Report on the Union natives on military service in East Africa, 27 June 1917.

547 Meinertzhagen, *Army diary, 1899-192*, 200; Miller, *Battle for the Bundu*, 233-234; Gardner, *German East: The story of the First World War in East Africa*, 144-145; Hancock, *Smuts I:*

Corps in the worst disease-ridden areas of East Africa has to be seen in conjunction with Smuts' earlier peculiar view, as noted, that coloured troops were presumed to be more resistant to malaria than whites. This false assumption, deliberate or otherwise, helps to explain the extraordinary losses of the Cape Corps in East Africa.

News of events in East Africa surfaced in the Union and elicited a sharp response. In Johannesburg, the local branch of the APO wrote to Governor General Buxton, making what they considered an obvious point: "that where men irrespective of caste, colour or creed, are fighting for their King and Country on the common field ... the Government should know one and only one policy alone". They continued: "[T]he policy ... of assigning to ... coloured troops areas regarded as dangerous to local white troops, is contrary to all the spirit of sacrifice and determination with which many sections of Her Majesty's subjects have responded to the call of their King and Country".[548] As far as could be ascertained Buxton did not respond, and it took a while for coloured troops to be removed from the unhealthy areas.

Upon their return to the Union, they were granted a period of rest in Kimberley. During this period, all members had to undergo blood tests for malaria and some were hospitalised. A sufficient number of fit men, augmented by new recruits, could though be mobilised for one battalion to fight against the Turks, Germany's allies in Palestine. In April 1918, they embarked from Durban, had specialised training in Egypt and then departed for the front in Palestine.

They were to form part of General E. Allenby's army and were involved in what turned out to be final mopping-up operations against the Turks. The high point of their expedition was to drive the Turks from what was known as Square Hill on 19 September 1918, with the loss of only one wounded and one member killed against the capture of 181 Turks. The following day though, in an attempt to inflict further harm on the Turks, they met with unexpected stiff opposition and of the 400 men who participated in the attack the corps lost 44, with 95 wounded. Despite this setback, General Allenby had the highest regard for the corps. They "fought with the utmost bravery and rendered splendid service'", he reported.[549] The pluck of the men in Palestine was destined to become part of Cape Corps tradition, with Square Hill, in particular, as a

---

The sanguine years, 1870-1919, 412-414.

548 G.G. 597/9/263/1, APO Johannesburg to Buxton, 6 December 1916.

549 Copy in Difford, *1st Battalion Cape Corps*, 443. For Cape Corps engagements in Palestine, see Difford, *1st Battalion Cape Corps*, 167-249; Lucas, *The Empire at war*, 499-500; Ploeger and Jacobs, "Kleurlinge in militêre verband", 42; Nasson, *Springboks on the Somme*, 158-159.

decisive battle to be remembered for generations to come. More prosaically though, an ordinary member A. Kammies recalled: "We fought hard, but one did not really have a choice; once you were in a battle you had to fight, else the enemy can kill one so much easier".[550]

Demobilisation

Many units of the Cape Corps were demobilised from Kimberley in the Northern Cape. A suitable military base for the corps was a longstanding quandary for the Defence Force authorities. Initially, it was thought that Cape Town would be a logical choice, but disciplinary problems brought on by the easy manner in which liquor could be obtained, as well as the ready availability of prostitutes which led to absenteeism, forced a rethink.[551] Several up-country towns were considered, but there was a concern to avoid predominantly Afrikaans-speaking places were "colour prejudice is very strong".[552] Eventually, Kimberley was decided upon as the city had a good proportion of English-speaking loyalists who, so it was argued, would be more tolerant. In addition, De Beers was prepared to provide a suitable camp site.[553]

In the event, Kimberley also proved to be problematical. Over the Christmas season of 1917, some recent returnees from East Africa were given leave to visit the town. They were less than welcome. Christmas cheer seems to have passed some local whites by and they objected to the presence of coloured soldiers in town. On Christmas Eve, the situation quickly got out of hand and unseemly street fights ensued as the two parties weighed into each other with gusto. The following day, close to 300 white men armed with knobkieries, iron pipes, chains and a few rifles patrolled a tense Kimberley. After troops had stones thrown at them, a fracas developed in which 30 people were injured. When word reached the camps that the corps was once again under attack, it was only with great difficult that the remaining men in the camp could be restrained from breaking out to assist their comrades. A troubled local police commissioner reported from his perspective that "the situation is critical and so long as the coloured troops are left in Kimberley, there will be friction ..."[554]

---

550 Interview with Mr. A. Kammies, Graaff-Reinet, 13 October 1980.

551 G.G. 548/9/93/155, Brigadier General A. Cavendish to Buxton, 29 August 1917.

552 WW I 1914/1918, Cape Corps, 1, Magistrate Potchefstroom to Secretary of Defence, 8 November 1917.

553 A.G. 42/18330, H. Bourne to Adjutant General, 27 August 1917; O.C. Records 15/2/39/5, Officer Commanding Records to Adjutant Cape Corps, 1 December 1917.

554 S.A.P. 1/250/17, Commissioner of Police Kimberley to Secretary of Police Pretoria,

Despite being a transparently one-sided view, it prevailed for a while. Over what was supposed to be the festive season, the military authorities removed the corps from the vicinity of the town and they decamped into the veld till white antipathies in town were considered to be less volatile.[555] The unedifying situation was ironic indeed and clearly a case of blaming the victims instead of the perpetrators. This happened despite the fact that the military authorities realised that the troops were not the prime instigators. "Gross insults were being hurled at both officers and men of the Cape Corps", their commanding officer testified and he described those who were guilty of such behaviour as "larrikins and hooligans". On their part, the troops "as a general rule, have shown great forbearance and have behaved in an exemplary manner, and it was only when they found that their comrades were being seriously injured that they retaliated".[556]

Even the conclusion of hostilities in Europe in November 1918 did not mean the end of local antagonisms in Kimberley. To his dismay, Brigadier General J.J. Collyer, acting secretary of defence, was informed that with the ceremonial festivities associated with the declaration of peace

> the unjustifiable and disgraceful behaviour of the white larrikins of Kimberley towards the Cape Corps soldiers continues. As the Cape Corps was marching down the street, one of these monstrosities stepped from the curb and hit a Cape Corps soldier on the jaw and disappeared.

This kind of behaviour persisted during the proceedings, and the anomaly of the situation was not lost on Collyer:

> While the Mayor was complimenting the corps on their behaviour in the field which had helped to bring about the very occasion which was being celebrated, the hooligan element was busy insulting and molesting the Cape Corps men in the ranks on the outskirts of the meeting.[557]

The events at Kimberley came somewhat as a surprise to the authorities, as the city was regarded as a white English-speaking loyalist bulwark, consisting in the main of South African Party or Unionist supporters with Afrikaans National Party adherents a

---

27 December 1917. See also *Diamond Fields Advertiser*, 3 January 1918 ("The recent riots"); *De Volkstem*, 28 December 1917 ("Handgevechten").

555 D.C. 1142/1239, Officer Commanding Cape Corps to Director General War Recruitment, 28 December 1917.

556 D.C. 1142/1239, Lieutenant Colonel A.J. Taylor to Director of War Recruitment, 27 December 1917.

557 D.C. 1142/1239, Collyer to Minister of Defence, 25 November 1918.

decided minority. Yet it was precisely from the English-orientated quarter, who was supposed to be more pro-war and also more tolerant towards coloured troops, that the protests and dissatisfaction emanated.[558]

At the root of this was obvious racism, but what is of interest in a wider sense is the way in which the war inadvertently acted as a catalyst for such behaviour. On their return, coloured troops were accused of "not knowing their place"[559] because of their contribution to the war effort. Those who harboured such ideas were most probably lower-order whites, described as "larrikins". Their behaviour had less to do with possible misdemeanours by the troops and more with a sense of apprehension that the pre-war social dispensation was being disturbed by wartime developments; hence it was necessary to return to pre-1914 conventions and for the socially threatened this meant that any further "worrisome" trends had to be arrested, regardless of how foul the means.

Not surprisingly, for the troops themselves these clashes left a sour taste. Regardless of the fact that they were fighting for the same cause as the white inhabitants, they were insulted and attacked. "The Cape Corps", it was reported "take up the position that they are quite good enough to be used to fight, but when they come back are, as stated by one, chased like mad dogs".[560]

Post-war dynamics and the politics of remembrance

Events in Kimberley, serious as they were, did not immediately dash any hopes of beneficial post-war change as far as the APO was concerned. What gave rise to this was that upon the return of the troops to Cape Town, General Smuts praised the corps; the controversies seemingly forgotten as well as Smuts' less than honourable role in their deployment. The APO was quick to respond that the sacrifices of the corps warranted some *quid pro quo* in terms of civil and economic rights.[561]

They also embarked on a lobbying campaign, petitioning the British government and the Peace Conference in Paris not to hand over control of South-West Africa to South

---

558 S.A.P. 1/250/17, Commissioner of Police Kimberley to Secretary of Police Pretoria, 28 December 1917.

559 S.A.P. 1/250/17, Commissioner of Police Kimberley – Secretary of Police Pretoria, 28 December 1917.

560 D.C. 1142/1239, Collyer – Minister of Defence, 1 January 1918.

561 Lewis, *Between the wire and the wall*, 88.

Africa until the rights of coloureds in the area had been guaranteed. These and other similar pleas to the Union government were brushed aside. Gradually, the realisation dawned that their wartime optimism might have been misguided. Abdurahman had to admit as much when he plaintively asked the delegates to the 1923 APO conference: "Can anyone mention any single advantage we gained for helping the cause of the Allies?"[562]

Although wartime participation failed to deliver what was hoped to be the fruits of victory, it did in a lower key and more generalised way contribute to opening up new horizons, a sharpened awareness of life beyond South Africa and their position as British subjects. Writing on the travails of the corps the historian Bill Nasson has noted:

> For virtually all of its ordinary servicemen, the war had given them a first-time experience of the empire, not only by tramping through Egypt, for instance, but by serving alongside British, Indian and other units and, in many cases, meeting men from these countries for the first time. For some, at least, the war could not help but make them more aware of an imaginative imperial citizenship as 'civilised' men.[563]

Outside the mainstream of channelled organisational politics and rarefied perceptions of empire, the wartime experience of certain members of the corps found expression in individual acts of defiance. When a former member of the corps was refused service at a whites-only café in Oudtshoorn, he responded: "What kind of place is this? I am allowed to fight for you, but I am not allowed to sit on your chairs."[564] In another countryside town, Robertson, the behaviour of certain corps veterans assumed a more openly militant form. Armed with army knives which they had retained after demobilisation, they attacked a white man after a verbal altercation. Subsequently, it was reported they conducted a reign of fear and threatened as to "how they are going to cut up Europeans".[565]

For others the meaning of their war experiences did not necessarily translate into a heightened sense of politically awareness or even aspirations, nor open defiance. It was rather to be found in a sense of personal growth. Sixty-two years after the

---

562 *Ibid.*

563 Nasson, *Springboks on the Somme*, 160.

564 Interview with Mr. C. van Vuuren at Oudsthoorn, 31 March 1979. Van Vuuren had come to know about the incident through oral transmission.

565 D.C. 377/132/40292, Town Clerk Robertson to Staff Officer Worcester, 5 July 1919.

war, A. Kammies from Graaff-Reinet recalled that his period of service in the corps represented a highpoint in his life and allowed him to look back with pride on his involvement. Regardless of the subjugation of coloured people, it was not necessary for him to feel inferior. He knew his own worth and "was able to hold his head high and could look whites foursquare in the eyes".[566] The war experience represented an achievement which could not be deleted or impinged upon by arbitrary discriminatory acts. Enhanced self-respect resided in the inner psyche, protected from the possible slings and arrows from a hostile outside world.

Particularly audible in the drum roll of Cape Corps remembrance history was the Battle of Square Hill. It was to become a synecdoche for the Cape Corps as a whole. "Talk about the Battle of Square Hill to any coloured man who knows the history of his people and chances are he will raise his shoulders an inch or two and look you proudly in the eye", the journalist and author Al J. Venter wrote in 1974.[567] While leaving room for some exaggeration, Venter's emphasis on the symbolic importance of coloured participation in the war was not too far off the mark. Although Square Hill did not assume the same proportions in the national historical consciousness as white South African losses at Delville Wood or the drowning of hundreds of black non-combatants when the troopship *SS Mendi* went down off the Isle of Wight, it did maintain its vitality even if not feted as much. In 2013, Bill Nasson could still inform a commemorative meeting at the Cape Town castle that "through these long decades", the image of the Cape Corps "still burns in our historical memory – of loyal, stocky soldiers, addicted to hobbies like darts and pigeon-racing as well as card games. Determined under fire, their bravery in the last year of the Great War was recognised by towns as well as rural 'dorps'."[568]

Memories of the war and the bonds that had been forged during the hostilities were also expressed in post-war relationships, not only between the men themselves but also between white officers and their former troops. In the countryside, former officers who had resigned from the Defence Force and entered into various business and farming ventures, were known to have a preference to employ Cape Corps veterans.[569] Wartime loyalty and tacit mutual understandings seemed to have help bridging the gap between military service and civilian life.

---

566   Interview with Mr. A. Kammies, Graaff-Reinet, 13 October 1980.

567   Venter, *Coloured: Profile of two million South Africans*, 257.

568   Nasson, "Reflections on the battle of Square Hill, September 1918".

569   Difford, *1st Battalion Cape Corps*, 27.

For some, involvement in the Cape Corps had a further dimension in that it was on a continuum with and reinforced other forms of service and civic duties. This was particular the case in Cape Town as far as the coloured elite was concerned. A shining example was that of Capetonian Jack Allies, a tradesmen who joined the corps as a private, fought in East Africa and Palestine, and was eventually promoted to sergeant. Upon his return to the Union after armistice, he became secretary of the Comrades of the Great War Association and took it upon himself to look into the needs of ex-servicemen, particularly men from Namaqualand who were hesitant to return home because of a prevailing drought. Allies kept his interest in the afterlife of the corps and was responsible for its 10th memorial service held in the City Hall in 1928. After the end of the Second World War in 1945, he was appointed as national president of the coloured ex-servicemen league. Steeped in military matters, his enthusiasm found a further outlet in organising the South African Coloured Boy Scouts. He rapidly went through the ranks of this paramilitary youth organisation to occupy one of the senior national positions. This kind of civic awareness, in which the original involvement with the Cape Corps echoed clearly, was simultaneously expressed in other areas of community life. Allies was also prominent in the Athlone and Crawford ratepayers association, he contributed to the running of food schemes and was a keen sportsman and organiser to boot.[570]

Jack Allies, Cape Corps stalwart in war and peace. [*Source*: See footnote 570]

Military service can then be viewed to be part and parcel of a wider social mosaic. It constituted part of the fabric of the wider public world through which some members of the coloured elite could express themselves in terms of civic awareness. This form of involvement, though it did carry a certain political freight, was not in the first instance primarily and overtly political, but was seen as conduits for responsible citizens to shoulder communal duties. In this sense, the constitutive elements of the

570 For details of Allies' career, see *The Sun*, 10 October 1947 ("Outstanding personalities").

Cape Corps as part of a community enterprise and commitment left a larger legacy insofar as these were transferred to and reflected in other endeavours.

Coloured involvement in the First World War furthermore resonated deep into the 20th century as it became one of the points of reference whenever the issue of military service for coloureds surfaced. Over time it assumed a most pliable form, twisted and massaged for whatever position was considered politically expedient at the time. During the Second World War (1939-1945), Smuts, in the heated political climate of the time, when the United Party narrowly won the vote for the Union to go to war, was anxious not to alienate anti-war Afrikaners, especially those whom he regarded as particularly colour sensitive. As a past master in political deception, he now argued in contradistinction to his earlier justification for arming coloured people in 1915, that coloureds should only be used as non-combatants as this "has been the old traditional system in this country. You have your fighters, your combatant force, and you have all the subsidiary services done by Natives and Coloured people and others."[571] In the event, coloureds were indeed armed and eventually deployed as sub-units in larger battalions in what was euphemistically called a policy of "dilution".[572]

With the advent of the National Party in 1948, and an explicit policy of apartheid, it was not too long before the Cape Corps was disbanded in 1949. Coloured people could now only be employed as labourers in the Defence Force on a loose footing and were not considered to be formally part thereof. Underlying this development was the argument that arming coloured people offended Afrikaner sensibilities, that it constituted a potential threat for whites and that in their military history, so it was claimed, Afrikaners were never dependent on the help of coloured people.[573] In what amounted to a thorough cleansing of what was now considered a relic of an unwanted past, the corps was not only demilitarised, but on a symbolic level the rupture also had to be publically visible. Coloured labourers in the army were therefore issued with a green uniform as opposed to the traditional khaki; the uniform was to have no epaulets and no military badges were allowed.[574] The outfit not only differed starkly from those worn by whites but also made it abundantly clear that coloured people

---

571 *House of Assembly Debates*, 13 May 1940. See also *House of Assembly Debates*, 15 April 1940.

572 Gleeson, *The unknown force*, 152; Orpen, "SA Coloured and Indian soldiers in World War II", 160-161.

573 Grundy, *Soldiers without politics*, 97-100.

574 *House of Assembly Debates*, 13 May 1949.

were not really an integral part of the new regime's army. The historical memory of the combatants of the Cape Corps who participated in predominantly white conflicts such as the two world wars and which the new rulers in any event frowned upon as wars fought on behalf of Britain, had to be obliterated.

Despite their exclusion from the Defence Force, or perhaps because of it, the notion of a coloured military tradition stayed alive. In particular, it was kept intact through organisations like the South African Coloured Ex-Servicemen Legion and annual commemorative services in honour of those who perished in the two world wars.[575] From 1951 to 1956, the legion was also involved in the futile campaign against the National Party's disenfranchisement of coloured voters. In part, their war background provided the inspiration for the new battle. The secretary of the legion, S.L. Leon, viewed it as a "fight against the removal of the fundamental rights that we fought for and many of our comrades gave their lives for".[576]

Over time though, the legion opposed apartheid's institutions less actively. In part, this was the result of an ageing membership, but also because some of the executive members gravitated towards controversial National Party institutions like the Coloured Representative Council, which was established in 1968 as a body to compensate for the loss of the coloured franchise.[577] This council was regarded as collaborationist and was shunned by committed activists and also by some more moderate men and women. The extent to which the South African Coloured Ex-Servicemen Legion was involved, can perhaps best be explained as a throwback to pre-1948 thinking when a measure of cooperation between white and coloured, albeit tentative, existed. For the Coloured Representative Council to be considered a stepping stone for greater involvement was, however, deemed by many in a harsher new apartheid environment as inappropriate.

Notwithstanding these tensions there still existed a strain of thought that considered the military tradition of the corps in the 20th century, dating back to the time of the First World, as worth reviving, even in an attenuated form. Thus, N. Kearns, chairman of the league, raised the possibility in 1961 of coloured people once again being inducted into the military. Initially the government was wary, but amidst black unrest

---

575 Compare *Springbok*, November 1970 ('They did not forget!').

576 University of South Africa, Documentation Centre, S.L. Leon Papers 237/35, "No surrender of our rights", 19 May 1951.

577 Compare S.L. Leon Papers 237/35 "Proceedings of the 33rd Annual Congress of the SA Cape Corps Ex-Servicemen's legion", December 1977.

and the banning of the African National Congress and the Pan Africanist Congress, as well as the policy of gradually expanding military service for white men, it was decided to enrol coloured men on a more organised basis. A unit known as the South African Coloured Corps was established in 1963.[578] Lest it be thought that this was a full revival of the Cape Corps, 'Cape' was dropped from the name and in line with apartheid thinking 'Coloured' had to be added. Moreover, the unit did not receive any weapons training; members served as clerks, quartermaster personnel, truck drivers, chefs and waiters.

Ten years later the status of coloureds in the Defence Force changed. With the escalation of the war in what was known as South-West Africa (currently Namibia), the need for more manpower meant that from 1973 coloured volunteers were being trained for gradual deployment in the operational area.[579] Changing times brought about new demands. Under the National Party regime the wheel has turned full circle; whereas they were excluded from the Defence Force in 1949, in 1973 they were once again integrated.

This development did not take place in an ideological vacuum. The revised role of coloured soldiers had to be underpinned and justified by a different set of assumptions. On an official level, the troops now had to be fulsomely recognised. In 1974, P.W. Botha, minister of defence, did not hesitate to express his "pride" in the men and was keen for "the idea to take root that the coloured population in growing numbers also regard the Defence Force as their protector".[580] In line with this kind of thinking, the military tradition of the corps was rediscovered. For P.J. Badenhorst, National Party member of parliament and later to be intimately involved with what would be known as coloured affairs, it was an almost unbroken tradition. In parliament, he argued: "Brown people have always been willing to die for South Africa. We think of the First World War when amongst other achievements eight coloured soldiers received decorations for bravery and in the Second World War 45 000 coloured soldiers served."[581]

The renewed recourse to tradition also called for changes in nomenclature. The South African Coloured Corps was now renamed back to the more traditional Cape Corps

---

578 Grundy, *Soldiers without politics*, 185-186; Cherry, "A feather in the cap? The South African Cape Corps: Ruling class ideology and community opposition", 121-122.

579 Grundy, *Soldiers without politics*, 185-186; Cherry, "A feather in the cap?", 121-122.

580 *House of Assembly Debates*, 9 September 1974.

581 *House of Assembly Debates*, 9 September 1974.

used in the First World War. In addition, the government sought to demonstrate its newfound goodwill in providing financial assistance for ex-servicemen to complete a memorial hall in Athlone. In 1974, the corps also received the Freedom of the City in Cape Town. Moreover, further praise was heaped on the corps when President Nico Diederichs in 1978 formally bestowed on the unit battle honours dating back from former wars.[582] On a symbolic level, continuity with the past was seen to be re-established.

Seen in a wider perspective, the permutations of Cape Corps tradition can be linked to the conditions which the renowned historian Eric Hobsbawn has identified as fertile for the emergence of invented traditions. He has identified periods of particular stress:

> We should expect it to occur more frequently when a rapid transformation of society weakens or destroy the social patterns for which the 'old' traditions had been designed, producing new ones to which they were not applicable, or when such old traditions and their institutional carriers and promulgators no longer prove sufficiently adaptable and flexible.[583]

Political and socio-economic crises rapidly gained momentum in South Africa during the 1970s and 1980s. These developments called for a reformulation of the ideological basis of a state intent on staying in power but in attempting to do so was forced to make concessions without appearing weak. It was then under such turbulent conditions, which included a need for armed manpower, that Cape Corps history had to be revisited with a view, according to an army spokesman, of contributing "towards dissipating the belief that until recently the SADF has always been a most exclusive organisation reserved for white citizens".[584]

The revival of the Cape Corps history was also opportunistically designed to serve as an agent for social cohesion within coloured communities. In the process, the past was once again invoked to establish a sense of continuity, even if it could be seen as contrived. In 1972, Staff Sergeant J. Cupido, later to become an officer in the corps, drew upon the history of the corps to convince the sceptical: "[T]he Cape Corps was the one unifying force amongst our people. It had no dividing lines, knew no political

---

582 Grundy, *Soldiers without politics*, 160-161; Cherry, "A feather in the cap?", 122; *Debates of the Coloured Representative Council*, 28 November 1974, Speech by Prime Minister B.J. Vorster.

583 Hobsbawn, "Introduction: Inventing traditions" in E. Hobsbawn and T. Rarenger (eds), *The invention of tradition*, 4.

584 Nöthling, "Blacks, coloureds and Indians in the SA Defence Force", 22.

affiliation and no social difference. It was a bond binding us all together in service to our country."[585]

Although, as we have seen, the corps had a certain pride of place in pre-1948 communities, it was somewhat ambitious, if not disingenuous, to think that the earlier reputation of the corps could simply and smoothly be transmitted to the apartheid dispensation as if nothing had happened in between. While communities generally used to revere the tradition of the old corps, they had serious reservations about the new one.[586] The ill-fated tricameral parliamentary system of the 1980s, and the rise of the United Democratic Front in opposition to it, made it increasingly difficult to project the corps as a unifying force. In the same way that coloureds in the tricameral system were rejected as junior partners to the National Party, the corps was seen as the handymen of the Defence Force. This association was neatly encapsulated by a young person when interviewed in Cape Town in 1984: "I don't vote for any dummy team and I wouldn't be fighting for the whites".[587]

Conclusion

Despite political slights and chicanery, participation in the First World War offered the Cape Corps an opportunity to establish a military tradition which in various ways fed into a sense of community. It could, however, also be yoked to apartheid projects which compromised its earlier dynamics. In this respect then, though unintended, the First World War helped to leave an enduring if ambiguous legacy.

585 *Paratus*, 8 Augustus 1972 ("Kaapse Korps herleef").

586 Grundy, *Soldiers without politics*, 177.

587 *Objector*, 5 August 1984 ("Objector on the street").

THE IMPACT OF THE FIRST WORLD WAR ON SOUTH AFRICA

A neglected catalyst for change?

Whereas the previous chapters have focused on certain South African participants in the war, an overarching question pertaining to the wider impact of the war and its standing as a factor in shaping or accelerating trends in South Africa in the second decade of the 20th-century remains.

In this context, it is useful to bring the Anglo-Boer War of 1899-1902 briefly into play. This war dramatically reshaped the political and socio-economic landscape in South Africa, besides leaving in its wake a cache of bitter memories which Afrikaner politicians and cultural entrepreneurs could access at various subsequent historical junctures, especially during the first half of the 20th century. The Anglo-Boer War was destined to become a central point of historical referral for a range of subsequent developments. Revealingly, none other than the former Free State president, M.T. Steyn, in July 1914 even linked it to the imminent First World War. He wrote to Smuts that

> the troubles in England are the result of the South African War. One sees still more. The war has driven England out of her 'splendid isolation' into her 'ententes' and her yellow alliances and today she has fallen foul of Continental entanglements. The mills of Providence grind slowly indeed![588]

Steyn's notion of causality might have been oversimplified, but it does demonstrate how large the Anglo-Boer War loomed in his perception of political developments.

---

588 Quoted in Van der Waag, "All splendid but horrible: The politics of South Africa's second 'little bit' and the war on the Western Front, 1915-1918", 75.

Whilst the importance of the Anglo-Boer War on several other socio-economic, cultural and political levels cannot be discounted, the question can nevertheless be raised whether the salience of this conflict has in our historical understanding not tend to dwarf the impact of other wars, including the First World War. Of course, one needs to make the rather obvious point that the devastating Anglo-Boer War took place on home soil and the fighting of the First World War for the most part conveniently elsewhere. This may explain the pre-eminence of the Anglo-Boer War in the historical imaginary and the way in which it tugged at the heartstrings of many, but is that sufficient reason to assume that the First War World at best had a peripheral impact on South African developments in South African society? To try and be more precise – did the absence of fighting in South Africa (apart from that of the Boer rebellion) also mean that the impact of the First World War passed the country by in other respects?

This question is addressed by probing certain admittedly selective trends. My interest is more in unguided, almost serendipitous, change as opposed to the fluctuations, machinations and positioning in formal party or organisational politics. This implies probing beyond surface events in an attempt to uncover broader subterranean strands and tendencies which emerged from 1914-1918 and which can causally be connected to the war. Such an approach would hopefully allow us to come to a more considered view of the wider significance of the war.

Central to the understanding of the issues at stake here is the dictum of Eric Hobsbawn, that wars "dramatize crucial aspects of the social structure" and "magnify phenomena for the benefit of the student".[589] One hopes to show that in the South African case the First World War can also be used as a lens to highlight previously hidden dimensions.

Legacies, 'platskiet' politics and overreach

With the outbreak of the First World War in 1914, it was barely four years that the Union of South Africa had been established as a political entity comprising the provinces of the Transvaal, the Free State, the Cape Colony and Natal. To a great extent it was a union in name only; underneath the brittle surface there were, besides other frictions, considerable divisions along language lines and between white and black. The challenge was to ensure the viability of union despite the many contending and disparate tendencies.

---

589 Hobsbawn, "From social history to the history of society", 20.

In this process, the war inadvertently created space for a more forceful pursuit of the integrity and power of the union than otherwise might have been the case. True, the armed suppression of the 1913-1914 white miners' strike on the Rand was a harbinger of things to come, but once South Africa became involved in the war on the side of Britain in 1914, the decision to participate in war had to be vindicated in forcefully suppressing dissidents with breakaway tendencies. This became clear with the effective crushing of the Boer Rebellion of 1914. The government of Louis Botha and Jan Smuts was not given to parley with the rebels, who initially sought to claim that they were only given to 'armed protest' without necessarily seeking to confront the state head-on. As soon as matters escalated, the ill-fated rebels quickly met their match when government forces rounded on them with intent. Occasioned by wartime developments, an assault on the state, however feeble, was successfully repulsed.

The war also allowed certain class fault lines in Afrikaner society to emerge. Although leaders of the 1914 rebellion might have been driven by political ideological motives, the concerns of a sizeable chunk of the rank and file were less clear-cut. There were a fair number of poor whites amongst the rebels, rural discontents who had become victims of so-called progressive capitalist farming practices which gave many a 'bywoner' [sharecropper] an increasingly tenuous hold on the land. In rebelling, some dissidents had fond hopes to turn the clock back to earlier republican days which they perceived to have been more accommodating to the landless poor. As the war loosened the props of society, it seemed to provide the space for a forceful expression of disgruntlement.[590] Moreover, the rebellion brought in its wake the Helpmekaar movement, founded to assist destitute rebels. It helped to foreground the plight of poor whites and was an early expression of Afrikaner concerns to rescue the poor for the 'volk' [Afrikaner people], which became such a hallmark of white nationalistic politics in the following decades. A Helpmekaar fund exists to this day, provides bursaries for tertiary education and has assets of about R100 million – in no uncertain terms the most tangible legacy which a band of ragged protesters could not have foreseen in their wildest dreams in 1914.[591]

In the aftermath of this rebellion, the event became part of Afrikaner nationalist sentiment. In this respect, the First World War can indirectly be seen as providing the

---

590 On the rebellion, see Grundlingh and Swart, *Radelose rebellie? Dinamika van die 1914-1915 Afrikanerrebellie*, 23-41.

591 I am indebted to Anton Ehlers, who is researching Helpmekaar, for providing me with these details.

opportunity for a nationalist spur to be fashioned. The historian S.E. Katzenellenbogen has also reminded us that Afrikaners were not alone in this. In 1973, he pointed out:

> Afrikaners would be most unwilling to accept that they had anything in common with African nationalists, but in addition to the desire to be free to develop their own culture – and to eliminate foreign political dominance and economic exploitation, black nationalists shared with Afrikaners the experience of the war of 1914-1918 as a significant turning point in their development.[592]

Intriguing as this statement may be, it needs to be qualified. The Anglo-Boer War was in terms of Afrikaner nationalism a much more pivotal event than the First World War, and also in terms of African nationalism the claim needs to be unpacked. As we have seen earlier, although a few members of the 21 000 strong SANLC, who worked as non-combatants in French forests and in harbours, came back with heightened political aspirations, the majority eased back into their pre-war lives and showed no signs of sustained political reawakening. And predictably the hopes of the ANC who sent a deputation to Lloyd George in an effort to gain some recognition in the post-war dispensation were dashed by a relatively sympathetic reception but no concrete commitments.

If one wishes to look at lasting political repercussions, these are once again to be found in the realm of unintended consequences. It was in the arena of historical memory that black participation left its most potent legacy. The sinking of the *Mendi* troopship off the Isle of Wight on 21 February 1917, with the loss of 615 lives, re-emerges in this context. In essence, the sinking of the ship was an accident at sea, but in subsequent retelling and embroidering of the event as a tale of heroism it became part of the warp and woof of nationalist myth-making, which exists to this day in the form of the ANC government's Order of Mendi for Bravery decorations.

In a lower key, though not in an altogether dissimilar manner, the Battle of Delville Wood, which saw the loss of 750 lives on the Western Front, was constructed as newly minted white South African heritage where English speakers and some Afrikaners fought side by side, supposedly forgetting the divisions of the Anglo-Boer War. This time round the war was linked to the notion of an emerging white South African identity. Over time it followed the predictable topsy-turvy trajectory of national historical memories. Whilst in the ensuing decades after the First World War, as

---

592 Katzenellenbogen, "Southern Africa and the war of 1914-1918", 117.

Afrikaner nationalism became more pervasive, Delville Wood as national symbol of unity receded and South African participation in the war was deemed as just another misguided venture on behalf of perfidious Albion. However, this did not deter the renowned Afrikaner leader of a besieged and tumultuous South Africa in the 1980s, President P.W. Botha, from invoking the heroics of Delville Wood to admonish an increasingly exasperated West, at the end of its tether with apartheid, that South Africa had in the past made great sacrifices on behalf of the Western world.[593]

Outside of the realm of historical memory and politics, the impact of the First World War also heralded a period of state violence in dealing with dissidents. This the Boer rebels had found to their cost, and others were to meet much the same fate. That much is evident from the suppression of the Bulhoek rising in the Eastern Cape in 1921, the Bondelwarts in South-West Africa in 1922 and, of course, the Rand strike of 1922. In the latter two cases, Smuts was not only content to unleash the police and military, but also brought the newly formed air force into play by bombing the mutineers into submission. Wartime technological developments like aerial bombing have in this instance clearly emerged in a different context in South Africa to be deployed against a civilian population. The war had indeed cast a long and deadly shadow.

The war furthermore released the genie of vaunting ambition. In a fit of sub-imperial convulsions, Smuts nurtured the idea of the establishment of a greater South Africa, incorporating Mozambique and East Africa. This turned out to be a chimera and a case of considerable overreach, but one that had its origins in the war as the world wide conquest of and reconfiguring of territories shaped new geo-political entities. This helped to fuel Smuts' territorial ambitions. If it happened elsewhere, why not here? And South Africa had in any case already acquired South-West Africa. It therefore might not have seen such an impossibility to expand the Union, and developments during the war provided the perfect opportunity for such an initiative. If it had succeeded, South Africa's overall history would have looked quite different in certain respects.[594]

The war not only encouraged such schemes, but the expansionist and gung-ho overreach was also wrapped up in a resurfacing of military masculinity, moulded and glorified during the war and enjoying a significant afterlife. General Smuts in particular, as the philosopher-soldier and premier from 1919, was an embodiment of

---

593 Nasson, *Springboks on the Somme*, 240.

594 Nasson, "A different dominion: Some reflections on South Africa in the Great War", Trinity College Dublin public lecture, 2013, 7, 11.

this kind of warrior. As his biographer indicated, he was often regarded as possessing an "icy coolness" and was fond of power which military prowess seemed to have formed a constitutive part.[595]

Black labour unrest, class divisions and women

The war years and their immediate aftermath were marked by one of the most sustained periods of black worker action in South African labour history, especially on the gold mines. In addition, there was a widespread boycott of mine concession shops in February 1917, affecting nearly all the mines on the East Rand. An important reason for this was that the mining industry was under the cosh during the war; as raw materials and machine tools were difficult to import, production started to slow down, the gold price remained fixed, profit margins began to shrink and, to their chagrin, these strains impacted on mine workers' already meagre pay packets.[596] Developments during the war foreshadowed the large-scale strike of 1920, which involved 71 000 workers (almost 40 percent of the black labour force) and affected 21 of the 35 mines on the Witwatersrand. Worker demands were firmly rejected, and it was only after the strike in 1920 that labourers were paid a small bonus.

Outside the mining industry, considerable labour unrest also occurred during 1918-1920: demands for higher wages in Bloemfontein in February 1919; the large-scale revolt against passes in Johannesburg in March and April 1919, which launched Clements Kadalie's Industrial and Commercial Workers' Union; and the agitation for wage increases in Port Elizabeth in January 1920.[597] The concern here is to explain how hostilities conducted mainly in Europe influenced black workers in a country 10 000 kilometres removed from the main war zone.

In this respect, it is essential to note the rapid secondary industrialisation which occurred during the war years. There was a brief decline in trade and industry at

595 Compare Hancock, *Smuts I: The sanguine years, 1870-1919*, 559, 561. See also Hyslop, "Martial law and military power in the construction of the South African State: Jan Smuts and the 'solid guarantee of force', 1899-1924", *Journal of Historical Sociology*, 22, 2, 2009.

596 For these developments, see U.G. 38/19, Annual Report of the Secretary for Mines and Industries and the Government Mining Engineer, 1918, 89-90; M.N.I. 514/1633/20, Report on the Native Mine Workers' Strike, 1920; Bonner, "The 1929 black mine workers' strike: A preliminary account", 273-297.

597 Bonner, "The Transvaal Native Congress, 1917-1920: The radicalisation of the black petty bourgeoisie on the Rand", 270-313; Johnstone, "The IWA on the Rand: Socialist organising unions among black workers on the Rand, 1917-1918", 248-272.

the outbreak of war, but soon after remarkable growth took place. The number of factories and other manufacturing enterprises increased from 3 998 in 1915-1916 to 6 890 in 1919-1920, an increase of 72 percent. The main areas of expansion were in the light consumer and processing industries and the metal building industry.[598]

Basically, these developments were related to the war in that South Africa was unable to import articles not produced locally, and local manufacturers were induced to take advantage of the opportunity created by diminishing foreign competition. Moreover, the natural protection which South African industries enjoyed as a result of being thousands of kilometres from Europe and America was increased during the war by the rise of freight, insurance and other import charges, as well as the substantially reduced commercial output of the belligerent nations.

The industrial upsurge was closely allied to accelerated urbanisation. During and immediately after the war, the number of unskilled workers (mainly Africans) employed in urban industries (excluding mines) rose dramatically by 83 percent: from 61 654 in 1915-1916 to 113 037 in 1919-1920.[599] The vast majority of these workers were concentrated in the industrial heartland of South Africa, the Witwatersrand area. The rapid proletarianisation clearly had important implications for labour unrest and indirectly the war provided the broad socio-economic context for strained industrial relations. This connection did not go unnoticed among officials of the Native Affairs Department. In a memorandum of May 1919, dealing with the position of Africans on the Witwatersrand, it was explicitly emphasised:

> The disorganisation of the commercial world ... has thrown the British Dominions on their own resources, and one is amazed at the strides that have been made in local manufacturing during the past four years. In short, the war has put the hand of time forward many years ... and this is perhaps most noticeable in regard to the natives ... They have been awakened by the roar and noise of a universal war ... Johannesburg has become the centre in which native thought has developed most during the war, and from which native political movements will radiate ... It is on the Witwatersrand that the native has had the opportunity of realising what industrial labour strikes mean.[600]

---

598 Houghton and Dagut, *Source material on the South African economy, 1860-1970*, 2, *1899-1919*, 209; Bloch, "The development of the manufacturing industry in South Africa, 1936-1969", 76.

599 Houghton and Dagut, *Source material on the South African economy*, 210, 226.

600 S.N.A. 1/4/26, Memorandum relating chiefly to Native political affairs on the Witwatersrand, 14 May 1919.

A further consideration in examining the links between the war and labour unrest is that of inflation. As a result of war conditions in Britain, the demand for goods exceeded supply and consequently prices increased drastically. Since South Africa had intimate trade links with Britain, this also affected the price structure in the Union. Banking and credit facilities were considerably extended during wartime industrialisation, and the unproductive debt almost doubled between 1910 and 1920. The cost of living, according to official statistics increased by 15,07 percent between 1914 and 1918, but there are indications that retail prices for this period rose between 31 and 39 percent.[601] Although white salaries were generally adjusted accordingly, black wages were either pegged at pre-war levels or only marginally increased. Not surprisingly, the issue of wages became a burning grievance and the focal point for industrial unrest.

Overall then, although one obviously had to bear in mind that labour unrest during this period also had their own specific dynamics, it is not too much to claim that war-induced changes, if they did not actually trigger strikes, provided the socio-economic frame which quickened growth and accelerated industrial action till well after the war. As a matter of fact, during this period the industrial landscape was arguably in broad terms consolidated and locked into a subsequent pattern of overall expansion, despite occasionally contractions, and also increasingly became a terrain open to contestation.

Specific conditions generated by the war furthermore highlighted the nature and ambiguities of African class formation and attitudes in the industrialised environment of the Rand. The growth of the African working class, and the labour unrest during and after the war, reveal the structural insecurity of the petty bourgeois and aspirant petty bourgeoisie elements. The latter's material position often differed little from that of the working class, but they enjoyed certain advantages, particularly in educational background, and self-consciously strove to set themselves apart from the rest of society. During the unrest, however, they had to contend with a movement whose membership, according to a contemporary white observer, consisted of persons "who had developed into a 'skebenga' [gangster] type – young men mostly, not even partially educated".[602] Once the *lumpenproletarian* section of society had asserted itself, the position of the petty bourgeoisie became distinctly contradictory. The war highlighted these points of difference and with the rise of the ICU during the 1920s they became even more apparent.

601 *Cape Times*, 18 January 1918 ("The cost of living").

602 *Rand Daily Mail*, 20 July 1918 ("Why the agitators failed").

Gender divisions of labour were not left untouched by the war. The entry of white women into the expanding manufacturing industry was hastened by the departure of men to the front. The number of white women employed on the Rand from 1915 to 1920 increased by 181 percent from an admittedly low base of 1 147 to a figure of 3 232.[603] Although the war had a marked impact on the employment pattern of white females, the same cannot be said for black women. The rate of urbanisation for black women was far slower than for whites. The numerical superiority of white females on the Rand, as well as prevailing employment practices in the manufacturing industry, ensured that black women were virtually excluded.[604]

Trends in agriculture

The war had a direct impact on agricultural production. It was quickly realised in white farming circles in South Africa that the severe dislocation in European and British agriculture caused by the war offered unique prospects. The war not only stimulated an internal market from which foreign competition was to a considerable degree eliminated, but also opened up to a larger export market. "With the vast armies in the field the consumption of food has increased enormously, and every one of these men has to be fed. It means not only an increase in price, but that we in South Africa have a glorious opportunity of producing more," was the euphoric comment of an agricultural journal in February 1915.[605] Despite a drought in 1916, as well as problems in importing certain farming implements and a sharp rise in freight rates during the war, these were boom years for white farmers. With the exception of three products – wattle bark, which suffered from the closing of the German market; fruit, which was handicapped by competition with meat for cold storage space on the ships; and ostrich feathers, which went out of fashion during the war years – "practically everything the farmer had to sell realised extremely high prices".[606] Cattle farmers, and to a slightly lesser extent maize and wool farmers, were the main beneficiaries of the changed conditions brought about by the war. After the initial disruption in trade, the value of South African agriculture and pastoral exports during the war years

603 Pollak, "Women in the Witwatersrand industries", 6.

604 Mariotti, "The incorporation of African women into wage employment in South Africa, 1920-1970", 278.

605 *The Agricultural Journal of South Africa*, February 1915, 170-171. See also U.G. 40-19, Annual report of the Department of Agriculture for the year ended 31 March 1919, 27.

606 U.G. 25-17, Annual report of the Department of Agriculture for the year ended 31 March 1916, 25-26.

showed an increase of approximately 62 percent in real terms. Not surprisingly, most white South African farmers could in 1919 look back upon a four-year period of "remarkable prosperity due to the war".[607]

The conditions brought about by the war, in turn affected class relations in the countryside. Its infusion of additional capital into agriculture as a result of the buoyant war conditions contributed to an intensification of the struggle between 'progressive' capitalising farmers on the one hand, and African sharecroppers and independent peasants on the other hand. There were considerable regional differences, but the general response from white capitalising farmers, in the Transvaal and the northern Orange Free State at least, was a renewed attempt to limit the already tenuous African access to land. The productive base of blacks, whether as sharecroppers or as independent peasant producers, had to be further eroded in order to turn them into dependent wage-earning farm labourers. To this end there were insistent calls that the relevant sections of the Natives' Land Act 27 of 1913, aimed at the removal of this type of African producer, should be applied more stringently and consistently. Indirectly the war thus helped to tighten pre-war screws.

Demographic change

Besides its impact on the socio-economic structure, the war also played a role in the demographic changes which occurred through the devastating influenza epidemic of the last few months of 1918. Wartime conditions abroad facilitated the spread of contagious disease; thousands of soldiers were crowded into military camps and then cooped up in the even more confined space of troopships which transported them to all the parts of the world.

Influenza appeared in South Africa around the middle of September 1918, with 11 726 whites and 127 745 black people dying in the ensuing epidemic which lasted until about the end of November. By a large margin many more South Africans died as a result of the flu than those who otherwise perished in the war. The ravages of the epidemic not only had an immediate and debilitating effect on communities, but in the long run had an appreciable effect on the country's demographic profile. The numbers were such, and the effect on subsequent birth rates so substantial, that the historian of the epidemic in South Africa is of the opinion that a whole generation has

---

607 *The Agricultural Journal of South Africa*, July 1919, 8.

been lost.[608] The impact of the flu is but one more example of the indirect manner in which war-induced change manifested itself.

Conclusion

In most general textbooks on South African history, one may find a passing reference to the First World War, usually mentioning the 1914 Boer Rebellion, the *Mendi* or perhaps Delville Wood and the SANNC delegation to Britain. The structural and other less visible changes wrought by the war are absent. This oversight should be seen as a result of the way in which war histories in South Africa, with some notable exceptions, are written. While it has been a characteristic of war and society studies abroad to map out the hidden ramifications of hostilities, in South Africa it has not been the case to the same extent.

To summarise then: the war impinged on South African society in almost imperceptible ways. Outwardly the country could still during this period appear to be locked into the familiar patterns of intra-white rivalry and white-black antagonism. Although one should of course not lose sight of these perennial dimensions, they should also not be allowed to overshadow less obvious but equally germane developments during this period. In broad political terms, the war had opened up tantalising prospects. For Boer rebels this took the illusionary form of a return to old republican ways. For Smuts, apart from the vision of a greater South Africa, the war brought new possibilities of warfare which could and indeed were used to suppress internal unrest. The more enduring effect of the war, however, can be found in the persistence and permutations of historical memory. Besides these, war-related factors had a knock-on effect in stimulating industry and agriculture, which in turn not only confirmed but also accelerated existing trends and patterns of interaction. These developments, often hidden from the general view, deserve in future to be foregrounded to a greater extent and perhaps even be upgraded to the status of a forgotten game changer.

---

608 Phillips, "South Africa's worst demographic disaster: The Spanish influenza epidemic of 1918", 69.

EPILOGUE

Although critics may argue that the period of the First World War is a "Eurocentric time capsule, artificially introduced into the African context",[609] it is hoped that this study has demonstrated that in many different and sometimes unexpected ways the war was very much a reality.

From the very outset Africans responded to the European conflagration and showed a keen awareness of the implications of the conflict. The black elite, as represented in part by the SANNC, argued, though not unanimously, that they should suspend their protest campaign against discrimination and support the war effort in the hope that such a policy would, at the conclusion of hostilities, be rewarded. Not surprisingly, this approach was encouraged by the government. It can be claimed that the SANNC, in aligning itself so closely with ruling class interests, sacrificed the opportunity of mounting a meaningful challenge at a time when the state was comparatively vulnerable. The SANNC certainly did not adopt a confrontational stance, demanding tangible concessions in return for support of the war effort. Whether a more assertive policy would have borne any fruit is, however, unlikely.

The SANNC nevertheless reflected only one strand of African political consciousness during the war. Outside the structures of formal black politics, some workers and peasants saw the war as an opportunity to voice their discontent forcefully and even to strike at the system of domination. In one case – the peasant uprising of late 1914 in the Matatiele district – consciousness was actually translated into collective action. South African blacks were not alone in reacting to the war in the way they did. Indeed, viewed from a wider perspective, there were marked similarities between the responses of black South Africans and those of Africans in the rest of the continent. While the educated elite in colonial Africa generally declared their loyalty to the imperial powers, some of the other classes regarded the war as an opportune time to come out in revolt as is evident from uprisings in Nyasaland (Malawi), Mozambique, and British and French West Africa.[610] As the Boer rebellion of 1914 in South Africa

---

609   The phrase quoted is from Rathbone, "World War I and Africa: Introduction", 9.

610   Rathbone, "World War I and Africa: Introduction", 5; Osuntokun, "West African armed revolts during the First World War", 6-17.

illustrates, this strategy was not confined to black people. Despite divergent motives, disaffected Boers and certain blacks nevertheless shared a common perception of the war as offering an opportunity for resistance.

As far as recruitment and the nature of military service are concerned, there were also some parallels between the experiences of South African black people and their counterparts elsewhere on the continent. Many recruits from the Union were, like Africans in the British, French, German and Portuguese colonies, deceived, cajoled, coerced or forcefully compelled to serve. Unlike the German askaris or the British King's African Rifles, who were armed, black South Africans served as general labourers and transport drivers in South-West Africa, and along with thousands of blacks from Britain's African colonies did duty in East Africa as carriers and porters. Indeed, in these debilitating, disease-ridden territories they literally carried the Allied forces into battle. The SANLC, however, had the dubious distinction of being the only sub-Saharan African force from the British Empire to be used in Europe where they helped to haul and load the armies to victory.[611] Perhaps the outstanding feature of the SANLC's service in France was the way in which the South African authorities sought to prevent members from getting ideas above their socio-political station in the domestic order. However, Africans resisted this policy and forced the government into an impasse so that, given its refusal to abandon the compound system, it was obliged to recall the contingent. As far as coloured troops were concerned, their sojourn in malaria-infested East Africa and the triumph of the Cape Corps at Square Hill were central to their war experiences.

Turning to the issue of increased political awareness on the part of the participants there is also a noticeable parallel with trends in other African colonies. The available evidence suggests that it is easy to overestimate the importance of veterans in post-war movements.[612] There is a contrast here with the post-war impact of black Americans who served in Europe in a non-combatant as well as combatant capacity. Immediately after the war these veterans were very much involved in the unrest that swept through America. While the general underlying causes of the riots in places like Charleston, South Carolina, Washington D.C., New York City and Chicago were socio-economic, political and psychological, it was the return of black veterans that seems to have triggered off bloody clashes during America's 'red summer' of 1919. In particular,

---

611 Killingray and Matthews, "Beasts of burden: British West African carriers in the First World War", 7-23; Page, "Fighting for their world: Black men in a white men's war", 9.

612 See, for instance, L.J. Greenstein, "The impact of military service in World War I on Africans: The Nandi of Kenya", 495-507; Killingray, "The colonial army in the Gold Coast", 375-415.

the lynching of black ex-soldiers by white racists, who believed that the veterans had come back with 'wrong ideas' about their social status after having served in Europe, sparked off retaliations by some veterans and widespread anger and counterattacks by the black community in general.[613] Thus, Afro-American veterans, driven by specific circumstances and local conditions, featured more prominently in immediate post-war developments than ex-servicemen on the African continent. It is nevertheless revealing to recall that events concerning the attacks on members of the Cape Corps in Kimberley upon their return to South Africa contained echoes of what happened in America, but the responses and consequences were not so dramatic.

In respect of the remembrance of the war, the *SS Mendi* accident was destined to dent historical memory for several decades. The afterlife of the Cape Corps was more muted, but still sufficiently tangible to be manipulated by different interest groups long after the guns of the war were silenced.

Finally, in an overall evaluation of the impact of the war, it has been argued that as a result of changing political and economic circumstances induced by the war, certain trends in the industrial life and agriculture for instance, were accelerated and provided the platform for developments during the 1920s. Whilst the involvement of black and coloured troops can certainly lay claim to be remembered historically, the impact of changes in South African socio-economic structures, though hitherto insufficiently recognised, can also be regarded as a memorable shift.

---

613 Barbeau and Henri, *The unknown soldiers: Black American troops in World War I*, 178; Mullen, *Blacks in America's Wars*, 50.

ACKNOWLEDGEMENTS

My family (Annamari, Mauritz, Marizanne and Mia) has as usual kept the home fires burning during my latest round in the trenches of historical writing. I trust my imminent return as a grizzly veteran will not be too much of a shock.

I have been fortunate in having Bill Nasson as a colleague. As a much decorated historian of war, he has encouraged me to revisit the unpredictable interplay between war and society. My other colleagues at Stellenbosch University (Anton Ehlers, Wessel Visser and Sandra Swart) have shown a keen interest. Bob Edgar, a long-standing acquaintance who has an encyclopaedic knowledge of South African history, has been generous in sharing early black newspaper cuttings. Finally, I am indebted to the National Research Foundation for providing me with essential research funds.

In part, this book is based on an earlier work which appeared in 1987 under the title *Fighting their own war* and has long been out of print. *Fighting their own war* also saw the light of day before the system of state subsidies for academic outputs had been put into place. The original book has been substantially revised and reconfigured in terms of style and substance. New work on the remembrance of the *SS Mendi* disaster has also been added (the first incarnation was published in 2011 in the *South African Historical Journal*, 63(1)). Moreover, other additional material now appears in print for the first time.

Albert Grundlingh
Stellenbosch University
August 2014

SOURCES

A. ARCHIVAL SOURCES

I. SOUTH AFRICA

1. Transvaal and Central Archives Depot, Pretoria

Accessions

A.20, Colonel W.H.M. Bamford.

A.75, T. Boydell.

A.120, L.B. Cross.

A.58, L. Esselen.

A.32, J.B.M. Hertzog.

A.34, General J.C.G. Kemp.

A.69, H. Oost.

A.90, Commandant N. Orpen.

A.787, Doctor G.S. Preller.

A.1, General J.C. Smuts.

Archives of the Magistrate Bethal (B.L.).

Archives of the Government Native Labour Bureau (G.N.L.B.).

Archives of the Governor-general (G.G.).

Archives of the Commissioner Native Affairs Johannesburg (K.J.B.).

Archives of the Secretary for the Department of Justice (J.).

Archives of the Secretary for the Department of Mines and Industries (M.N.I.).

Archives of the Secretary for the Department of Native Affairs (N.A.).

Archives of the Secretary for the Department of the Prime Minister (P.M.).

Archives of the South African Police (S.A.P.).

2. South African Defence Force Documentation Centre, Pretoria

Archives of the Adjutant-general (A.G.).

Archives of the Chief Staff Officer (C.S.O.).

Archives of the Commandant-general (C.G.).

Archives of the Secretary for the Department of Defence (D.C.).

Archives of the Officer Commanding Records (O.C. Records).

South African Native Labour Contingent Attestation Forms (SANLC).

Union War Histories Group (U.W.H.).

WWI 1914/1918 Group (WWI 1914/1918).

WWI German South-West Africa Group, 1914/1918 (WWI G.S.W.A. 1914/1918).

WWI Imperial Service Details, 1914/1918 (WWI I.S.D.).

3. Cape Archives Depot, Cape Town

Accessions

A.608, H.E.S. Fremantle.
A.583, F.S. Malan.
Archives of the Magistrate East London (1/E.L.N.).
Archives of the Magistrate Ladysmith (1/L.S.M.).
Archives of the Magistrate Tabankulu (1/T.B.U.).
Archives of the Chief Magistrate Transkei (C.M.T.).
Archives of the Magistrate Umtata (1/U.T.A.).

4. Natal Archives Depot, Pietermaritzburg

Accessions

H.E. Colenso.
Natal Wesleyan Mission.
Zulu Society Papers.
Archives of the Chief Native Commissioner (C.N.C.).
Archives of the Secretary for Native Affairs, Natal (S.N.A.).

5. Albany Museum, Grahamstown

D.L. Smit Papers.

6. Rhodes University, Cory Library, Grahamstown

Lovedale Collection.
Methodist Church Collection.
W.B. Rubusana Collection.

7. Killie Campbell Library, Durban

G.H. Nicholls Papers.
J. Hertslet Papers.
J.S. Marwick Papers.

8. South African Public Library, Cape Town

J.X. Merriman Papers.
W.P. Schreiner Papers.

9. University of Cape Town, Jagger Library, Cape Town

W.E. Stanford Papers.

10. University of South Africa, Sanlam Library, Pretoria

S.L. Leon Papers.
S.T. Plaatje Papers/S. Molema Papers.

11. University of the Witwatersrand, Library, Johannesburg

J. Howard Pim Papers.

II. LESOTHO

1. Lesotho National Archives, Maseru

Archives of the Secretary to the Government (S.).

III. BRITAIN

1. Public Record Office, Kew, London

Colonial Office Records (C.O.).
Cabinet Papers (C.A.B.).
Ministry of Munitions (M.U.N.).
Board of Trade Records (T.).
War Office Records (W.O.).

2. House Of Lords Record Office, Westminister, London

A. Bonar Law Papers.

3. Imperial War Museum, London

Major General E. Northey Papers.
Archival Film on the SANLC, 1917.

4. University of London, School of Oriental and African Studies, London

H.S. Msimang, unpublished 'Autobiography'.

5. University of London, King's College, Liddell Hart Centre, London

Brigadier General G. Aston Papers.

6. Oxford University, Bodleian Library, Oxford

L. Harcourt Papers.
A. Milner Papers.

7. Oxford University, Rhodes House, Oxford

Aborigines' Protection Society Papers (A.P.S.).

8. Cambridge University, Churchill College, Cambridge

M. Hankey Papers.

9. Wiltshire County Record Office, County Hall, Trowbridge, Wiltshire

W.H. Long Papers.

10. Newtimber Place, Hassocks, Sussex

S.C. Buxton Papers.

B. OFFICIAL GOVERNMENT PUBLICATIONS

I. SOUTH AFRICA

Acts of the Union of South Africa, 1912.

Debates of the Coloured Representative Council, 1974.

Official history: Union of South Africa and the Great War, Pretoria, 1924.

S.C. 1-15, *Report of the Select Committee on the Rebellion.*

S.C. 3-15, *Union of South Africa, Senate, Report of the Government's Special Commissioner.*

S.C. 1-19, *Report of the Commissioner appointed to enquire into and report upon the causes which led up to the partial cessation of the municipal sanitary services at Johannesburg,* June 1918, 6-8.

U.G. 37-14, *Report of the Native Grievances Inquiry 1913-1914.*

U.G. 10-15, *Report on the Outbreak of the Rebellion and the policy of the Government with regard to its suppression.*

U.G. 13-16, *Report of Commission of Enquiry into the treatment of Prisoners of War by the German Protectorate Authorities during the late hostilities.*

U.G. 14-16, *Report on the work done by the Inspection Staff on War Expenditure in connection with the Rebellion and the German South-West African campaign up to the end of October 1915.*

U.G. 19-16, *Report of the Native Land Commission.*

U.G. 22-16, *Report of the Native Land Commission: Minutes of Evidence.*

U.G. 24-16, *Report of the Board of the South African Railways and Harbours.*

U.G. 40-16, *Report of the Rebellion Losses Commission.*

U.G. 42-16, *Judicial Commission of Inquiry into the Causes and Circumstances relating to the recent Rebellion in South Africa: Minutes of Evidence.*

U.G. 46-16, *Report of the Judicial Commission of Inquiry into the Causes and Circumstances relating to the Recent Rebellion in South Africa.*

U.G. 25-17, *Annual Report of the Department of Agriculture for the year ended 31 March 1916.*

U.G. 32-18, *Minutes of Evidence of the Eastern Transvaal Natives Land Committee.*

U.G. 7-19, *Report of the Department of Native Affairs/or the years 1913 to 1918.*

U.G. 15-19, *Report of the Influenza Epidemic Commission,* 1919.

U.G. 38-19, *Annual Report of the Secretary for Mines and Industries and the Government Mining Engineer,* 1918.

U.G. 40-19, *Annual Report of the Department of Agriculture for the year ended 31 March 1919.*

U.G. 45-19, *Interim Rapport van de Lage Graad Mijnen Kommissie,* 1919.

U.G. 34-20, *Final Report of the Low Grade Mines Commission,* 1919.

U.G. 34-22, *Report of the Department of Native Affairs for the years 1913 to 1918.*

U.G. 39-25, *Report of the Native Churches Commission.*

Union of South Africa. House of Assembly Debates, 1911, 1912, 1914-1915, 1974.

Union of South Africa. Union Statistics for Fifty Years. Jubilee Issue, 1960.

II. BRITAIN

Parliamentary Debates (House of Commons), 1916.

C. OTHER OFFICIAL PUBLICATIONS

Annual Address of the President of the Transvaal Chamber of Mines, 1915.
Annual Address of the President of the Transvaal Chamber of Mines, 1916.
Annual Address of the President of the Transvaal Chamber of Mines, 1917.
Annual Address of the President of the Transvaal Chamber of Mines, 1918.
Annual Address of the President of the Transvaal Chamber of Mines, 1919.
Annual Report of the Witwatersrand Native Labour Association, 1914.
Annual Report of the Witwatersrand Native Labour Association, 1915.
Annual Report of the Witwatersrand Native Labour Association, 1916.
Annual Report of the Witwatersrand Native Labour Association, 1918.
Annual Report of the Witwatersrand Native Labour Association, 1919.
Juta's Daily Reporter: Decisions of the Cape Provincial Division of the Supreme Court of South Africa, 1918.

D. SOURCE PUBLICATIONS

Barnes, J. and Nicholson, D. (eds). *The Leo Amery diaries I, 1896-1929*, London, 1980.

Hancock, W.K. and Van der Poel, J. (eds). *Selections from the Smuts Papers III, 1910-1919; IV, 1918-1919; V, 1919-1934*, Cambridge, 1966 and 1973.

Houghton, D.H. and Dagut, J. (eds). *Source material on the South African Economy, 1860-1970*: 2, *1899-1919*, Cape Town, 1972.

Karis, R. and Carter, G.M. (eds). *From protest to challenge: A documentary history of African politics in South Africa, 1882-1964, I, Protest and hope, 1882-1934*: 4, *Political profiles, 1882-1964*, Stanford, 1972 and 1977.

Lewsen, P. *Selections from the correspondence of John X Merriman, 1905-1924*, Van Riebeeck Society, 50, Cape Town, 1969.

Meinertzhagen, R. *Army diary, 1899-1926*, London, 1960.

E. NEWSPAPERS AND PERIODICALS

Abantu-Batho, 1917-1919, 1923.
African Times and Orient Review, 1917.
African World, 1914-1916.
Agricultural Journal of South Africa, 1914-1920.
Alice Times, 1916-1918.
APO, 1914-1915, 1919.
Cape Times, 1914-1921, 1936, 2014.
Cape Times Annual, 1919.
Church Times, 1914-1916.
City Press, 1984.

Contact, 1960.
Daily Chronicle, 1916.
De Burger, 1916-1918.
De Volkstem, 1914-1919.
Diamond Fields Advertiser, 1914-1918.
East London Daily Dispatch, 1914-1917.
Farmer's Weekly, 1914-1920.
Het Volksblad, 1916.
History Today, 2007.
Ilanga Lase Natal, 1914-1920.
Imvo Zabantsundu, 1914-1920.
Inkundla ya Bantu, 1944.
Izwe Ia Kiti, 1914-1915.
Izwe Lase Afrika, 1941-1942.
Le Monde, 2014.
Mail & Guardian, 2007.
Natal Advertiser, 1916-1917.
Natal Mercury, 1914-1919.
Native Teachers' Journal, 1920.
Objector, 1984.
Ons Vaderland, 1915-1916.
Paratus, 1972.
Pretoria News, 1916-1917.
Rand Daily Mail, 1914-1920.
Round Table, 1914-1918.
South Africa, 1916-1919.
Sowetan, 1984.
Springbok, 1970.
Sunday Express, 1938.
Sunday Times, 1914-1918.
Territorial News, 1914-1918.
The African Defender, 1938.
The African World, 1914, 1916.
The Bantu World, 1946.
The Christian Express, 1914-1920.
The Church Abroad, 1917.
The Friend, 1914, 1916.
The Imperialist, 1914-1918.
The South African Review, 1918.
The Star, 1914, 1916-1919, 1952, 1967.
The Times, 1916.
The Weekly Mail, 1993
The World Today, 2014

This Day, 2004.
Transvaal Leader, 1914-1915.
Tsala ea Batho, 1914-1915.
Umteteli wa Bantu, 1932.
Zululand Times, 1916-1917.

F. BOOKS, JOURNAL ARTICLES, PAMPHLETS, UNPUBLISHED THESES AND PAPERS

Abrams, P. "The failure of social reform". *Past and Present* 26, 1963.

Adhikari, M. *Not white enough, not black enough: Racial identity in the South African coloured community*. Cape Town, 2005.

Adler, F.B., Lorch, A.E. and Curson, H.H. *The South African Field Artillery in German East Africa and Palestine, 1915-1919*. Pretoria, 1958.

Allport, G.W. *The nature of prejudice*. New York, 1958.

Allport, G.W. and Postman, L. *The psychology of rumour*. New York, 1947.

Andrew, C.M. and Kanya-Forstener, A.S. "France, Africa and the First World War". *Journal of African History*, XIX(1), 1978.

A.P.S. pamphlet, *British Africans in Europe and the Work of the Welfare Committee*. London, 1917.

Ballinger, M. *From Union to Apartheid*. Cape Town, 1969.

Barbeau, A.E. and Henri, F. *The unknown soldiers: Black American troops in World War I*. New York, 1974.

Beaton, A.J. "Railway construction during the campaign of 1914-1915 in German South-West Africa". *Transactions of the South African Society of Civil Engineers*, July 1916.

Beinart, W. *The political economy of Pondoland, 1860-1930*. Cambridge and Johannesburg, 1982.

Beinart, W. and Bundy, C. "State intervention and rural resistance in the Transkei, 1900-1915". In Klein, M.A. (ed.), *Peasants in Africa: Historical and contemporary perspectives*. London, 1980.

Ben-Zeev, K. "Public encounters: The negotiation of ritual. Risk and relevance in the performance of Johannesburg's National Remembrance Sunday ceremonies". Unpublished MA dissertation, University of the Witwatersrand, 2008.

Bevan, E. *Brothers all: The war and the race question*. London, 1915.

Bisset, W.M. "Unexplored aspects of South Africa's First World War history". *Militaria*, 613, 1976.

Blignaut, C.J. "Die reënval van die Pietersburg-plato". Unpublished MA dissertation, University of Pretoria, 1952.

Bloch, G. "The development of the manufacturing industry in South Africa, 1939-1969". Unpublished MA dissertation, University of Cape Town, 1980.

Boell, L. *Die Operationen in Ostafrika: Weltkrieg, 1914-1918*. Hamburg, 1951.

Bond, B. and Roy, I. (eds), *War and society, I & II*. London, 1975 and 1977.

Bonner, P.L. "The 1920 black mineworkers' strike: A preliminary account". In Bozzoli, B. (ed.), *Labour, townships and protest: Studies in the social history of the Witwatersrand*. Johannesburg, 1979.

Bonner, P.L. "The Transvaal Native congress, 1917-1920: The radicalisation of the black petty bourgeoisie on the Rand". In Marks, S. and Rathbone, R. (eds), *Industrialisation and social change in South Africa: African class formation, culture and consciousness*. London, 1982.

Bouch, R.J. "The railways and the war effort, 1914-1915". *Militaria*, 41(3), 1972.

Bottomley, J. "The South African Rebellion of 1914: The influence of industrialisation, poverty and poor whiteism". Seminar paper, African Studies Institute, University of the Witwatersrand, June 1982.

Bozzoli, B. *The political nature of a ruling class: Capital and ideology in South Africa, 1890-1933*. London, 1981.

Bozzoli, B. (ed.), *Town and countryside in the Transvaal: Capitalist penetration and popular response*. Johannesburg, 1983.

Bradford, H. "Mass movements and the petty bourgeoisie: The social origins of I.C.U. leadership, 1924-1929". *Journal of African History*, 25, 1984.

Brown, I.C. *Understanding race relations*. New York, 1973.

Brownlee, W.T. *Reminiscences of a Transkeian*. Pietermaritzburg, 1975.

Buchan, J. *History of the South African Forces in France*, London, 1921.

Buchanan, A.R. *Black Americans in World War II*. Santa Barbara, 1977.

Buell, R.L. *The Native problem in Africa: I & II*. New York, 1928.

Bundy, C. *The rise and fall of the South African peasantry*. London, 1979.

Bundy, C. "Dissidents, detectives, and the dipping revolt: Social control and collaboration in East Griqualand in 1914". Seminar paper, Centre for Southern African Studies, University of York, 1982.

Buxton, S.C. *General Louis Botha*. London, 1924.

Callaway, G. "Umlungu: or the European in South Africa". *East and West*, February, 1917.

Cell, J.W. *The highest stage of white supremacy: The origins of segregation in South Africa and the American south*. Cambridge, 1982.

Chanock, M. *Unconsummated Union: Britain, Rhodesia, and South Africa, 1900-1945*. Manchester, 1977.

Cherry, J. "A feather in the cap? The South African Cape Corps: Ruling class ideology and community opposition". In Cooper, L. and Kaplan, D. (eds), *Reform and resistance: Selected research papers on aspects of contemporary South Africa*. Cape Town, 1986.

Chilvers, H.A. *The story of De Beers*. London, 1939.

Clothier, N. *Black valour: The South African Native Labour Contingent, 1916-1918 and the sinking of the* Mendi. Pietermaritzburg, 1987.

Cock, J. and Nathan, L. (eds), *War and society: The militarisation of South Africa*. Johannesburg, 1989.

Cobley. A.G. *Class and consciousness: The black petty bourgeoisie in South Africa, 1924 to 1950*. New York, 1990.

Coetzee, D.J.J. "Die onafhanklikheidstrewe van die Nasionale Party". In Marais, A.H. and Geyser, O. (eds), *Die geskiedenis van die Nasionale Party 1910-1924, I: Agtergrond, stigting en konsolidasie*. Cape Town, 1975.

Collyer, J.J. *The campaign in German South-West Africa, 1914-1915*. Pretoria, 1937.

Cope, J. and Krige, U. (eds), *The Penguin Book of South African verse*. London, 1968.

Crowder, M. "The impact of two world wars on Africa". *History Today*, 34, January 1984.

Crowe, J.H.B. *General Smuts' campaign in East Africa*. London, 1918.

Dalby, D. and Harrison Church, R.J. (eds), *Drought in Africa*. London, 1977.

Davenport, T.R.H. *The beginnings of urban segregation in South Africa: The Natives (Urban Areas) Act of 1923 and its background*. Occasional Papers, 15, Rhodes University, Grahamstown, 1971.

De Kock, M.H. *Selected subjects in the economic history of South Africa*. Cape Town, 1924.

Desmore, A.J.B. *With the 2nd Cape Corps thro' Central Africa*. Cape Town, 1920.

De Villiers, J. "Die Kaapse Regiment, 1806-1817". *South African Historical Journal*, 7, 1975.

De Wet, J.M. *'n Lewenskets van Jopie Fourie*. Cape Town, 1946.

Dieterlen, H. *Bahlankana ba Fora* [The Sons of France]. Morija, 1918.

Difford, I.D. *The story of the 1st Battalion Cape Corps, 1915-1919*. Cape Town, 1920.

Donajgrodzki, A.P. (ed.), *Social control in Nineteenth Century Britain*. London, 1977.

Donaldson, K. (ed.), *South Afsrican Who's Who, 1919-1920*. Cape Town, 1921.

Downes, W.D. *With the Nigerians in German East Africa*. London, 1919.

Doxey, G.V. *The industrial colour bar in South Africa*. Cape Town, 1961.

Dubow, S. "Race, civilisation and culture: The elaboration of segregationist discourse in the in the interwar years". Seminar paper, African Studies Institute, University of the Witwatersrand, 1986.

Dubow, S. *Racial segregation and the origins of apartheid in South Africa, 1919-36*. Oxford, 1989.

Duff, H. "White men's war in black men's countries". *The National Review*, LXXXIV, February, 1925.

Duminy, A. and Ballard, C. (eds), *The Anglo-Zulu War: New perspectives*. Pietermaritzburg, 1981.

Edgar, R.R. "A.P. Mda: The making of an African nationalist, 1935-1944". History workshop paper, University of the Witwatersrand, 1990.

Edgar, R.R. "Garveyism in Africa: Dr. Wellington and the American movement in the Transkei". *Ufahamu*, VI(3), 1976.

Edgar, R.R. "The fifth seal: Enoch Mgijima, the Israelites and the Bulhoek Massacre, 1921". Unpublished PhD dissertation, University of California, Los Angeles, 1977.

Edgar, R.R. "Lesotho and the First World War: Recruiting, resistance and the South African Native Labour Contingent". *Mohlomi: Journal of Southern African Historical Studies*, III, IV, V, 1981.

Edgar, R. "Changing the old guard: A.P. Mda and the ANC Youth League, 1944-1949". In Dubow, S. (ed.), *South Africa's 1940s: Worlds of possibilities*. Cape Town, 2005.

Ellinwood, D.C. and Pradhan, S.D. (eds), *India and World War 1*. Columbia, 1978.

Enloe, C.H. *Ethnic soldiers: State security in a divided society*. New York, 1980.

Evans, M.S. *Black and white in South East Africa*. London, 1911.

Flemmer, M. "Sir William H. Beaumont and the Natives Land Commission, 1913-1916". Unpublished MA dissertation, University of Natal, 1976.

Foot, M.R.D. (ed.), *War and society*. London, 1973.

Frankel, P.H. *Pretoria's Praetorians: Civil-military relations in South Africa*. Cambridge, 1984.

Gardner, B. *German East: The story of the First World War in East Africa*. London, 1963.

Garson, N.G. "Party politics and the plural society: South Africa, 1910-1929". Collected Seminar Papers on the Societies of Southern Africa in the 19th and 20th Centuries, 10, Institute of Commonwealth Studies, University of London, London, 1970.

Garson, N.G. "South Africa and World War I". *The Journal of Imperial and Commonwealth History*, 8(i), 1979.

Genis, G. "South African Great War Poetry, 1914-1918: A literary-historiographical analysis". Unpublished PhD dissertation, University of South Africa, 2014.

Gevisser, M. *The dream deferred: Thabo Mbeki*. Johannesburg, 2007.

Gish, S.D. *Alfred B. Xuma, African, American, South African*. New York 2000.

Gleeson, I. *The unknown force: Black, Indian and Coloured soldiers through two world wars*. Cape Town, 1994.

Greenstein, L.J. "Military service and the Nandi of Kenya". *Journal of Modern African Studies*, 16(3), 1978.

Gregory, A. *The silence of memory: Armistice Day, 1919-1946*. Oxford, 1994.

Grundlingh, A.M. "Some trends in South African academic history". In Jeppie, S. (ed.) *Rethinking history*, Cape Town, 2005.

Grundlingh, A.M. and Swart, S. *Radelose rebellie? Dinamika van die 1914-15 Afrikanerrebellie*. Pretoria, 2009.

Grundy, K.W. *Soldiers without politics: Blacks in the South African armed forces*. Berkeley, 1983.

Hancock, W.K. *Smuts I: The sanguine years, 1870-1919*. Cambridge, 1962.

Hancock, W.K. *Smuts II: The fields of force, 1919-1950*. Cambridge, 1968.

Harris, J.H. "Native races and peace terms". *Contemporary Review*, 606, June 1916.

Hellman, E. "Non-Europeans in the army". *Race Relations*, X(2), 1943.

Henige, D. "Impossible to disprove yet impossible to believe: The unforgiving epistemology of deep-time oral tradition". *History in Africa*, 36, 2009.

Henri, F. *Bitter victory: A history of black soldiers in World War I*. New York, 1970.

Henriksen, T.H. *Mocambique: A history*. London, 1978.

Hernton, C.C. *Sex and racism*. New York, 1969.

Hobsbawn, E.J. "From social history to the history of society". In Gilbert, F. and Graubard, S.R. (eds), *Historical studies today*. New York, 1972.

Hobsbawn, E.J. and Ranger, T. (eds), *The invention of tradition*. London 1983.

Hodges, G.W.T. "African manpower statistics for the British forces in East Africa". *Journal of African History*, XIX(1), 1978.

Holbrook, W.P. "The impact of the Second World War on the Gold Coast, 1939-1945". Unpublished PhD dissertation, Princeton University, 1978.

Hopkins, H. *The strange death of Private White: A Victorian scandal that made history*. London, 1977.

Hordern, C. *Military operations in East Africa, 1914-1916*. London, 1941.

Horwitz, S. "The non-European war record in South Africa". In Hellman, E. and Abrahams, L. (eds), *Handbook on race relations in South Africa*. London, 1949.

Howard, M. *War and the liberal conscience*. Oxford, 1978.

Howard, M. *War in European history*. Oxford, 1976.

Humphrey, A.M.D. "South African agriculture in a period of transition, 1913-1924". Unpublished Honours dissertation, University of the Witwatersrand, 1978.

Hyslop, J. "Martial law and military power in the construction of the South African state: Jan Smuts and the 'solid guarantee of force', 1899-1924". *Journal of Historical Sociology*, 22, 2, 2009.

Innes, D. *Anglo American and the rise of modern South Africa*. Johannesburg, 1984.

Jabavu, D.D.T. *The black problem*. Lovedale, 1920.

Jabavu, D.D.T. "Native unrest in South Africa". *International Review of Missions*, 1922.

Jeffreys, M.D.W. "The *Mendi* and after". *Africana Notes and News*, 15(5), March 1963.

Johnstone, H. *The black man's part in the war*. London, 1917.

Johnstone, F.A. *Class, race and gold: A study of class relations and racial discrimination in South Africa*. London, 1976.

Johnstone, F.A. "The IWA on the Rand: Socialist organising unions among black workers on the Rand, 1917-1918". In Bozzoli, B. (ed.), *Labour, township and protest: Studies in the social history of the Witwatersrand*. Johannesburg: Ravan Press, 1979.

Kagan, N. "African settlements in the Johannesburg area, 1903-1923". Unpublished MA dissertation, University of the Witwatersrand, 1978.

Kallaway, P. "F.S. Malan, the Cape liberal tradition and South African politics". *Journal of African History*, XV(1), 1974.

Kaplan, D.E. "The South African state: The origins of a racially exclusive democracy". *The Insurgent Sociologist*, X(2), Fall 1980.

Karsten, P. *Soldiers and society: The effect of military service and war on American life*. Westport, 1978.

Katzenellenbogen, S.E. "Southern Africa and the war of 1914-1918". In Foot, M.R.D. (ed.), *War and society*. London, 1973.

Keable, R. "African priests in France". *The East and West*, January 1918.

Keable, R. *Standing by: War time reflections in France and Flanders*. London, 1919.

Keegan, T. "Lapsed whites and moral panic: An aspect of the South African ideological crisis". Seminar paper, University of Cape Town, 1979.

Keegan, T. "The sharecropping economy, African class formation and the 1913 Natives' Land Act in the Highveld maize belt". In Marks, S. and Rathbone, R. (eds), *Industrialisation and social change*. London, 1982.

Keiser, R.D. "The South African governor-general, 1910-1919". Unpublished PhD dissertation, University of Oxford, 1975.

Keith, A.B. *War government of the British dominions*. London, 1921.

Kiernan, V.G. "Colonial Africa and its Armies". In Bond, B. and Roy, I. (eds), *War and Society II*. London, 1977.

Killingray, D. "Repercussions of World War I in the Gold Coast". *Journal of African History*, XIX(1), 1978.

Killingray, D. "War and society in British colonial Africa: Themes and prospects". In Ray, P.L., Shinnie, P. and Williams, D. (eds), *Into the 80s: The proceedings of the Eleventh Annual Conference of the Canadian Association of African Studies*. Calgary, 1981.

Killingray, D. "The colonial army in the Gold Coast: Official policy and local response, 1890-1947". PhD dissertation, University of London, 1982.

Killingray, D. and Matthews, J. "Beasts of burden: British West African carriers in the First World War". *Canadian Journal of African Studies*, 13(1-2), 1979.

Kramer, A. "Recent historiography of the First World War". *Journal of Modern European History*, 12(2), 2014.

Lacey, M. *Working for Boroko: The origins of a coercive labour system in South Africa*. Johannesburg, 1981.

Lambert, J. "Britishness, South Africanness and the First World War". In Buckner, P. and Francis, D. (eds), *Rediscovering the British world*. London, 2005.

Lewis, G. *Between the wire and the wall: A history of South African 'Coloured' politics*. Cape Town, 1987.

Limb, P. *The ANC's early years: Nation, class and race in South Africa before 1940*. Pretoria, 2010.

Limb, P. (ed.), *The people's paper: A centenary history and anthology of Abantu-Batho*. Johannesburg, 2012.

Lodge, T. *Black politics in South Africa since 1945*. Johannesburg, 1985.

Louis, W.R. *Great Britain and Germany's lost colonies*. Oxford, 1969.

Lucas, C.P. (ed.), *The Empire at war: Volume IV*. London: Oxford University Press, 1924.

Marais, A.H. "Die derde rebellie". *Acta Diurna Historica*, 1(4), December 1972.

Mariotti, A.M. "The incorporation of African women into wage employment in South Africa, 1920-1970". Unpublished PhD dissertation, University of Connecticut, 1980.

Marks, S. and Rathbone, R. (eds), *Industrialisation and social change in South Africa: African class formation and consciousness, 1870-1930*. London, 1982.

Marks, S. *Reluctant rebellion: The 1906-1908 disturbances in Natal*. London, 1970.

Marwick, A. *War and social change in the twentieth century: A comparative study of Britain, France, Germany, Russia and the United States*. London, 1974.

Marwick, A. *Women at war, 1914-1918*. London, 1977.

Matloff, M. "The nature and scope of military history". In Weigley, R.F. (ed.), *New dimensions in military history*. New York, 1975.

Matthews, J.K. "World War I and the rise of African nationalism: Nigerian veterans as catalysts of change". *Journal of Modern African Studies*, 20(3), September 1982.

Mayer, P. "The origin and decline of two rural resistance ideologies". In Mayer, P. (ed.), *Black villagers in an industrial society: Anthropological perspectives on labour migration in South Africa*. Cape Town, 1980.

Mayer, S.L. and Koenig, W.J. *The two world wars: A guide to manuscript collections in the United Kingdom*. London, 1976.

McLaughlin, P. *Ragtime soldiers: The Rhodesian experience in the First World War*. Bulawayo, 1980.

Mda, Z. *Black diamond*. Johannesburg, 2009.

Meyer, J. (ed.), *British popular culture and the First World War*. Leiden, 2008.

Miller, C. *Battle for the Bundu: The First World War in East Africa*. London, 1974.

Milward, A.S. *The economic effects of the world wars on Britain*. London, 1970.

Molema, S.M. *The Bantu: Past and present*. Edinburgh, 1920.

Moroney, S. "Mine worker protest on the Witwatersrand, 1901-1912". In Webster, E. (ed.), *Essays in Southern African labour history*. Johannesburg, 1978.

Mosse, G.L. *Fallen soldiers: Reshaping the memory of the world wars*. Oxford, 1990.

Mullen, R.W. *Blacks in America's wars*. New York, 1973.

Nasson, W.R. "Delville Wood and South African Great War commemorations". *English Historical Review*, 119(480): 85-86.

Nasson, W.R. "Doing down their masters: Africans, Boers, and treason in the Cape Colony, 1899-1902". *Journal of Imperial and Commonwealth History*, 12(1), 1983.

Nasson, W.R. "Moving Lord Kitchener: Black military transport and supply work in the South African War, 1899-1902, with particular reference to the Cape Colony". *Journal of Southern African Studies*, 11(1), October 1984.

Nasson, W.R. "Reflections on the battle of Square Hill, September 1918". Address at Cape Corps commemorative assembly, Castle of Good Hope, September 2013.

Nasson, W.R. "War opinion in South Africa, 1914". *Journal of Imperial and Commonwealth History*, 23(2), 2008.

Nasson, W.R. *Springboks on the Somme: South Africa in the Great War, 1914-1918*. Johannesburg, 2007.

Nasson, W.R. *A different dominion: some reflections on South Africa and the Great War*, Trinity College Dublin, Public lecture, 2013.

Nattrass, J. *The South African economy: Its growth and change*. Cape Town, 1981.

Ncwana, Bennet S.M. *Souvenir of the Mendi disaster*. Cape Town, 1940.

Nelson, K.L. "Black horror on the Rhine: Race as a factor in postWorld War I diplomacy". *Journal of Modern History*, 42(4), December 1970.

Nettleship, M.A., Givens, R.D. and Nettleship, A. (eds), *War, its causes and correlates*. The Hague, 1975.

Ngubo, A. "The development of African political protest in South Africa, 1882-1910: An analytical approach". Unpublished PhD dissertation, University of California, 1973.

Nöthling, C.J. "Blacks, coloureds and Indians in the SA Defence Force". *South Africa International*, 2(1), July 1980.

Nzula, A.T., and others, *Forced labour in colonial Africa*. London, 1979.

Odendaal, A. *Vukani Bantu! The beginnings of black protest politics in South Africa to 1912*. Cape Town, 1984.

Odendaal, A. *The founders: Origins of the ANC and the struggle for democracy in South Africa*. Cape Town, 2012

Ogot, B.A. (ed.), *War and society in Africa*. London, 1972.

Oost, H. *Wie is die skuldiges?* Johannesburg, 1958.

Osuntokun, A. *Nigeria in the First World War*. London, 1979.

Opland, J. "Praise poems as historical sources". In Saunders, C. and Derricourt, R. (eds), *Beyond the Cape frontier: Studies in the history of the Transkei and Ciskei*. Cape Town: Longman, 1974.

Opland, J. "Introduction". In Opland, J. and Nyamende, A. (eds), *Isaac Williams Wauchope: Selected writings, 1874-1916*. Cape Town, 2008.

Orpen, N. 'SA Coloured and Indian soldiers in World War II – A comment". *South Africa International*, II(3), January 1981.

Osuntokun, A. "West African armed revolts during the First World War". *Tarikh*, 5(3), August 1979.

Osur, A.M. *Blacks in the Army Air Forces during World War II: The problem of race relations*. New York, 1977.

Page, M.E. "Malawians in the Great War and after, 1914-1925". Unpublished PhD dissertation, Michigan State University, 1977.

Page, M.E. "Fighting for their world: Black men in a white man's war". Seminar paper, African Studies Association Conference, Washington, D.C., 1982.

Park, R.E. "The social function of war". In Bramson, L. and Goethals, G.E. (eds), *War: studies from psychology, sociology and anthropology*. New York, 1964.

Pearsall, C.W. "Some aspects of the development of secondary industry in the Union of South Africa'. *The South African Journal of Economics*, 5, 1937.

Peires, J. "Preface". In Opland, J. (ed.), *Abantu Besizwe: Historical and biographical writings, 1902-1944*. Johannesburg, 2009.

Peregrino, F.Z.S. *His Majesty's black labourers: A treatise on the camp life of the SANLC* Cape Town, 1917.

Perry, J. and Perry, C. (eds), *A chief is a chief by the people: The autobiography of Stimela Jason Jingoes*. Oxford, 1975.

Phillips, H. "South Africa's worst demographic disaster: The Spanish influenza epidemic of 1918". *South African Historical Journal*, 20, 1988.

Pirio, G.A. "The role of Garveyism in the making of Southern African working classes and Namibian nationalism'. Seminar paper, South Africa in the comparative study of class, race and nationalism conference, New York, 1982.

Plaatje, S.T. *Native life in South Africa*. 2nd edition. London, 1917.

Ploeger, J.J. and F.J. Jacobs. "Kleurlinge in militêre verband". *Militaria*, 4(2), 1971.

Pollak, H. "Women in the Witwatersrand industries". Unpublished MA dissertation, University of the Witwatersrand, 1932.

Potgieter, A.J. "Die swartes aan die Witwatersrand, 1900-1933". Unpublished PhD dissertation, Rand Afrikaans University, 1978.

Qualter, T.H. *Propaganda and psychological warfare*. New York, 1965.

Qangule, M. "Samuel Edward Krune Mqhayi". In Ndletyana, M. (ed.), *African intellectuals in 19th and early 20th century South Africa*. Pretoria, 2008.

Rathbone, R. "World War I and Africa: Introduction". *Journal of African History*, XIX(1), 1978.

Rayner, W.S. and O'Shaughnessy, W.W. *How Botha and Smuts conquered German South West*. London, 1916.

Reinders, R.C. "Racialism on the left: E.D. Morel and the 'Black Horror on the Rhine'". *International Review of Social History*, 13, 1968.

Robinson, J.P.K. *With Botha's army*. London, 1916.

Roux, E. *Time longer than rope: A history of the black man's struggle for freedom in South Africa*. Madison, 1972.

Rowbotham, S. *Hidden from history: Rediscovering women from the 17th century to the present*. New York, 1974.

Samson, A. *World War I in Africa: The forgotten conflict among the European powers*. London, 2013

Samuel, R. and Thompson, P. "Introduction". In Samuel, R. and Thompson, P. (eds), *The myths we live by*. Routledge, London, 1990.

Saunders, C. "F.Z.S. Peregrino and the South African Spectator. *Quarterly Bulletin of the South African Public Library*, XXXII(3), March 1978.

Schleh, E.P.A. "Post-service careers of African World War Two veterans: British East and West Africa with particular reference to Ghana and Uganda". Unpublished PhD dissertation, Yale University, 1968.

Scholtz, G.D. *Die rebellie, 1914-15*. Johannesburg, 1942.

Scully, W.C. "The colour problem in South Africa". *The Edinburgh Review, or Critical Journal*, July 1919.

Shepherd, R.H.W. *Lovedale, South Africa: The story of a century*, 1941.

Shepperson, G.A. "External factors in the development of African nationalism, with particular reference to British Central Africa". *Phylon*, 22(3), 1961.

Shepperson, G.A. "Nyasaland and the millennium". In Thrupp, S. (ed.), *Millenial dreams in action*. The Hague, 1962.

Shepperson, G.A. "The comparative study of millenarian movements". In Thrupp, S. (ed.), *Millenial dreams in action*. The Hague, 1962.

Shepperson, G.A. and Price, T. *Independent Africa: John Chilembwe and the origins, settings and significance of the Nyasaland native rising of 1915*. Edinburgh, 1958.

Shiroya, O.J.E. "The impact of World War II on Kenya: The role of ex-servicemen in Kenyan nationalism". Unpublished PhD dissertation, Michigan State University, 1968.

Silburn, P.A. *The colonies and imperial defence*. London, 1909.

Simons, H.J. and Simons, R.E. *Class and colour in South Africa, 1850-1950*. Harmondsworth, 1969.

Skota, T.D.M. *African yearly register*. Johannesburg, 1931.

Smurthwaite, A.G. "The policy of the Smuts government towards Africans 1919-1924". Unpublished MA dissertation, University of South Africa, 1975.

Spiers, E.M. *The Army and society*. London, 1980.

Spies, S.B. *Methods of barbarism? Roberts and Kitchener and civilians in the Boer Republics, January 1900-May 1902*. Cape Town and Pretoria, 1977.

Spies, S.B. "The outbreak of the First World War and the Botha government". *South African Historical Journal*, 1, 1969.

Stedman Jones, G. "Class expression versus social control? A critique of recent trends in the social history of 'leisure'". *History Workshop*, 4 (Autumn), 1977.

Stember, E. *Sexual racism*. New York, 1976.

Sloley, H. "The African Native Labour Contingent and the Welfare Committee". *Journal of African Society*, 17, 1918.

Strachan, H. "The First World War as a global war". *First World War Studies*, 1 (March), 2010.

Stuart, J. *A history of the Zulu rebellion, 1906*. London, 1913.

Suttner, R. *The ANC underground in South Africa*. Johannesburg, 2008.

Stuart-Stephens, D. "Our million black army". *The English Review*, October 1916.

Switzer, L. and Switzer, D. (eds), *The black press in South Africa and Lesotho*. Chicago, 1978.

Tate, M. "The war aims of World War I and World War II and their relation to the darker peoples of the world". *Journal of Negro Education*, 19, 1943.

Tatz, C.M. *Shadow and substance in South Africa*. Pietermaritzburg, 1962.

Thompson, L.M. *The unification of South Africa, 1902-1910*. Oxford, 1960.

Ticktin, D. "The war issue and the collapse of the South African Labour Party, 1914-15". *South African Historical Journal*, 1, 1969.

Trapido, S. "White conflict and non-white participation in the politics of the Cape of Good Hope, 1853-1910". Unpublished PhD dissertation, University of London, 1970.

Trew, H.F. *Botha treks*. London, 1936.

Tylden, G. *The Armed Forces of South Africa with an appendix on the commandos*. Johannesburg, 1954.

Vahed, G. "'Give till it hurts': Durban Indians and the First World War". *Journal of Natal and Zulu History*, 2001, 41-61.

Van der Horst, S.T. *Native labour in South Africa*. Cape Town, 1942.

Van der Waag, I. "All splendid but horrible: The politics of South Africa's second 'little bit' and the war on the Western Front, 1915-1918". *Scientia Militaria*, 40(3), 2012.

Van Onselen, C. *Chibaro: African mine labour in Southern Rhodesia, 1900-1933*. London, 1976.

Van Onselen, C. *Studies in the social and economic history of the Witwatersrand, 1886-1914: Vol. I. New Babylon, Vol. 2, New Nineveh*. London and Johannesburg, 1982.

Von Lettow-Vorbeck, P.E. *My reminiscences of East Africa*. London, 1920.

Von Lettow-Vorbeck, P.E. *East African campaigns*. New York, 1957.

Venter, A,J. *Coloured: Profile of two million South Africans*. Cape Town, 1974.

Vinson, R.T. *The Americans are coming! Dreams of African American liberation in segregationist South Africa*. Athens, Ohio, 2012.

Walshe, P. *The rise of African nationalism in South Africa: The African National Congress, 1912-1952*. London, 1970.

Warwick, P. *Black people and the South African War, 1899-1902*. Cambridge and Johannesburg, 1983.

Warwick, P. and Spies, S.B. (eds), *The South African War, 1899-1902*. London, 1980.

Webster, E. "Background to the supply and control of labour in the gold mines". In Webster, E. (ed.), *Essays in Southern Africa labour history*. Johannesburg, 1978.

Whittal, W. *With Botha and Smuts in Africa*. London, 1917.

Wickins, P.L. *The Industrial and Commercial Workers' Union of Africa*. Cape Town, 1978.

Willan, B.P. "The Anti-Slavery and Aborigines' Protection Society and the South African Natives' Land Act of 1913". *Journal of African History*, 20(1),1979.

Willan, B.P. *Sol Plaatje: A biography*. Johannesburg, 1984.

Willan, B.P. "The South African Native Labour Contingent, 1916-1918". *Journal of African History*, 19(1), 1978.

Wilson, F. "Farming, 1866-1966". In Wilson, M. and Thompson, L.M. (eds), *The Oxford History of South Africa, 1870-1966, II*. London, 1969.

Wilson, F. *Labour in South African gold mines, 1911-1969*. Cambridge, 1972.

Winter, J. (ed.), *War and economic development*. Cambridge, 1975.

Winter, J. *Sites of memory, sites of mourning: The Great War in European cultural history*. Cambridge, 1995.

Winter, J. and Sivan, E. *War and remembrance in the twentieth century*. London.1999.

Winter, J. and Prost, A. *The Great War in history: Debates and controversies, 1914 to the present*. Cambridge 2005.

Wynn, N.A. *The Afro-American and the Second World War*. London, 1976.

Young, A.D.T. "British policy towards the Union of South Africa, 1919-1929". Unpublished PhD dissertation, Bristol University, 1974.

Yudelman, D. *The emergence of modern South Africa: State, capital and the incorporation of organised labour on the South African gold fields, 1902-1939*. Cape Town, 1984.

G. COMMUNICATIONS AND ORAL INTERVIEWS

1. Letter from Howard Phillips, Department of History, University of Cape Town, 28 September 1981 in connection with the influenza epidemic of 1918.

2. Transcripts of oral interviews with P. Mabatoana (17 and 22 April 1980) and R. Mohapeloa (7 May 1980) at Maseru. (I am indebted to Prof. R.R. Edgar, Howard University, Washington, D.C. for copies of these interviews.)

3. Oral History Project, African Studies Institute, University of the Witwatersrand. Transcripts of interviews with K.S. Modipa (17 October 1979), P.M. Masike (24 February 1980), T. Manoto (26 February 1980), K. Maine (17 September 1980), M. Moloko (20 November 1979) and S. Phala (6 September 1979). (I am indebted to Charles van Onselen for drawing my attention to these interviews.)

4. Interview with Mr. A. Kammies, a former member of the Cape Corps at Graaff-Reinet on 13 October 1980.

5. Interview with Mr. C. van Vuuren at Oudsthoorn, 31 March 1979.

H. INTERNET SOURCES

ANC Daily News Briefing, 25 June 2002 [Accessed 21 April 2009].

http://www.info.gov.za/speeches/2007/07080810451001.htm [Accessed 19 May 2008].

http://www.info.gov.za/speeches/2007/11080810451001.htm [Accessed 19 May 2008].

http://www.info.gov.za/speeches/2007/07080810451001.htm [Accessed 19 May 2008].

http://www.info.gov.za/speeches/2007/07080810451001.htm [Accessed 19 May 2008].

http://www.kaganof.com/kagablog/2007/10/03/sek-mqhayi-a-call-to-arms/ [Accessed 31 March 2010].

http://www.navy.mil.za/newnavy/syrface/mendi040918-mendi-home-article.htm [Accessed 31 March 2010].

http://www.news24.com/SouthAfrica/News/Ramaphosa-Mtethwa-to-attend-WWI [Accessed 4 July 2014].

INDEX

Printed in Great Britain
by Amazon

86614439R00122